NEWSWRITING AND REPORTING

Newswriting

JAMES M. NEAL AND SUZANNE S. BROWN

and Reporting

The Iowa State University Press / Ames

JAMES M. NEAL is associate professor of journalism at the University of Nebraska—Lincoln, where he teaches beginning and advanced reporting classes. A 1949 graduate of the University of Colorado School of Journalism, he spent nearly nineteen years as a newspaperman. He has been news editor of the *Colorado Springs Free Press,* the *Scottsbluff* (Neb.) *Star-Herald,* and the *Norman* (Okla.) *Transcript.* He also has served on the city desk of the *Daily Oklahoman* and the central copydesk of the *Hartford Courant,* and for eight years he was wire editor of the *Rapid City* (S.D.) *Journal.* A former state chairman of the South Dakota Associated Press Managing Editors Association, he began teaching in 1967 at South Dakota State University and received the M.A. degree in journalism there in 1970. He is author of a college course in Introduction to the Mass Media, written for the Extension Division of the University of Nebraska.

SUZANNE S. BROWN is a former associate editor in the curriculum department of the University of Nebraska Extension Division. She has the B.S. degree in speech (radio-television) from Northwestern University (1959) and the M.A. degree in English from the University of Arizona (1963). She has worked for KMBC radio and television in Kansas City and has taught English composition and literature at Rockhurst College, the University of Arizona, and the University of Kansas. She is the author and instructor of a college course in Introduction to the Novel for the University of Kansas Extramural Independent Study Center.

© 1976 The Iowa State University Press Ames, Iowa 50010. All rights reserved

Composed and printed by The Iowa State University Press

First edition, 1976
Second printing, 1977

Library of Congress Cataloging in Publication Data

Neal, James M   1925–
    Newswriting and reporting.
    1. Reporters and reporting. I. Brown, Suzanne S.,
1937–   joint author. II. Title.
PN4781.N27   070.4′3   75-26545
ISBN 0-8138-1320-4

CONTENTS

INTRODUCTION / THE WHO, WHAT, WHY, AND HOW OF THIS BOOK

This is a "how-to" book for the beginning reporter. It is primarily for college journalism sophomores who are only beginning to learn the difference between expressing themselves and fulfilling the demands of a variety of readers. If you are such a student, this book will show you how to recognize the makings of a story, how to get mandatory information, how to evaluate it and put it together, how to polish it, and how to avoid the major legal pitfalls. We hope that this book also will build a small fire under you—inspire you to dig beneath the surface of daily events, to gather fragments that often pass for news and weave them into the broader context of history, and to search for meaning as well as for facts.

By clipping examples from your daily newspaper and following the suggested assignments at the end of each chapter, you could profit from this text without the help of an instructor. We don't advise it, however, unless you have the help of a professional journalist or you are merely using the book to sharpen techniques you are already familiar with. Each of the 12 chapters is a self-contained study unit. From the beginning, we have conceived the book as an aid to the classroom instructor as well as to the student. No textbook, especially one about writing, can take the place of a teacher's or an editor's constructive criticism. Nor can it take the place of actual practice. But this book can help sharpen your perception, give you basic information about the reporter's work, and make you aware of the purposes and principles of journalism. And it will give you many examples of clear, lively prose.

The techniques we describe can be applied to any assignment, whether it is a two-minute telephone interview or a weeks-long investigation of official malfeasance. Every story, big or small, demands the same things: the ability to formulate the right questions, the persuasiveness and persistence to get the answers, and the skill to put these answers together in a way that makes sense to the public. This applies as much to broadcast journalism as to newspaper work. Therefore, we have concentrated more on the *process* of reporting than on its application to particular beats or assignments—or a particular medium.

Our goal is to help you learn to write simple but polished news stories within a short time. And by "news stories," we mean timely, original stories packed with information that you yourself gather, not exercises from a workbook. But before you head for your typewriter, you should have some idea of what is expected and how to get it. Therefore, we have placed the basics of reporting before writing. We also have placed the organization of the whole story before a detailed examination of its parts. The theory behind the sequence of the first eight chapters is to provide information in the order that you must see it. Chapter 8 is a miniature handbook of English usage, designed both as a text and as a reference section. The last four chapters deal with human interest and the depth report, advanced reporting problems, newsroom organization and practice, and law and ethics—all of which can wait until you have learned to write a simple story.

Although this sequence has proved effective in the classroom, many instructors may prefer to begin with the mechanics of language (Chapter 8) or lead writing (Chapter 7). For that matter, some may want to begin with ethics and law (Chaper 12). We think you can begin anywhere, because each chapter is "Chapter 1" in the sense that each treats a distinctly separate aspect of reporting or writing.

Although major points are illustrated throughout with examples from many sources, we have tried to avoid making the book a patchwork of yesterday's news. The examples most effective in stimulating class discussion and individual analysis, we believe, are those you yourself clip from your daily newspaper. Because they are timely and local, they should be far more interesting than anything that we could provide. Therefore, many of the suggested assignments require clippings which you must supply.

Our goal throughout has been depth treatment of fundamentals. This applies particularly to the basic mechanics of writing. We don't assume that you already have had intensive instruction in English composition. On the contrary, we are fairly certain that you haven't. And this is why we have written a textbook with a new approach. Many of the newswriting textbooks in current use were written decades ago. They were excellent books then, and they still are. But the student audience has changed. Despite many revisions, the older standard texts remain founded on an assumption that is no longer valid—the assumption that, before a student enters a newswriting class, someone else already has taught him how to spell, punctuate, and put a simple sentence together.

This isn't the case. Mass higher education has so overburdened college English departments that freshman composition is in danger of disappearing—at least as a universal requirement. At some schools, the composition course has been cut to one semester. At others, it has given way entirely to a reading course. No university, it seems, has sufficient staff to teach composition to several thousand unwilling freshman, and many English professors believe it is useless to try. Until some remedy is found, newswriting instructors must continue to teach much of what once was taught in freshman English.

So this is a *writing* textbook, but one in which we have tried to minimize the artificial separation of "writing" and "reporting." Both, after all, are communication, and both require the use of language.

Because it deals with professional skills, certainly this is a practical book. Nonetheless, it is both difficult and undesirable to draw too fine a line between the "practical" and the "theoretical." So, although we have devoted only one chapter (Chapter 1) specifically to communication theory, we have tried to relate theory and practice throughout. We also have applied theory to the language in which this book is written. The tone is conversational, as it is in a classroom or a newsroom. We are deliberately repetitious at times in order to emphasize basic principles, and we have written much of the book in the second person to remind you that it is written for *you*.

Before you turn to Chapter 1, a word of warning: you will find several contradictions in this text. First we tell you writing is easy; later we say it isn't. At one point we urge you to write as fast as possible; at another we suggest that you think first. Here we stress imaginative approaches; there we insist on the need for restraint. Don't be dismayed. Newswriting, after all, is a reflection of life, and it is almost as complex as life itself. And like most statements about life, most statements about newswriting may be equally true.

JAMES M. NEAL
SUZANNE S. BROWN

NEWSWRITING AND REPORTING

CHAPTER ONE / REPORTERS: WHO THEY ARE AND HOW THEY FUNCTION

As a student reporter, you are preparing to become a professional communicator. You will have plenty of company. Everyone is communicating all the time, verbally or nonverbally, and millions are making a profession of it: teachers, clergymen, salespeople, psychotherapists, data processors, politicians, and military drill instructors. Modern society has, in fact, so many professional communicators that reporters can hardly be blamed if they object to being placed in such a broad classification. It lumps them with persuaders, propagandists, and technicians—groups with which they hardly belong. It says nothing about the functions and qualities which set journalists apart.

The mere fact that reporters communicate hardly makes them unique. All of us constantly are receiving messages through our senses, selecting and interpreting what we see, hear, feel, smell or dream, and frequently passing along portions of this information verbally. When the information is timely, factual, and interesting to others, we're functioning as reporters on a personal and limited scale. Other than pay, what sets the professionals apart from the average person is (1) the size of their audience, (2) the utility and interest of their messages, and (3) the knowledge and attitude brought to the job.

Whereas most of us speak only to the relatively few people we meet face-to-face, reporters address an audience that ranges from a few hundred to several million. The average person can select subjects and wording to fit an individual listener, but the reporter ordinarily must write about actions and situations that interest large groups. And reporters must tell most of their stories in words that any reasonably literate person can understand.

Professional reporters are the hired eyes, ears, legs, and brain of the reader, viewer, or listener. Everything they do is guided by the individual reader's interests. They are paid to survey a small fraction of the world's activities each day and tell the public what they find: what's happening, what's scheduled to happen, what people are saying about it, and (when they can be reasonably sure) what it means. If they do their job well, they supply much of the current information that each person needs to develop a workable picture of reality. If they do it poorly, they become responsible for part of the public's ignorance and prejudice.

Continual awareness of this responsibility to the public marks the attitude of professional reporters. Reporters are individuals, but they also are vital elements in the social process of communication. By helping decide what constitutes news, how it should be written and to what length, they function as human valves and amplifiers in the vast machinery of mass communication. They select, reject, compile, interpret, explain, and highlight. But in so doing, they are geared more to the product than to the process. They don't serve simply as an open conduit between the reader and reality, as mechanical sifters of fact and opinion. If they are functioning properly, they are constantly attuned to the receiver. A reporter is a *thinking* agent of the reader.

A DEFINITION OF COMMUNICATION

Perhaps understandably, reporters tend to concentrate on the special subjects they cover, with little attention to the overall process of communication. Indeed, a solid theoretical background may seem unnecessary. Communication is learned so early that we tend to regard it as a basic human tool that anyone can use with little or no conscious thought. Like the air we breathe, it's all around us, and we use it without seeing it. We concentrate on the message— whatever it is that we want to say, write, read, view, or hear—with little attention to the complex processes of listening, speaking, receiving, or conveying messages.

Yet if reporters are to be professionals, they at least must understand the basic process of communication, where they fit into it, and what problems they can expect to encounter.

Communication is defined as *the transmission or exchange of information or ideas or feelings by means of sounds, signs, or symbols.* The basic elements are a sender or source, a message, a medium, and a receiver or audience. The information may be either rational or emotional (usually it's a mixture of both), and the means or medium may be spoken or printed words, gestures, musical or mathematical symbols, semaphore, or smoke signals—anything that conveys meaning. Communication, especially that of spoken and written words, is the cement that holds society together. Without it we would have no schools, no political institutions, no system of trade, no culture. Communication is all that makes people human.

Mass communication, obviously, is the transmission of information to large numbers of persons, usually over a considerable geographical area. The basic media are print, film, and electricity. But in popular usage, "media" means specifically newspapers, television, radio, motion pictures, magazines, and books. And journalism, the timely accounting of newsworthy activities, is only one of their functions.

Despite their ever present activity, the mass media carry only a tiny fraction of the world's total volume of messages each day. Consider your own experience. Most of the messages you send and receive are delivered orally, in person or by telephone, to people you know. A few go by mail. Most have a limited circulation and a short life span. They go only as far as the next person or to a small group and often seem to die there within seconds. It's usually no great loss; they are only mundane remarks about subjects of only passing interest.

At the other extreme are many messages, transmitted both by print and word of mouth, that have been circulating for generations—some for centuries. The works of Plato, Aristotle, Dante, Chaucer, Shakespeare, Goethe, Tolstoy, and Marx are only a few examples of communication that has spanned many lifetimes and reached audiences of millions. Both in content and usually in form, these messages have universal significance. Only the richest, rarest, and most profound communications of any era achieve this stature.

Many of the classics of Western literature, philosophy, and history, along with the Bible—by far the most enduring and far-reaching of them all—embody and preserve oral traditions that extend even further into the past. No doubt these messages of folklore and religion have been circulating in one form or another since the beginning of human speech. Some seem to have reached all of humanity.

The messages of journalism appear to lie somewhere near the midpoint between the transience of everyday communication and the permanence of the communication which forms our cultural heritage. Although most news stories have a limited range, some circulate widely, a few reaching nearly everyone in the civilized world. And the life span of many is considerably longer than that of ordinary conversation. "Nothing is as dead as yesterday's news," editors may say, yet today's newspaper becomes a major source of information for tomorrow's history books. News has reached a high degree of permanence through print, film, and tape. Unfortunately, longevity isn't restricted to only those stories of merit. Trivia and misinformation also may seem to live forever in the clipping files.

THE ROLE OF THE COMMUNICATOR

Mass communication and education, more than any other institutions, act as clearinghouses and conveyor belts for the continuing flow of human messages. Yet every person plays at least a minor role in transmitting the facts and fictions of the past and present to future generations. All of us originate many messages based on our experiences and observations. Perhaps more often, however, we pass along messages originated by someone else—second-hand information, some current and some that began circulating so long ago that nobody remembers the source.

All of us, then, function as relays in the ongoing process of communication that links continent to continent and the past to the future. All of us reject some messages and accept others, ignoring or forgetting many, and in some way changing whatever passes through us. We evaluate and interpret, add some elements and delete others, compile or confuse portions of several messages, then rephrase the whole hodgepodge and, intentionally or not, give it our own emotional tone. How we communicate affects, at least slightly, people around us and generations to come. The quality of our civilization depends on how well each of us performs this function—what we are able to observe and choose to observe, how we interpret and synthesize it, how accurately we remember it, how clearly we pass it on, and what emotional tone we give it.

As professional communicators, reporters are likely to have a much greater influence than most people on both the present and the future. Whatever they write has the potential of affecting people thousands of miles away and people many years hence—their children and grandchildren. Will the news clippings be full of trivia and misinformation? Or will they leave a reasonably accurate picture of reality?

A PUBLIC TRUST

The reporter's responsibility for accuracy becomes clear when you realize that much of what we "know" is only second-hand information. We don't in fact know it at all. We accept it largely on faith. A teacher tells us that the world is round, and we hear that seamen, fliers, and astronauts agree. But we don't really know unless we circle the globe ourselves. As long as authorities agree and the concept seems to work, we have little reason to question it.

When authorities disagree, it's a different story. A clergyman tells us one thing, our parents say otherwise, and the professor offers still a third view. Whom, we wonder, can we trust?

Some people accept the answer given by Will Rogers in an oft-quoted remark: "All I know," the cowboy humorist said, "is what I read in the papers." Rogers uttered this hyperbole before the advent of television, and probably more people today would credit that medium as a source of all they know. But if newspapers and TV were our only sources of reliable knowledge, nobody would learn to swim, drive a car, play volleyball—or twirl a rope as Rogers did. Nor would anyone learn much philosophy or ancient history. All of us learn many things from experience and the instruction we receive from parents and teachers.

Nevertheless, Rogers' comment suggests three important points: (1) many people do rely on the mass media for a large portion of their factual information, an increasing amount as they grow older; (2) they tend to believe what they read and see, and (3) most people manufacture their view of the world largely from raw material supplied by the mass media.

This second-hand picture of reality is inescapable. Nobody can be everywhere or see, hear, and understand everything. That's why we have professional reporters. And, like Will Rogers, each reader must accept what the reporter tells him largely on faith. Readers have neither the time nor the resources to get the story or to check its accuracy. That's the reporters' job. And they must perform it in such a way that they merit the public's trust.

EXPOSURE, PERCEPTION, AND RETENTION

What the reader wants first is trustworthy information. And to get it, reporters first must be *exposed* to it. Simple exposure—access to information—is a basic problem. If reporters can't get to the scene of the action, if they can't reach someone who did, if they can't see the right documents or reach the person who has special information, they can't get the story. They often spend an inordinate amount of time trying to discover who has the information and how it can be dislodged.

Exposure, however, still isn't enough. Reporters also must see, hear, and understand; they must *perceive* whatever they have been exposed to. Exposure is no help if the information is presented in words, statistics, or some other form that the reporters don't understand. Reporters can't take the easy way out and merely pass along raw information. If *they* can't understand it, neither will readers.

Finally, the reporters must *retain* the information, at least long enough to get it on paper. This is where memory, skilled notetaking, speedwriting or shorthand, and a tape recorder are valuable.

Physical limitations handicap reporters in every step of this process. Reporters, like anybody else, can't be everywhere. They can't see, hear, or understand all that they do encounter. Nor can they retain all of what they do see, hear, and understand. Broadcast reporters may come close to retaining it all if they are shooting sound-on-film motion pictures, but even a camera is severely limited. It can't face in all directions at once, nor can it reach into the past. It can capture only a limited part of the action at a specific time and place.

Moreover, research indicates that psychological as well as physical limitations affect our exposure to and perception and retention of information. People apparently have a tendency to expose themselves mostly to information that appeals to them or reinforces their beliefs (Some select the *Scientific American,* others a football game on television.) And they have a tendency to see and hear only what they expect or want to see and hear. Retention works the same way: we remember best whatever fits our beliefs and expectations. Unconscious psychological selectivity is a problem which affects reporters, their sources, and their readers—everyone in the communication process. It must be recognized as one of the major barriers to clear, complete, and accurate communication.

EXERCISING SELECTIVE JUDGMENT

One way reporters overcome the problems of unconscious selectivity is through conscious selectivity. In order to fulfill the public trust, they must report only the information they are sure of. Verifying facts—by observation, interviews, checking records, making phone calls—is a regular part of the reporter's daily routine.

When the story is simple and noncontroversial (for example, an announcement of a public meeting) and the source is known to be reliable, reporters have little difficulty. They simply read back their notes to the source to make certain they have the correct hour, day, and place. But when a story is at all controversial or complex, reporters select their facts carefully, trying to write nothing they couldn't prove in court. They use as many sources of information as possible—oral, written, or printed—as well as what their own senses tell them, searching for both corroboration and contradiction. When information can't be confirmed, they either must clearly label it as "an unconfirmed report" or leave it out of the story.

The only safe course is prescribed in the newsroom proverb: "When in doubt, leave it out." Attributing doubtful information to its source is a weak and risky device. An attributed lie is no better than an unattributed lie.

But more often than not, the selective judgment involved in getting the facts and getting them straight is fairly mechanical. Accuracy, like proficiency in spelling and punctuation, is merely where reporters begin. To become professionals, they must also exercise considerable judgment in the selection of what information they use: which stories are worth their attention, which facts belong in the stories that do merit writing.

Reporters don't write everything they know. Some facts are trivial, irrelevant, inflammatory, or libelous. Many so-called stories aren't even news in that they add nothing of interest to the reader's knowledge. Others may be interesting but are better treated as advertising.

Usually beginners' news judgment is shaped by prevailing journalistic practice, the policies of their newspaper, and the specific demands of their city editor. But these guides, however valuable, are only the foundation. Any literate person can become a hack by following orders or by reading the newspaper regularly and supplying the same kinds of stories it already has published. To progress beyond this stage, you must learn to (1) determine which facts are pertinent to a story and limit the story to those facts, and (2) recognize stories in situations others have ignored.

WHAT DO WE AMPLIFY?

If reporters act as valves, regulating the amount and kinds of information readers receive, they also act as amplifiers, magnifying some events, situations, and personalities, while ignoring or minimizing others. The result is an incomplete and therefore distorted picture of reality. It can't be helped. Distortion is inherent in any process of selection and amplification. Reporters can only try to maintain a reasonable perspective. They must cover all the legitimate news they can and try to avoid overmagnifying any person, event, or situation.

By whatever they write, reporters confer the status of public recognition on something or somebody—more often somebody. A name that appears regularly in the news becomes familiar to readers. And readers reason, perhaps unconsciously, that the person who bears the name must be important. The result can be a blossoming career, sometimes unjustified, for an entertainer, athlete, or politician.

Status conferral isn't limited to personalities. It applies as much to institutions and agencies (Harvard, Yale, the Central Intelligence Agency, and the United Way) as it does to the careers of Charles

Lindbergh, John F. Kennedy, or Elvis Presley. It applies to ideas, cults, activities, and stereotypes (relativity, Zen, Wall Street, hippies)— anything mentioned frequently in the news. Responsible reporters try to make certain that the status they automatically confer is earned.

Perhaps the most common status-conferral problem arises from monotonously quoting the same official sources day after day. Sometimes nothing can be done about it. The information is legitimate news, the source must be identified, and the information always comes from the same source. The only alternative to publicizing the same person regularly is to get the information from someone else. When this is possible, it's not a bad alternative. You may not be getting all the facts from your regular source. And at least you will get a different viewpoint and provide the reader with some variety.

FROM INFORMATION TO ACTION

Inaccuracy and overmagnification are dangerous because people tend to act on the basis of their information. Theoretically, they will act wisely if their information is complete and accurate, unwisely if it isn't.

Stimulating action, of course, isn't the reporter's job. Neither is it the business of the reporter to prevent action, unless it threatens to become violent. Reporters should merely get the facts, organize them meaningfully, and present them clearly. What the public does with the information is, in a democracy, the public's business.

Nevertheless, reporters must recognize that any information— rumor, gossip, or a simple factual story—has the potential to trigger action, sometimes sensible and sometimes violent. A story may stimulate social reform or it may lead to a riot, a war, criminal prosecution, or suicide. Sometimes reporters themselves are the targets of the action. Threats, complaints, verbal abuse, and libel suits plague the lot of newspeople. Reporters have been beaten, kidnaped, and shot for things they wrote. Journalism is neither a popularity contest nor a calling for the faint-hearted.

Luckily, most people act on the basis of their *total* information, rather than isolated scraps. And they usually act slowly. The Big Story that generates so much excitement in the newsroom may cause nothing but bored yawns among most readers. People who are uninterested, stubborn, lazy—or genuinely thoughtful—may require a mountain of information before they move. It is perhaps well that the general public tends to be lethargic. If everyone reacted immediately to every sensational event, we would be in a constant state of panic.

With all we know about readers, we can never be absolutely

certain how they will react, either as individuals or as a group, to any isolated story—or even if they will react at all. We know only that they are not like computers; we can't send them a signal and trigger a predetermined response. A single message transmitted millions of miles to a spacecraft can indeed command it to change course, but individuals and society are seldom moved so easily.

Still the action-triggering potential of news is worth remembering. If you tell the readers what the city council is planning to do for them (or *to* them) at 8 P.M. Monday, you just may draw a crowd. You can't be sure—but you *can* be certain that nobody will be present unless people have been informed. They must be told what is expected to happen, when, and where.

REPORTERS ARE ONLY HUMAN

Much of our factual information is brought to us by television cameras, radio and tape recorders, telephone and computer. As a result, a large body of communications theory has grown out of discoveries in the physical sciences and their application by electrical engineers. Mathematician Norbert Wiener has applied this knowledge to the operation of the human nervous system (another form of electronic computer) and even to organized society in what he calls the science of cybernetics. Wiener attempts to unite the physical, biological, and social sciences and explain all communications in terms that apply to electrical circuits. One such term that has become part of the popular vocabulary is *feedback*. To electronics technicians, it means a voltage fed back from the output of a circuit to control the input. It can be measured precisely. To public relations practitioners, whose measuring instruments are far less accurate, feedback means simply listening to the audience and shaping the message accordingly.

Much of the mathematical theory of communications conceivably could be applied to the individual reporter. But it would be both impractical and an oversimplification. We cannot view reporters simply as conduits or amplifiers in the intricate network of mass communications. We must treat them as human beings, not as abstractions or pieces of electrical equipment.

Unlike computers, reporters make mistakes. Their eyes and ears play tricks on them, or they misunderstand the meaning of a story or misjudge its importance. A reporter can misspell a name, copy down a figure wrong, get the complaining witness confused with the defendant, or identify persons in a photograph from right to left instead of left to right. Beginners soon learn to double-check everything at every stage: when they are getting the information, while they are writing it, and after they have finished. They use directories, dictionaries, almanacs, reference works, and printed sources of all kinds, and the question they probably ask most often is, "How do you spell that?"

We also must recognize that reporters, unlike cameras or microphones, have attitudes, opinions—even prejudices—which they must suppress as fully as possible in the interest of professionalism. They must approach each story with an open mind. Rather than search only for those facts that fit some preconceived notion, they try to get the facts before they determine what the story is. They learn to question not only the popular beliefs of the day, but their own beliefs as well.

THE "REPORTER PERSONALITY"

Every journalist, working in whatever medium at whatever level, is basically a reporter. For better or for worse, the reporter is likely to be white, middle-class, and college-educated. And although radicals of both the left and the right have found their way into the profession, the reporter is most likely to be somewhere in the middle of the road. As an individual, the reporter is probably a mixture of realist and romantic, optimist and cynic, specialist and jack-of-all-knowledge. A reporter may be many things: a cool-headed investigator, a passionate dramatist, a student of history, a "cop-shop lawyer," a social scientist, a hack, or a person of letters. But whatever the individual differences in talent and temperament, the reporter is the heart of journalism.

Historically, the reporter has worn many hats. Some—Mark Twain, Walt Whitman, William Cullen Bryant, Richard Harding Davis, and Ernest Hemingway—have been primarily men of letters. Others—Winston Churchill, John F. Kennedy—have earned enduring reputations as political leaders. A few, like Walter Lippmann or Arthur Krock and C. L. Sulzberger of *The New York Times,* have dealt almost entirely with the broad sweep of world history. And there are those, like Walter Winchell and Earl Wilson, who have traded largely in personal gossip.

Reams have been written about the "typical reporter" or the "reporter personality," much of it questionable. Reporters vary widely in their attitudes, interests, backgrounds, and methods of operation. Perhaps the only safe generalization is that most are curious about a wide variety of activities and persistent in their quest for facts. They also tend to be skeptics, systematic doubters who believe nothing without proof. In this respect, the reporter is more closely related to the scientist or legal investigator than to the poet or dramatist.

Every city editor knows that there are all kinds on the staff—

human interest writers who fail miserably on complicated legal issues, reporters renowned for accuracy and notorious for wooden prose, some so brash they offend news sources, and others so shy that they can approach some persons only by telephone. Many are experts in a special subject, others experts only at writing. And a few "legmen" can hardly write at all but are extremely adept at ferreting out facts. The newspaper is whatever it is because of this variety of talents and the way the city editor uses them.

A DEMANDING CAREER

As a way of life, reporting the news is something less than a rose garden—except for the number of thorns. It demands a strong body, a tough mind, and a high tolerance for tension. It requires speed, dependability, punctuality, and a better-than-average liberal education. And it usually requires settling for less than prosperity or lasting fame.

Reporters write about the here and now for readers in their own time. They have little prospect of wealth, and it's unlikely that anything they write will outlive them. They know that today's best effort will be used to wrap tomorrow's garbage, that they will be fortunate if they save enough money to send their children to college. And still, if reporters are professional, they put all their talent and energy into each day's work.

The job often requires more stamina than talent. The workday may stretch far into the night, and a developing story may require that the reporter live with it for days. Even when the reporter quits at the end of a normal shift, he or she may be called back for a special assignment. The world never sleeps, and often reporters can't either. They are on call 24 hours a day. They can't simply stop being reporters at the end of 8 hours.

Life in the newsroom can be frustrating. Beginners are frustrated by the tedium of routine stories they must survive to prove themselves worthy of better assignments. Veterans may be frustrated by unexpected emergencies that are always taking them away from their families at odd hours. And all are frustrated by the lack of space and time. Every reporter knows that each story would be better if there were four more inches of space and another half hour to write it.

One might suspect that reporters are either inordinately in love with their job or slightly insane. Why else would they choose a career in which the pace is so often frenetic, the hours frequently long and irregular, the material rewards meager, and ulcers an occupational hazard? Why else would they stay with a job that wins them few real friends and so often forces them to be observers rather than participants in social and political life?

One of the attractions, of course, is the very difficulty of the job, the challenge of trying to make order out of some portion of a disorderly world each day before deadline. Another is the knowledge that the reporter performs a useful role in society: warning readers of dangers, alerting them to opportunities, holding up a mirror to reality. And some beginners are attracted by the supposed glamour of journalism. Here, they are told, is where the action is. This is where you meet the most interesting people.

The "glamour" of reporting must be taken with at least a grain of salt. Although it's not quite like any other occupation, reporting is still a job. Much of the work is conducted at a desk, with reporters using the telephone and pounding a typewriter. The most dramatic action they ever see may be in the newsroom itself, and the most interesting people they meet probably will be other news personnel.

Beginners soon learn that most of the exciting action stories they write concern events that they never see. Accidents, disasters, fires, and riots seldom give warning. Reporters are no more likely to witness them than anyone else. If they get to the scene at all, it will probably be after the action has ended, and they will have to get the story by interviewing those who saw it. Many times, under pressure of deadline, reporters must round up the facts by telephone, without ever leaving the office. They are often merchants of secondhand information.

For each exciting story, most reporters must write a dozen others that are nothing but work: meeting notices, community promotions, tedious statistics, long lists of names. Every newspaper has its routine obituaries, its daily weather story, its pile of publicity releases to be verified and rewritten. Such stories fill legitimate needs. Each will be read by someone, and reporters must write them. But it's too much to expect them to enjoy them all.

With all the monotony of routine assignments, however, reporters still go where others can't, open doors that are closed to the general public, and see people and documents that are inaccessible to the average citizen. Only reporters are privileged to see so much of the daily workings of society, so many of the triumphs, disappointments, farces, and tragedies of life in their own time. They are still the first to know the news—and the stories behind it. They have a front-row seat at the human comedy.

STATUS WITH DRAWBACKS

Reporters also have the status of public recognition. Their names become familiar to the reader and their faces are recognized by judges, senators, policemen, public officials, and celebrities of many kinds. This, combined with access to the reader's mind through the news columns, is something of a mixed blessing. Reporters are prime targets for every publicist and politician, every person with a cause, a complaint, or an ax to grind—everyone who wants to reach the public with a message. Through flattery, cajolery, or pressure, people try to use reporters. If you join a club, you probably will be asked to serve as publicity chairman (a position you normally must decline as a conflict of interest), and if you attend a wedding, you may be asked to take photographs. People stop you on the street or telephone you at home with "great ideas" for stories the newspaper should run. Sometimes the tips are valuable, but often they are worthless. But you must listen, just in case.

Reporters may tend to become cynical about many of the "interesting people" they meet. They discover that those people often have the same weaknesses that they have and that many are motivated primarily by self-interest. Reporters may respect the achievements of these people, but they quickly cease to be awed by them as individuals. And they learn to resist their flattery.

Many people try to buy reporters' goodwill, if not their actual services. They offer free meals, free drinks, and free tickets to circuses, sports events, plays, and concerts—usually in the name of friendship and with no visible strings attached. Most reporters accept simple hospitality but not gifts or gratuities. And they give nothing in return. They never promise to write anything that isn't legitimate news, nor do they agree to suppress any information they consider in the public interest. Reporters act as agents of the reader, not of the sources of information. They can have friends among their sources, but they can't play favorites. The day may come when the reporter must write something detrimental to his or her best source.

INSULATION CAN BE OVERDONE

In the interest of maintaining their independence, many reporters avoid unnecessary social contact with news sources. Sometimes this extends to nearly everyone outside journalism. Newspeople often seem to associate only with other journalists, as if they were a special breed set apart from the rest of society. They work together, eat together, drink together, and often live together. The newsroom's bachelor boys and girls date each other and often marry.

In extreme cases, this social isolation can result in intellectual incest. Unless they know many people—in different occupations, with different life-styles, and with different points of view—reporters are likely to lose touch with the larger reality. They must know how others live and how they think in order to serve the reader. A reporter's world should be larger than just that of fellow workers and the persons who regularly provide information.

For some, the danger of intellectual incest begins at birth. Sons and daughters of newspeople grow up to become students in schools of journalism—where the professors also are to some extent products of the newsgathering establishment. Often, what beginners learn in college or on their first job reinforces what they already have learned at home. They may be told early that there is a "right" (approved) and a "wrong" (forbidden) way to do many things, and unless they have learned to think for themselves, they may already be conditioned to accept a tradition-bound editor's definitions of right and wrong without challenge.

The fact is that journalism as a whole has few absolute rules— other than accuracy and fairness. Every newsroom, it is true, has certain prescribed practices, but these vary from one organization to another. And exceptions are allowed nearly everywhere.

If beginners accept *all* of their newsroom's traditions without challenge, they are making a mistake. The reporters' job is to question everything, to believe nothing they hear and only half of what they see without further evidence. This extends to the organization's policies and practices and to the conventional wisdom of journalism as a whole. It also extends to the arguments of those who criticize policy and tradition. What alternatives do they have to offer? In short, reporters should question all beliefs, ideas, proposals, criticism, and praise. They must reject any belief or attitude that inhibits their ability to see clearly and seek the facts.

A TRAINING GROUND

Not all beginners, of course, are exposed to journalism's traditions long enough to risk infection. Many view a reporter's job only as a stepping-stone to something else—a career in politics, advertising, education, business, or public relations. Some will return to the campus to enter graduate school and eventually become professors. Others will stay in the newsroom but seek the relative tranquility of the copydesk and perhaps move into administrative jobs. And a few will become novelists, dramatists, or magazine writers. For many, the newsroom is only a training ground, a place where they can study the world while they sharpen their writing skills.

The turnover rate of young reporters is often quite high. This has advantages as well as disadvantages. Beginners generally have more energy, enthusiasm, and imagination than older staff members, but less judgment and craftsmanship. A steady supply of young reporters can be insurance against trite thinking, but an oversupply can weaken the total product.

Because a reporter of 29 may be considered a veteran in some newsrooms, many people think of reporting as only a young person's job. Yet the nation's top reporters usually are middle-aged, and some political writers are past normal retirement age. Most editors try to maintain a cadre of such experienced reporters.

A SKIMMER AND A SCHOLAR

What makes the newsroom an excellent training ground is that reporters must learn to *learn,* as well as to write. This is a skill which can be transferred to any occupation.

In a practical sense, reporters are professional students. They set out each day to learn something new, something that adds to the reader's knowledge, and they use the same techniques a classroom student uses. They look, listen, ask questions, take notes, and consult documents and reference works. They move around more than most students, use more human sources, ask far more questions, and work much faster. They pay less attention to abstractions, more attention to realities. They also tend to be more skeptical. They don't trust the professor or anyone else.

Some of the learning is necessarily superficial. An important story may break too late in the day to allow detailed investigation, or a story may have too little reader interest to warrant exploration in depth. In such instances, reporters must learn the bare essentials as quickly as possible. Even then they usually learn much more than they write. Several pages of notes may result in a story only four paragraphs long.

Since the advent of television, however, the trend in newspapers has been toward depth reporting. Having lost the battle to be first and most graphic, editors try to offer more detail and more explanation than other daily media. This often casts newspaper reporters in the role of scholarly investigators. Like magazine writers, they may spend weeks investigating a situation from every conceivable angle—researching it, conducting dozens of interviews, even living with it. Reporters have lived with explorers, combat infantrymen, and poverty-stricken families. They have posed as convicts, mental patients, and naive customers to expose injustices. And they often must read books and stacks of documents to compile depth reports. The collected facts may be equivalent to a master's thesis, and the entire story may require a series of several articles. Many such projects are expanded later into books.

Much of the day-to-day learning consists only of the facts necessary for a specific story. But to be successful, reporters also must have a large store of general knowledge. They must be lifelong students of individuals, institutions, and language. Formally or not, they must study law, political and social organization, psychology, and history. They must learn enough about humans in general to know what the reader needs and wants. And they also must learn how to write clearly. All these things are part of who the reporter is—and form the essential basis for how a reporter functions.

SUGGESTED ASSIGNMENTS

Exercises in Observation

One of the qualities that distinguishes outstanding reporters is their ability to see, hear, and feel more than the average person. Thus, to begin your training in this field, you might try a few simple exercises in observation. Once you have done these, others will readily occur to you. You should regularly test and practice your powers of observation.

1. Look at the person sitting beside you for 30 seconds. Now close your eyes and try to tell everything you saw. What about the person's size? Physical shape? Hair color? Complexion? Eye color? Can you describe his clothing? Could you estimate his age? Was the person wearing a wedding ring? What distinguishing marks or characteristics set this person apart as an individual?

   Now open your eyes and confirm your observations. Did you really see the person completely and clearly, or did you get a lot of details wrong? Now ask the person his age, height, and weight, and see how close you came.

2. Try to describe everything happening in the classroom as your professor lectures. Ignore the lecture for a moment—concentrate on the entire scene. Is the person beside you taking notes, or just doodling? How many are having trouble staying awake? Notice the student who reacts to the lecturer's every word, nodding his head, raising his eyebrows, looking puzzled. Notice those who stare straight at the professor, without changing expression or body position. Is the room too hot? Does the professor drone, come on strong, make jokes, or move around while speaking? Could you write a human interest story, without a single direct quote, based on what happens in a classroom?

3. Position yourself in a corner of the campus coffee shop for 15 minutes. Watch the students enter and leave. Observe them carefully, how they look, how they move, where and how they sit. Eavesdrop on fragments of conversation. Take all the notes you can, then hurry to your typewriter and try to recreate the scene as you saw and heard it, this time with any dialogue you might have heard. Write it without any proper names; if you recognized any of the students, don't name them. Try to limit yourself to

reporting only what you saw and heard at that time, with no background information.

4. Write a story about a lecture. Arrange ahead of time for a number of students or the entire class to report on the same lecture. Nobody should ask questions. Then compare your different versions.

After completing these exercises or similar ones of your own devising, you should have learned two things:

1. *The power of observation can be developed by conscious practice.*
2. *Mere passive observation seldom yields enough information for a complete news story.* You may be able to recreate a scene or record a lecture, but unless something unusual happened during these exercises, it wouldn't be news. And even if you did see or hear something unusual, you'd still have to ask questions, get names and ages, and confirm the accuracy of what you saw and heard.

The lesson simply is that your eyes and ears aren't enough, no matter how carefully you train them. But don't quit trying to train them. Personal observation still is fundamental.

CHAPTER TWO / RECOGNIZING AND EVALUATING A NEWS STORY

You know intuitively what a story is. Ever since you were old enough to speak, you have been telling stories and listening to stories. As soon as you could, you began reading them—mostly children's fiction at first, then factual stories as you grew older and began to read school books, magazines, and newspapers.

So you've been conditioned all your life to recognize stories. But when it comes to analyzing the components or putting together a story yourself, how well do you fare? Can you dash it off as quickly as you can tell it to a friend? Or do you freeze when you sit down at the typewriter?

If you are a would-be writer who freezes, chances are you have one or more of these problems:

1. You don't have all the necessary facts. You can't supply the specific who, what, where, when, why, and how that are the essential ingredients of every story.
2. You're a poor typist, and you're thinking less about the story than about where to put your fingers.
3. You have no clear picture of the person you are addressing (as you do when telling a story face-to-face). You can't identify his interests.
4. You don't understand fully enough the concept of "story."

Each point is important. Reporters always should have more information than they think necessary. They also must know what is important to the audience and have enough typing skill that manual awkwardness won't interfere with clear thinking. But above all reporters must have a good idea of what constitutes a story.

True, not all news appears in story form. Every newspaper publishes a lot of information as statistics or lists—stock market reports, weather readings, football and baseball standings, lists of births and divorces. News broadcasters, having less time than the newspaper has space, devote less attention to lists of names and numbers, but they too deal with a certain amount of nonstory material. News of this kind, however, can be gathered and recorded by anyone, regardless of talent or training. The reporter who expects to be more than a clerk must learn to put news in story form.

STORIES: FICTIONAL AND FACTUAL

The beginning reporter, exercising caution, can learn something about "story" from fiction. News stories and works of fiction differ, of course. News consists only of actual persons and events, with nothing invented, whereas fiction consists of imagined characters and scenes. The reporter's goals, too, usually differ from the fiction writer's. Most news stories are designed to inform or explain, whereas fiction is written to entertain, evoke emotion, or stimulate thought.

But the essential elements of the "story" are the same: people and action. Journalists can use the analogy to fiction as long as they remember that the people they deal with are real and the actions they report are only those that could be proved in court.

Teachers of fiction define story as *struggle*. Call it conflict or merely action; the important thing is that something must happen. Without action, we have no story.

The simplest fiction plot involves one central character struggling to solve one basic problem. As the action (story) progresses, the character encounters obstacles which require further action. In a good plot, the protagonist may move two steps backward for each step forward. At any rate, he or she keeps moving, struggling against obstacles or opposing forces. Struggle is the essence, and the story ends when the protagonist wins, loses, or quits. The reader is interested as much in the struggle itself as in its outcome.

In fiction or drama, the conflict may be either internal or external. The central character may struggle against a personal foe, against the forces of nature, against society or some segment of it, or against his own selfish impulses. In sophisticated fiction, the opposing force is seldom personified. It is only a situation, with no heroes or villains, against which a fallible human being struggles. This is the brand of fiction that most closely resembles reality.

Fiction stories must include motivation and sequel—causes and effects. So should news stories. But perhaps the most important thing that reporters can learn from fiction is that all stories involve *people*—individually or in groups—in *action*. Events never happen in a vacuum. People are always involved in them, and—except for natural disasters—people usually cause them. The struggle may be anything but dramatic, the obstacles not even obvious, but struggles and obstacles are present in news as in fiction.

In its totality, news is the daily chronicle of mankind—people talking, arguing, fighting, trading, planning, building and destroying, winning and losing, making love and making war. It is the story of individuals and nations, humanity and inhumanity; and any definition that omits the human element misses the point entirely. All news concerns human beings. Even when a story is primarily about natural phenomena—storms, eclipses, droughts, floods, or earthquakes—we write about their effects on people or how people view them. We are human beings writing about human beings for human beings.

From all this, we can derive three rules for the beginning writer:

1. Put proper names into your story—names of individuals and organizations.
2. Use strong verbs—as strong as the action justifies.
3. Write mostly in the active voice, which stresses the actor. Most events don't just happen; people cause them.

Avoid Overdramatizing

Before you charge off in a cloud of purple prose, bent on turning every story into a drama, a word of caution. No story is more than an abstraction from reality. It is never life itself. Until it is written, it isn't even a story. It is merely an event, an idea, or a set of circumstances that becomes a story only through the reporter's perception and skill. And ethical reporters must always ask themselves whether they are seeing the "story" clearly and coolly or whether they are exaggerating the conflict and overdramatizing. Journalism has no place for the writer who "never lets facts stand in the way of a good story."

Life, unlike fiction, is seldom melodramatic. It has few clearly defined heroes or villains, and even those can't be labeled as such. They can be characterized only through fair, objective reporting of their deeds and words. The "villain" in real life is seldom an individual or even an identifiable group. More often it is a situation that has developed over such a long period that the early causative factors—and the persons responsible for them—have been long forgotten. Society itself—the circumstances under which it exists, its customs, and its restrictions—is at the root of many evils. Thus, the reporters who look for a specific culprit usually are either wasting their time or distorting reality.

Nor should the reporter seek out controversy. Like violence, controversy usually will make itself known. It is true, without *conflict* no story exists. But conflict doesn't necessarily imply either violence or controversy. For example, a scientist searching for a cure to cancer is engaged in a conflict—against the forces of nature and the frustration of failures. This is by no means a controversy. Even when a controversy exists, the reporter must take pains to avoid portraying a simple difference of opinion as a confrontation.

Other Storytelling Limitations

As tellers of stories, journalists have several limitations. They have neither the time nor the space to develop a story as thoroughly and "realistically" as the fiction writer. Much of the minor action and physical description the fiction writer uses to make a scene vivid must be omitted as unimportant; the reader of news is more interested in the outcome than in the events leading up to it. Therefore, reporters seldom tell the story chronologically. Instead of keeping the audience in suspense, they begin where fiction writers would end—with the climactic action and its net effect.

Nor do journalists have the fiction writer's freedom of expression. They can't comment on the action or enter the characters' minds. They write only what is said or done, not what a person thinks or feels, which means that they often must present action without fully explaining its motivation.

In fiction, the story usually ends when the protagonist wins, loses, or quits. In news, it's not that easy. First, we have no protagonist in the fiction sense, because reporters don't take sides. Second, there are few winners and few losers (except in the sports report), and sometimes you can't tell one from the other. Further, the action refuses to stop at a convenient place. Some human struggles seem to continue without end, and the only way journalists can approach the fiction writer's "satisfactory ending" is by quitting when they have presented all the facts available at the moment.

NEWS IS MORE THAN STORY

To the writer of fiction, the story is in a sense its own end. But to the journalist, the story is only a container, a form in which news is presented. And it is easier to define the container than its contents. People generally agree on what constitutes a story, but they differ widely over what constitutes news.

News must be timely, factual information which has some value to the reader or listener. It may be enlightening, instructive, or only entertaining. It may be only an interesting tidbit to store away in the mind, something that adds to a person's general knowledge, or it may be information that can be put to use immediately, such as announcements of future events. Regardless of its nature, it can be considered news only if the reader sees some benefit in it.

Indirectly, of course, the public may benefit from almost any current, factual information. The more a person knows, the more he or she can talk about. People who gossip know this instinctively. And some people—salesmen, politicians, and others whose success depends partly on conversational ability—approach the news consciously with the goal of having something to talk about. (Reporters, too, can benefit from this approach. If they are well informed in several news areas in addition to their own, they seldom lack an "ice-breaker" to open an interview.)

News has been defined as:

Anything you didn't know yesterday—If it doesn't somehow add to what you already know, it isn't news.

Whatever interests the reader—If it doesn't interest somebody, it's not news. On the other hand, some highly interesting information—gossip, for example—may not be news because it lacks significance.

Tomorrow's history today—This is a good definition of the outstanding stories and even of some less attention-getting stories that are laden with statistics. But it gives news more importance than the bulk of it deserves.

Any change in the status quo—This approach is based on the notion that something must happen, or there's no story.

The status quo itself—The prevailing situation, which the public may ignore or take for granted, can be important news when it is made visible and analyzed.

A timely, factual report of events, ideas, and situations that interest the public—This may be the best definition of all. It combines timeliness and audience interest, and it is slightly less vague about subject matter. And, unlike the other definitions, it says that news isn't news until it is reported.

The list could go on for several pages. But perhaps the best advice to beginners is that if it's timely, something the general public hasn't heard or noticed before, if it interests you or an identifiable portion of your audience, then it's news.

MANY PUBLICS, MOSTLY LOCAL

Telling a story implies an audience. Defining news—which is the content of the journalist's story—involves determining the relationship between events and the interests of your public. Thus the concepts of *story* and *news* are inseparable from an awareness of audience or reader.

You may dream of writing the Big Story that will be read by everyone in the world, but it's only a dream. Even the most important international stories reach only a fraction of the world's population. And usually reporters write for a far more limited audience: the readers, listeners, or viewers in a precisely defined geographical area. The newspaper or broadcast station's first goal is to serve its own trade area. Most stories, therefore, are primarily of local or regional interest. The community—its economy, geography, history, traditions, and ethnic composition—plays a large role in determining what constitutes news. For example, a story from Cuba presumably is more important to people in nearby Miami than it would be to Kansans. And a story from Oslo or Stockholm will attract more readers in Minneapolis, with that city's large population of Scandinavian descent, than it would in Houston, New Orleans, or Santa Fe. Similarly, a change in the price of gold automatically is top priority news in Lead, South Dakota, whose only industry is the Homestake Gold Mine. And the price of corn means more in Iowa than in California.

No community, of course, is an entirely homogeneous group of people. Instead, it consists of many small publics within the general public. Each of these special groups is united by a common bond of interest. And to build and hold mass circulation, newspapers must recognize the particular interests of each group—blue-collar workers, farmers, businessmen, the aged, ethnic minorities, the poor, sports fans, youth, housewives, parents of school children, the family and friends of the bride. Reporters soon learn to write for numerous publics with interests they may not share.

Interests Shared by All

Regardless of their different interests, all our readers and listeners are human beings, and they are alike in all ways that one human being is like another. No study of the reporter's audience is complete, therefore, without some examination of what writers call "the human condition."

Lawrence Durrell wrote four novels, known collectively as *The Alexandria Quartet,* in which he attempted to demonstrate that in the final analysis all things will be shown to be true of all people. Perhaps Durrell's is an overstatement, but psychologists agree that all humans *are* much alike, that they are both rational and emotional, that they live in a constant state of conflict between self and society, that they are always struggling to reduce the tension of this conflict. Humans are basically selfish, yearning for freedom yet realizing that without social order no individual can be free. They know they are mortal, that someday they must die, a truth against which they constantly rebel. Since they can't attain physical immortality, their alternative goal is to live as long and as well as they can. Most people want love and affection, recognition for their achievements, and status among their peers. All want to be healthy, and most want to prosper.

To summarize, all humans want a longer, healthier, and happier life both for themselves and their children, who may be their only ticket to immortality. And, perhaps unconsciously, they expect the media to supply information that will help them attain these goals. Primarily, people want stories that will:

1. *Warn of imminent physical danger*—an outbreak of war or local violence, an approaching storm, an epidemic, an unsafe product, or adulterated food.
2. *Report developments that promise to extend life*—a peace agreement, a medical discovery, improvements in hospital facilities, a new system of keeping physically fit.
3. *Expose threats to individual freedom*—political oppression, economic injustice, infringements of civil rights.
4. *Help them improve their economic or political position*—simple informative stories about business developments and the employment situation, or explanatory or even instructive stories about managing investments, preparing for retirement, juggling the family budget, or preparing the tax returns. A political or economic feature even may be a success story about a person the reader dreams of emulating.
5. *Describe improvements or deterioration in the quality of living*—urban decay, the crime rate, vanishing wildlife, advancements in housing and recreation, changing mores, improvements in clothing and cooking.
6. *Tell what is happening or is expected to happen to their children*—readers want to know what kind of world their children will live in and how educators are preparing them for it.

The Reporter as Watchdog

To help protect their audience, many reporters view their role as that of a public watchdog. They stand ready to detect and report anything dangerous to the public's physical, economic, or political security—a hazardous drug, unsafe toys, business collapses, waste of public funds, political blunders, pollution of the environment, racial discrimination, violence and injustices of many kinds. They try to provide information that will "keep the establishment honest."

Because of this watchdog function, the press often is criticized as a purveyor of only bad news. Yet without this "bad" news, how would the public be warned? How could the average person acquire the information he needs to act with enlightened self-interest? The thoughtful editor realizes that "bad" news is one of his more important commodities, that somehow he must keep the reader informed without becoming a chronic alarmist.

The first step toward balanced news judgment is to recognize that the press has a responsibility to report progress as well as threats. Arms limitations, cancer treatments, reduced taxes, and shorter work weeks are at least as important as the more depressing stories. Any event or situation that affects the reader's security in any manner, favorably or unfavorably, is top priority news.

Working Classifications

Not all stories deal with life, death, taxes, food, clothing, and shelter. And of those that do, not all are concerned with immediate action. Reporters write many "idea" stories about religion and philosophy which deal with universal interests but which are hardly "gut issues." In addition to such stories that appeal to the intellect, they write many that appeal largely to the readers' emotions—their vanity (they like to see their names in print), their curiosity about neighbors, their desire for a thrill, a shudder, or a laugh.

How can we classify such a wealth of subject matter with so many different goals? We could, perhaps, talk of "hard" news (that which is immediately useful) versus "soft" news (that which has delayed value). Or "spot" news (highly perishable because of the time element) versus "feature" copy (usable anytime this season). Or we could departmentalize news into sports, home and family, city, state, national, and international. Or we could distinguish between the investigative story, which can require weeks of digging, and the publicity release which arrives without any effort on the reporter's part. We could even classify stories by whether they deal with events, ideas, or situations, or by whether they are informative, explanatory, or entertaining.

Perhaps the wise course would be to avoid categorization completely. But to understand how professionals think, let's examine a classification system often used by working journalists. This divides stories into three categories: straight news, interpretation, and human interest. Like all classification, this system is arbitrary, artificial, and often difficult to apply. Indeed, it is a rare story of any length that is entirely "straight" with no interpretation or human interest. Nevertheless, these three categories are used so commonly that the beginner at least should be aware of them.

STRAIGHT NEWS

This often deals only with events. Straight news results from simple surveillance. Most routine stories—obituaries, meeting notices, traffic accidents, crime reports, and weather roundups—fall into this category. When city editors tells reporters to "play it straight," they mean to confine the story strictly to the facts and avoid any attempt to determine motivation or long-range consequences or arouse any emotional response in the reader. On most simple stories, reporters encounter no problem; they play it straight automatically. But on some sensitive developments, editors may have to warn them against interpretation because motivation or consequence can't be determined immediately or because of the danger of arousing violent public response. In reporting straight news, the reporter summarizes the action but takes special pains to avoid inferences, as in this example:

NEW YORK (Reuters)—The Franklin National Bank reported Sunday that it has incurred losses possibly reaching $25 million in foreign currency trading since March 31.

A bank spokesman said that, because of the losses, the bank has asked the Securities and Exchange Commission to briefly suspend trading in Franklin's securities.

Earlier Sunday the Federal Reserve Board in Washington had announced that it was prepared to advance funds to the bank. This followed an announcement on Friday by Franklin's holding company that it would recommend against declaring a regular quarterly dividend.

Franklin Chairman Hal V. Gleason Sunday announced plans to increase the bank's capital by $50 million through two offerings by Franklin New York Corp. to its shareholders, the first for $30 million and the second for the remainder at terms to be determined.

A spokesman for the New York-based bank—the nation's 20th largest—reported also that its foreign currency exchange department had incurred losses since March 31 of approximately $2 million.

"In addition it has recently been discovered that because of a trader in that department operating beyond his authority and without the bank's knowledge, it will have sustained losses as of May 12, 1974, of $12 million and has potential losses of $25 million at May 10, 1974, rates."

He added: "The appropriate authorities and the bank's insurance company have been notified and the bank believes that its insurance will provide coverage for a substantial portion of the loss."

Last month, Franklin National obtained a $30 million loan from the Manufacturers Hanover Trust Co. to increase its capital.

Notice that the reporter says nothing on his own authority in this example. He tells only what bank spokesmen and the Federal Reserve Board have announced.

INTERPRETATION

This is an effort to tell what the facts mean in terms of causes and effects. Even the word "interpretive" is enough to start a controversy in some newsrooms, where editors may argue long and inconclusively over the definition of objectivity. For this reason, many working journalists never speak of "interpretive" pieces. They call them "backgrounders," "situationers" or "depth reports," if only to avoid arguments.

Interpretation, by whatever name it goes, deals more often with situations and ideas than with isolated events. It is *explanatory* writing, usually arising from analytical coverage of government, the economy, education, or social problems. It requires expert knowledge of the subject and an imposing array of facts, plus the ability to put a complex situation or idea into simple, understandable language. Reporters try to tell what the facts mean without resorting to speculation. Occasionally, when the meaning isn't clear, reporters may be forced to quote the speculation of other observers. If so, they must know the subject well enough to pick sources who can speculate with some authority.

Here is an example of interpretation based on knowledge of background information—facts that have been published before:

ROME (Reuters)—Italians have voted overwhelmingly to maintain the three-year-old law instituting divorce here in a politically charged referendum.

Final returns gave the pro-divorce

forces 59.1 per cent of the ballots cast to the abolitionists' 40.9 per cent. The vote was 19,093,929 favoring divorce to 13,188,184 against.

A carnival atmosphere reigned in Rome, with crowds of divorce advocates parading through the streets, chanting "victory, victory."

The result is a serious defeat for Amintore Fanfani, secretary of the large Christian Democrat Party, who had promoted the referendum in the hope of uniting his Catholic-based party behind him and dealing a hard blow to the Communists, Italy's second major political force.

The Christian Democrats had led the fight to repeal the divorce law, and the Communists spearheaded the campaign to keep it.

The outcome is also a sharp blow for the Roman Catholic Church, which had told the predominantly Catholic 37 million voters that they were conscience-bound to vote to abolish divorce.

The scale of the pro-divorce victory was unexpected, although the figures confirmed the findings of public opinion polls. Few had expected that the church and the Christian Democrats who have led the country politically since World War II would not be able to sway Italians into at least a close vote.

Because the line between interpretation and editorializing is so fine, editors often discourage beginners from any attempt to "interpret." They prefer to assign interpretive stories to reporters who already have demonstrated the necessary knowledge, judgment, and skill to present interpretation fairly and clearly.

HUMAN INTEREST

In this kind of news, which usually focuses on an individual rather than a group, the actual subject is a feeling or an emotion. Writers, however, don't editorialize or express subjective reaction. They achieve their effect best by "putting the reader there," by showing the event or situation that arouses emotions or a sense of humor. This is sensory writing, close kin to fiction, and reporters often use narrative organization and other literary devices. They round out the story with color, description, anecdote, dramatic quotes, or dialogue; but as in any other reporting, they never go beyond the provable facts.

Many human interest stories focus on an odd or unusual event, as in this example:

> OKEECHOBEE, Fla. (UPI)—An 11-year-old boy, using a new "super-glue," accidentally glued his eye shut while building a model airplane, and a doctor had to reopen the eye surgically.
>
> Mike Harris said he rubbed his left eye after several drops of the glue squirted into it last Sunday and found his eyelids would not move.
>
> "I was scared at first because Daddy didn't believe me," Mike recalled today.
>
> Mike's father, Robert Harris, soon was convinced his son's eye was glued shut after a series of hot compresses failed to loosen the glue.
>
> Harris drove Mike to a local hospital, but was told no eye surgeon was available and to take Mike to Fort Lauderdale, 150 miles away.
>
> An eye surgeon in Fort Lauderdale debated briefly about using a super-glue solvent, but decided against it for fear it might damage the boy's eye.
>
> The surgeon finally put Mike in the operating room, trimmed Mike's eyelashes, then opened the eyelid surgically. Mike was released from the hospital yesterday.
>
> Mike's father said he had been told the glue, a chemical compound known as "cyanoacrylate," is used in Europe by surgeons in place of stitches, but is not approved for that use in American medical circles.

A story of this sort, if it had been written without names, probably would have been rejected. Newsreporters tend to be extremely skeptical about "great human interest" stories. The more they sound like good fiction, the more likely they are to *be* fiction.

Featurizing and the Feature Article

Every reporter likes to write the story that is thorough, satisfying, and interesting from beginning to end, the story that will still be usable next week or even next month because it has a semi-timeless quality. Stories of this sort, which must rely on something other than immediacy for their appeal, are known as feature articles. The subject may be anything—a person, an idea, a situation, a hobby, a process, or a historic anniversary. The purpose may be to inform, to explain, to instruct, or only to entertain. The only qualities that set the feature apart from other stories are its lack of immediacy and its depth treatment of an interesting or provocative subject. For good examples, see the inside pages of your Sunday newspaper.

A feature should have a "news peg"; that is, it should be related to a topic recently in the news. Sometimes the news peg is implicit; sometimes it is expressed clearly near the beginning. The "peg" is the writer's way of telling readers why the article is being published—why they should bother reading it. Often a feature may have no more news peg than the reader's assumed interest in a relatively current subject, as exemplified by this beginning:

> When a woman is granted a divorce, she not only loses her husband, but can lose her credit rating.
>
> In many instances a divorced woman has a rude awakening when she goes to a store to buy something on credit and is told that her credit is limited because she now is divorced.

The rest of the story quotes businessmen, a banker, a lawyer, and several women on the divorcee's plight. At no point does it cite the date of any specific action. It appears, therefore, that it could have been written several weeks before publication.

Although human interest is not an absolute requirement, most effective features contain a considerable amount. The reason is simple: human interest, expressed in color, description, anecdote, and dialogue, is a proven means of keeping the reader's attention throughout a long story. This aspect of most features has caused some confusion in terminology. When editors tell reporters to "featurize" a spot news story, they usually mean to play up the human interest, to focus on whatever is amusing, odd, or unusual. They seldom mean to turn it into a genuine depth article.

THE CLASSIC YARDSTICKS

All news judgments are relative. Whenever editors say "This is news," they mean "for this newspaper in this community today." Tomorrow the story may be dead because it has lost its timeliness.

Or it may be crowded out of the paper by stories of greater significance. We can never judge a news story except in relation to other stories at the same moment.

Even then, the evaluation of news is a highly subjective process. One editor may view the events of the day in the broad context of world history while another hews to the old-fashioned notion that "a dog fight on Main Street is worth more than a revolution in Latin America." The first accuses the other of provincialism; the second retorts that the first is guilty of afghanistanism. Editors are no more agreed on news value than are readers.

Still, no matter how they apply them, all editors measure news values by the same yardsticks. These are:

Significance—whether the event promises or threatens to change the course of history. An event's significance is determined by how many persons it will affect, to what extent, and for how long. The reporter asks *what will be the consequences.*

Magnitude—how much, how many, how big, how fast. Everything else being equal, a million is bigger news than a thousand. A plane crash that kills 120 is bigger news than one that kills five, and a hurricane with 200-mile-an-hour winds is bigger news than one that barely qualifies. The reporter asks *how many are dead* and *how much will it cost.*

Timeliness—the reader wants information that's new. The reporter asks *when did it happen,* and ordinarily tries to work the day into the first sentence to let the reader know that it's new. Priority usually goes to the latest action, but even an action that happened long ago may still be spot news if it is only now being disclosed. For example, any new information about Noah's Ark would be news.

Proximity—a two-dollar word for the local angle. If all else is equal, here is greater than there. Readers are interested most in those events closest to them. The reporter asks *where.*

Prominence—names make news. These are generally names of persons or institutions that already have aroused public interest. The name might be that of the president or a senator, a celebrity in sports or show business, or an institution such as Harvard, the U.S. Marine Corps, or the Central Intelligence Agency. The reporter asks *who.*

Human Interest—a quality that every reader can relate to personal experience or recognize as a universal aspect of life. Does the story hit home? Here the reporter can examine only his or her own reaction.

To observe how significance, magnitude, timeliness, and proximity are woven together, examine this portion of a story from the *Kansas City Star:*

A program to reach and feed the elderly of metropolitan Kansas City—including nearly 10,000 in Platte, Clay and Jackson counties—will be mapped out by a special task force on the aging in its first meeting next month.

The task force, appointed by the new Metropolitan Commission on the Aging, will tackle the problem of nutritional needs of the 142,000 persons over 65 years of age who live in Clay, Jackson and Platte counties and Kansas City. It will be the beginning of what officials say is the first coordinated project to find and serve the aged, many of whom are isolated and live alone in this area.

Jim Bergfalk, an administrative assistant for the Jackson County Court, said the 35-member task force "will be called together within the next three weeks and immediately expanded to include representatives from Platte and Clay counties."

"We need to pull everyone together in a united form," Bergfalk said. "Our goal is to break down the isolation of the elderly in our society and we'll use hot meals as a means to do it."

He said the task force will outline an extensive program of how to feed the elderly, probably using a volunteer organization, and then seek more than $500,000 under a $100-million nutrition program passed by Congress.

Bergfalk said about $2.5 million had been allocated for Missouri and that Kansas City could expect to receive $500,000 to $600,000.

He estimated that based on the 1970 census, one-fourth of the 10,000 elderly in Platte and Clay were living alone.

Clay County has 7,530 persons who are 65 years or older. Platte County has 2,275. In Platte the elderly constitute 7 per cent of the total population. In Clay the figure is 6 per cent. That is considerably under

> Jackson County, where the aged make up 11 per cent of the population, and Kansas City, where the percentage is about 12.

Notice how important numbers are in expressing both the magnitude and the significance of this story.

CONCLUSION

If we were reduced to only one yardstick for measuring the news value of an event, idea, or situation, whatever the medium we're working with, it would have to be *audience involvement*. Did the reader or listener participate physically in the action? Did he observe it? Does he know somebody who did? Will he be affected by it? Will he be involved emotionally if we report it? Can he use the information? Will it cause him to think? Unless he can answer "yes" to at least one of those questions, the story has no value to that particular person.

To present news in story form, beginners should investigate causes and effects, personal motivation, problems, complications, and solutions. And they should never forget that all stories, no matter how undramatic they may be, involve actors and actions.

SUGGESTED ASSIGNMENTS

1. Clip 10 stories from a daily newspaper. Paste each story to a separate sheet of paper and answer these questions about it:
   a. Who are the actors and what is the action?
   b. What kind of story—straight news, interpretive, or human interest—is this?
   c. Which of the classic yardsticks make it newsworthy?
   d. Who will read it? How will they be involved? How will they benefit?
   e. Does it answer all the questions the reader might be expected to ask? If not, what information is missing?
   f. What or who is the source of the information?
   g. Does the story suggest a later follow-up on the same subject? If so, what should be the angle to take in the later story?

CHAPTER THREE / ANALYZING THE COMPONENTS

As you gather and organize facts, bear in mind Kipling's famous rhyme:

> I keep six honest serving men
> (They taught me all I knew)
> Their names are *what* and *why* and *when*
> And *how* and *where* and *who*.

These are the components of every news story, the raw material you must collect, interpret, organize, and transmit. On the surface, they may seem simple, merely a list of the questions an inquisitive child might ask about almost anything. But they are precisely the questions many people stop asking when they outgrow childhood. And they are not as simple as they first appear. Getting the five W's and H accurately and completely is a daily difficulty. Learning to express them clearly, gracefully, and objectively can be a lifelong project.

The purpose of this chapter is to refine your understanding of Kipling's components. To do this, we must examine attribution, identification, backgrounding, motivation, consequence, descriptive detail, style, and word usage—everything a reporter puts into a story. For some of these subjects, this chapter can serve only as an introduction to be expanded in later chapters.

WHAT'S HAPPENING? AND SO WHAT?

"Let's see what's happening in the world today . . ." With these words, millions of readers pick up their newspapers each day expecting to find the answer—not everything that happened, of course, but everything of interest to them. And they expect the reporter to provide the answer as quickly as possible in each story, preferably in the first dozen words, as in this example:

> SAIGON—The last American combat troops left South Vietnam today.

What happened or *what is scheduled to happen* is the essence of the story, the central fact that gives it unity. And this is how most news stories begin. We satisfy the reader's curiosity and establish the story's point in the first sentence:

> *WHAT HAPPENED:* DALLAS—President John F. Kennedy was shot and killed today by a hidden assassin armed with a high-powered rifle.

> *WHAT'S SCHEDULED:* WASHINGTON—Live television coverage is scheduled for Thursday night when Nelson A. Rockefeller is expected to be sworn in as the nation's 41st vice-president.

Theoretically, the introduction (known as the *lead*) can be built around any of Kipling's serving men. But in practice, most stories focus immediately on *what* or *who,* the action or the person or group involved. And usually the action is the more important. The simple lead usually focuses on the significance or magnitude of a specific action—the most important thing that happened, plus what it means to the reader. The reporter anticipates the reader's "So what?":

> A new postal regulation could cost taxpayers money if its violators aren't informed soon, says a Lincoln postal official.
> On Nov. 18, the U.S. Post Office stopped delivering letters without postage. Instead, the letters are returned to the sender or channeled to the dead letter office.
> However, the increase in volume of dead letters may offset the regulation's worth, said Bob Wittstruck, customer relations supervisor at the main post office. He said the increased cost of handling eventually will be passed on to taxpayers through increases in taxes or postal rates.

The lead paragraph traditionally is only a single sentence, although exceptions are common. The idea is to make a point in the

first sentence, then expand upon it throughout the story. The point—
the most important action and its significance—usually is summarized
in a simple, declarative sentence of fewer than 25 words.

The lead usually makes a positive statement. The story is seldom
concerned with a *lack* of action (if nothing happens, usually there's
no story), nor is it often concerned with *routine* activities. An organization's day-to-day functions, for example, seldom constitute news;
the reader can legitimately ask "So what?" or "Who cares?"

> *NEGATIVE:* Storm clouds of partisan fervor *don't seem*
> *to be rising* over the State Capitol after
> a proposal to operate the Legislature
> along party lines.
>
> *POSITIVE:* Statehouse sources *indicated little support* to-
> day for a plan to reorganize the Legisla-
> ture along party lines.
>
> *WHO CARES?:* The Baptist Women's Society met Thurs-
> day afternoon at the home of Mrs. Fred
> Winter.
>
> *SLIGHTLY BETTER:* Bandages supplied by the Baptist
> Women's Society have been sent to for-
> eign missions, members of the organiza-
> tion were told Thursday.

Emphasis on newsworthy action continues throughout the story.
And action is expressed in verbs, which is why Stanley Walker, city
editor of the old New York *Herald-Tribune,* urged reporters to "give
me the verbs—the little verbs that cut and whip and leap and soar."
He could hardly have picked shorter, livelier examples. He might
have added, however, that cutting and whipping don't happen by
themselves; somebody causes them. Each action requires an actor.
And to make the sentence active, place the actor before the verb; tell
who or what cuts or whips, leaps, or soars. For example:

> *PASSIVE:* It is hoped that construction can be started by
> September.
>
> *ACTIVE:* Jones said he hoped *the firm* can start construc-
> tion by September.

Despite editors' preference for active voice, a passive lead sentence sometimes is more successful in getting the reader's attention
if it places the most important action closer to the beginning of the
sentence. This is often accomplished by construction that places the
source of the information at the end. For example:

> *ACTIVE:* According to Sen. John O'Malley, the govern-
> ment today awarded a $5-million contract
> for a new post office in Pumpkin Corners.

> *PASSIVE, BUT MORE EFFECTIVE:* A $5-million contract has been awarded for a new post office in Pumpkin Corners, Sen. John O'Malley announced today.

The rule is to place the most important information at the beginning of the lead. In the example above, the contract award is more important than either the person who announced it or the party who made the award.

"What Happened" May Be Words

Action, of course, can be either physical or mental. We can tell what a person or group did or how people were physically affected by something that happened. Often, however, mental actions—what people think, feel, or believe, their ideas, imaginings, or illusions—are more important in the long run than immediate physical action. Obviously, a reporter's only access to this kind of action is through what is said or written. The "what" of many stories, then, will be what a person or group *said*—an idea, a proposal, an expression of opinion, or a report of scientific findings. A few examples:

> WASHINGTON—The possibility that Greece or Turkey might seize American tactical nuclear weapons based on their territory and risk an atomic war over their Cyprus dispute is being raised by Sen. Stuart Symington, D-Mo.

> WASHINGTON—A staff report by the U.S. Commission on Civil Rights strongly endorses increased busing as a necessary tool for dismantling segregated northern school districts.

> State Democrats say the veto-proof Congress is a figment of somebody's imagnation.
> Democratic Gov. J. James Exon said there is no such thing as a veto-proof Congress because party members seldom vote together.

> A proposed merger of city and county law enforcement has hit an early snag.
> Sheriff Merle Karnopp says he "unalterably opposes" a plan that would extend police patrolling and criminal investigation outside the city, now duties of the sheriff's office.

Reporters sometimes are accused of paying too much attention to what persons say and not enough to what they do. This is particularly true in coverage of politics and business, areas in which actions may contradict public statements. Too often a newswriter reports a speaker's words accurately without taking the time to determine whether they are true. And a cynical reader learns to dismiss many such stories as "only words."

Yet words can be important news, *even when they are false.* History and social psychology demonstrate that what people say and write, their symbolic actions, often are the most important things they do. Words can start or end wars and perhaps be a major factor in turning defeat into victory, as exemplified in the careers of Hitler, Churchill, and Franklin Roosevelt. True or false, wise or foolish, words are deeds, and generally the reporter must regard them as a powerful form of action. Often false or foolish words are reported mainly for what they tell about the person who uttered them.

The problem lies in determining which words are worth reporting. This becomes a never ending exercise in judgment, with no absolute rules to guide you. But we can speculate that words are worth reporting when:

1. They add something new to man's total knowledge.
2. They come from an expert on the subject or a person with access to important facts.
3. They come from a person of political or economic power capable of translating words into action.
4. They express the opinion of a significant number of people.

In summary, the news value of words often depends as much on who says them as on the words themselves. The reporter considers the source: Is he or she an expert? A person in a position of power? One with access to the facts? Does the individual represent the consensus of a large group? How reliable has the person been in the past? What, if anything, does he or she have to gain by these remarks?

If we apply these yardsticks to two prominent news sources of this century, Ralph Nader and Wisconsin's Senator Joseph McCarthy, we can see how difficult it becomes to determine what constitutes legitimate news. Many liberal editors (and others) have denounced the press for reporting at face value McCarthy's irresponsible charges of Communist infiltration of the State Department in the early 1950s. Reporters should have investigated the truth behind the words, they say, or at least delayed reporting the charges until they could be answered. This is valid criticism. Words presented as fact should always be investigated. Yet some of the same critics had no qualms about reporting Ralph Nader's attacks on various industries and bureaucracies in the 1960s and 1970s, and few bothered to investigate his allegations.

Just as McCarthy did, Nader often dealt in hyperbole. Many of Nader's early charges were well documented and later substantiated. But others were not. Unlike McCarthy, Nader was hardly able to translate words into action—at least, not at the beginning. Nor could he be expected to have as much access to factual information as a United States senator has. His reliability, when he first collided with General Motors over the safety of the Corvair, was untested. Why, then, were Nader's words accepted with so little question?

Perhaps the best explanation is that most editors perceived Nader as having nothing to gain personally by his allegations, whereas McCarthy potentially had the presidency of the United States to gain. Nader's apparent lack of self-interest was his best recommendation. His later record of reliability, although far from 100 percent, was sufficient to enhance his stature.

No matter how reliable a news source may be, much of what is said must be evaluated carefully. The simple fact that the source is speaking for publication will influence both what is said and how it is said. If the person is talking about himself, for example, he will normally portray his actions favorably. This is a distorting factor which reporters can mitigate by careful selection and paraphrase. Also they must consider which of the facts and opinions expressed are of interest to readers—as well as to the speaker. Instead of reporting direct quotations, reporters more often summarize the speaker's thoughts in their own words, a technique that enables them to eliminate the irrelevant or prejudicial. But in selecting, summarizing, paraphrasing, or even quoting the speaker directly, reporters constantly must guard against distortion of the original meaning, tone, or emphasis of the remarks being reported.

WHO: IDENTIFICATION AND ATTRIBUTION

Every person mentioned in a news story must be identified clearly and adequately. At the minimum, this means first and last names, role in the news, title or occupation, and sometimes age and address. Reporters collect much of the same personal information that is required on a job application. Whenever possible, they get it directly from the person they are identifying, but they also make extensive use of directories, clipping files, and secondary personal sources.

Reporters use the term "identification" as much as law enforcement officers do. In this sense, identification means supplying enough factual information about a person to differentiate him from any other person with the same name. We can't, for example, identify a person as "Ole Olson of Minneapolis" (Minneapolis has at least two). We must tell where where Ole works or where he lives, how old he is, or whatever else is necessary to present him as a unique human being. We try to write about individual persons, rather than meaningless names or labels. Reciting professional credentials is often necessary to indicate why the person is being named.

The beginner can best learn the common methods of identification by reading obituaries, personality profiles, and police stories. Each of these requires thorough identification and each approaches the problem in a slightly different way.

The only news in an *obituary* is the fact of death and when and where the funeral services will be held. Otherwise, the entire story is identification. We give the person's name, age, address, and occupation; relationship to others; education; civic, fraternal, and professional membership; and especially his or her achievements. We identify persons by everything important they have done and when and where they did it. The more obvious means of identification that are likely to be omitted from the ordinary obituary are criminal convictions and physical description. But even these appear in obituaries of prominent persons. The most common sources for the items in an obituary are the funeral director and biographical files. An example of a routine obituary:

> Services for Mrs. Ruth T. Freund, 71, will be held at 1 p.m. Thursday at the Harris Funeral Home, 1471 West McNichols. Mrs. Freund died Monday in the Arnold Home.
>
> A lifelong resident of Detroit, she taught English in the Detroit school system for 35 years until her retirement. Her career included many years at Cass Technical School. She was the widow of Dr. Hugo A. Freund.
>
> Surviving are a brother, Carl M. Taylor, and a sister, Mrs. Grace Redding. Burial will be in White Chapel Cemetery, Troy.

Minor details of identification that appear in the obituary are likely to be ignored in the *personality sketch*. In this form the writer tries to portray the subject as a living human being, showing him or her in some newsworthy light. This usually requires at least minimal physical description and considerable direct quotation. We bring people to life by showing what they do and telling what they say, characterizing them by their opinions, activities, and habits of speech

and gesture. The techniques are well illustrated in this portion of a
student's prize-winning story:

By IVY HARPER

RAPID CITY, S.D.—A smile softens
George McGovern's face. The Hot
Springs Elks Club organist recognizes
him—the balding, slender candidate for
re-election to the U.S. Senate—and strikes
up McGovern's theme, "This Land Is
Your Land."

People at the bar turn in their chairs
and stare, but no one moves.

McGovern approaches his fellow South
Dakotans one by one and puts out his
hand.

"That time of year again, George," a
man yells.

McGovern laughs, and for a moment,
the sound of his laughter blending with
the theme song recalls a night more than
two years before. July 12, 1972, was a
night of triumph, victory at the Democratic convention, of national attention
and of hundreds of cheering workers sing-
ing the tune now being played in a tiny
South Dakota bar,

McGovern moves through the crowd.
A birthday group starts a hip-hip-hooray-
for-McGovern chant, and the chant
spreads.

In the fall of 1972, such a friendly
scene would have been unlikely. On Nov.
7 of that year McGovern learned that
even the voters of his native state had rejected him in his defeat by Richard
Nixon.

"Losing my own state was the most
difficult thing for me to accept in 1972,"
McGovern says today. "I have always felt
that I understand the people in this part
of the country, and it was painful not to
have them understand me."

Today, few reporters trail him. His
campaign trips are as likely to be by
car as by jet. There is no massive campaign staff, no TV crews.

At first, McGovern says, he missed the
national attention, "but that has long

since gone."

"I don't miss the television cameras—they always got in the way so that I couldn't talk to the people on a one-to-one basis," he says. "I have enjoyed this campaign."

And although a Senate campaign in South Dakota is tiring, the pace is considerably slower than a presidential race.

"I like a relaxed campaign," McGovern says.

And that's the way it is. No big advertising campaigns, no advance men (South Dakotans would resent planned events, McGovern says), no movie stars ("We've managed to keep Shirley MacLaine out so far," one aide said).

It's just McGovern casually walking down the main streets, dropping in at grocery stores, bowling alleys, American Legion halls, trying to persuade the voters to return him to Washington and to reject his Republican opponent, ex-Vietnam prisoner of war Leo Thorsness.

McGovern today is the same man who stumped the nation in 1972. His hair is shorter, he is less tanned and a little thinner. But he says his positions on the issues are the same.

The safest position on identification is that it's always better to have too much, rather than not enough. This is particularly true of *police news* or other stories that involve the possibility of defamation. Identification is an important element in libel law, and the reporter can't afford to make a mistake or even to be ambiguous. We must make certain that the identification is clear, that nobody else by the same name could argue that he has been defamed.

Here is a typical example of identification, properly attributed to the police, in an arrest story:

A 34-year-old unemployed securities salesman was arrested today and charged with murder in the shooting of broker Franklin Smith.

Police identified the suspect as Arthur Jones, 2212 N. Oak Ave. Jones had worked for Smith's brokerage firm until last August.

> Detectives arrested the lanky, balding suspect at the Municipal Airport as he was preparing to board a commercial airliner for a flight to Los Angeles.

Note that the first mention identifies the suspect only by age and occupation. This is a technique commonly used in the lead to avoid starting the story with an unfamiliar name. But it is far too general; in a city of any size, several 34-year-old securities salesmen are likely to be unemployed at any particular moment. Therefore we name the suspect and give his address in the second paragraph. This pins him down much closer. But on the off chance that two Arthur Joneses of the same age live at the same address, we further identify the suspect as the Arthur Jones who once worked for the victim—a fact that of course contributes to the story in other ways as well. Then, to help eliminate any remaining doubt, we include physical description and the circumstances of the arrest.

Notice also in the arrest story that the suspect's name is attributed to police. Reporters customarily use this protective device because suspects frequently give false names—or police make errors in relaying them to the press. A further protection required in many newsrooms is the inclusion of the middle initial in all men's names, no matter what the story. By requiring the middle initial, the city editor usually forces the reporter to use a directory and check the spelling and address as well.

Special Problems

Identification of women has long posed special problems. It probably will continue to do so as long as women change their names when they marry—and refuse to give their correct ages when arrested. At this writing, most newspapers identify women by both sex and marital status, neither of which is explicit in the identification of men. Many women object to this practice as discriminatory, and rules have been modified in several newsrooms. Some have adopted "Ms." for all women, regardless of marital status. Many more, however, have decided to honor the individual's preference.

The most common styles for identification of women:

Married or Widowed—First mention, Mrs. Samuel Jones; subsequent reference, Mrs. Jones. A married woman always is identified by her husband's first name. If widowed, technically she remains Mrs. Samuel Jones until she remarries. Strict adherence to this rule creates three problems: (1) The rule may conflict with a widow's personal preference (or, for that matter, the personal preference of more and more married women), (2) in reporting club news, the source of the information may not know the name of some woman's husband—or even be certain whether she is married, and (3) police seldom include marital status in routine reporting forms and they use the woman's first name, not her husband's, if she is married.

Divorced—First mention, Mrs. Shirley Smith; subsequent reference, Mrs. Smith. The divorcee is identified by her own first name. Again, this is a rule which often is modified to follow personal preference.

Unmarried—First mention, Anne Johnson; subsequent reference, Miss Johnson. The "Miss" is omitted on first mention. This rule may create problems with elderly spinsters, some of whom still regard their single status as a stigma or at least a social handicap. It also raises the question of the minimum age a girl must attain to qualify for the title. Practice often varies considerably within a single newspaper. A girl of 14 seldom is "Miss" in the general news columns, but a flower girl of 5 often receives the title in a wedding story. To most editors, a girl becomes "Miss" at 17 or 18, the age at which she usually ceases to be subject to juvenile laws.

Male teenagers present another problem. At what age does a boy become a man? Editors once were guided by the legal voting age, but that was when the age was 21. Now the law has created a no-man's-land. A person may vote at 18, but in many states the unmarried male remains a legal infant until 21—unable to buy liquor, not responsible for debts, still subject to juvenile courts. A 19-year-old male often can be referred to only as "a youth," no matter how editors despise the term.

"Youth" is only one of the age bracket tags editors attempt to avoid. Others are *oldster, senior citizen, middle-aged, tot, toddler,* and *youngster.* Such tags are both trite and imprecise. Whenever age is an important factor in identification, the reporter should get the exact number of years.

Children normally are identified on first mention by first and last name and exact age. On subsequent reference, only the first name is used. Occasionally a first name may be one that is used by either sex—for example, Shirley, Leslie, Dale, Val, or Joyce—but the reporter usually can avoid confusion by immediate use of "he" or "she." Children also are normally identified as the son or daughter of "Mr. and Mrs. Robert Smith of 1532 Camden Drive," which further helps avoid confusion.

A story that focuses on one individual may require so much identification that it amounts to a small biography. When this happens, reporters face a problem of placement. Should they interrupt the narration near the beginning with a capsule biography of three or four sentences? Or should they spread out the information through several paragraphs by using appositives? The answer depends on how much information is necessary. The greater the amount, the more likely it should be spread out.

Pitfalls of Identification

In their haste to identify individuals, reporters often distort stories by the way they use labels. These may be titles *(Dr., Col.)*, common nouns of occupation *(salesman, banker, dishwasher)*, or adjectives *(blond, black, conservative, radical)*. Some such labels are unavoidable; without them, the story would lack meaning. But they always must be used with discretion. The reporter not only must make certain that the label is accurate, but he also must determine (1) whether it reflects adversely on the individual, (2) whether it reflects adversely on some larger group, and (3) whether it is pertinent to this particular story.

At worst the labeling noun can be libelous. Any identification that imputes crime or moral turpitude is libelous *per se* and must be avoided unless the newsgathering organization is prepared to defend it. Tags of this kind include *killer, prostitute, thief, black-mailer, traitor, racketeer, lecher,* and *deadbeat.* Luckily, most journalists are aware of the danger in name-calling at this level. They avoid such tags entirely unless a person has been convicted of the specific crime. And even after conviction, the tag must be approached with caution. How many persons must an individual kill before we are justified in calling him a killer? How much, and how often, must a person steal before we can call him a thief?

Name-calling is easy to avoid. A more difficult problem, however, is the subtle stereotyping that may result when we classify a wrong-doer as a *black militant,* a *veteran,* a *student activist,* a *draft protester,* or even an *unemployed dishwasher.* By implication we may be convicting the group as well as the individual. Is it important to the story to give the person's race or occupation? Somtimes yes, sometimes no. In any case, however, we can't assume that all blacks are militants nor that all students are activists. Nor can we assume that all black militants or student activists are wrongdoers.

Another common danger is the adjective of inference. Examples include *conservative, reactionary, liberal, radical, outspoken, boisterous, modest, shy, beautiful,* and *rugged.* Each of these adjectives involves a subjective evaluation by the writer. The traits they suggest have been inferred, a process that must be classified as editorializing.

With rare exceptions, such adjectives should be eliminated from all news copy.

Even the concrete descriptive adjective in identification can cause trouble. Is it important that a defendant is long-haired and pimply-faced? Or is it irrelevant and potentially prejudicial? Some editors avoid the issue by eliminating virtually all adjectives, objective or otherwise, in every story. This is an extreme position which leads to dull, lifeless copy, but in certain sensitive stories it is perhaps the best approach. In handling adjectives, the reporter must be guided by his subject matter.

The subject of the story—the nature of the action—also influences identification by title. A professor, military officer, or medical doctor may trade on his title to gain public acceptance for views totally unrelated to his field of expertise. For example, a physician who is also a city councilman may express opinions on a proposed ordinance that has nothing to do with medicine. Because he is a councilman, his views are legitimate news. But should he be identified as "Dr."? Some editors say no; others are willing to accord him the title on first mention, then drop it thereafter. Perhaps the best way is to identify him only as a councilman, the role in which he is speaking.

Identifying Organizations and Concepts

Organizations, like individuals, must be identified sufficiently to make them understandable to the reader. At the lowest level, this requires spelling out the names of "alphabet" agencies on first mention (United Nations, Rural Electrification Administration, Railway Express Agency, Rodeo Cowboys Association, Radio Corporation of America, Federal Housing Administration, Future Homemakers of America). One reason for this will be obvious to the careful reader: some organizations share the same initial letters.

Merely giving the name, however, often isn't enough. Proper nouns tell us very little. What is the purpose of this agency or organization? How does it function? How is it financed? Who is in charge? Who are the members? What are their views? Who influences them? Many stories do little more than answer these questions in detail about organizations that the average person reads about daily but never really understands. The reader recognizes a familiar name and often curiosity ends at that point. Investigative reporters dig beneath the noun to get at the verb. They are interested more in what the organization *does* than in what it is called.

An organization is nothing more than a group of persons united in a common activity. A simple appositive phrase or nonrestrictive clause is often sufficient to identify an organization by its activity, its membership, or both. For example:

> The Black Hills, Badlands and Lakes Association, which promotes tourism in South Dakota, . . .

> The Rural Electrification Administration, which lends money at low interest to rural power cooperatives, . . .

Every reporter quickly discovers that many organizations are not all they appear to be. Some espouse one purpose but practice another. Often their goals can be clarified only by a careful study of the individuals who compose their leadership. Other organizations exist primarily on paper. They have an imposing letterhead and an impressive list of officers—who may never have met. Such "organizations" may consist only of a file folder at the back of some person's desk drawer. Before a reporter accepts a news release from any organization, he or she should at least verify its existence and determine its goals.

Abstract concepts are difficult to identify for the same basic reasons that organizations are. In each instance, something complex has been reduced to a label which robs it of meaning. We categorize an activity or an idea by giving it a name, tell ourselves that we understand it, then quickly forget everything but the label. This is a form of mental shorthand that is sometimes helpful but often crippling. If reporters expect to convey meaning clearly, they must frequently look at the contents behind the label.

Some concepts have a relatively specific meaning. Parity, for example, was routinely defined for years by the Associated Press as "a price calculated to give the farmer a fair return on his products in terms of prices he must pay." (One might argue that this is an inadequate explanation, but the AP at least recognized that some explanation was necessary.) The theory of relativity, too, can be defined, although an adequate definition might take several pages.

More abstract concepts—democracy, communism, human rights, dignity of man—have only whatever meaning the user chooses to give them. As a reporter, you should avoid them, except when you are forced to use them in direct quotations. When news sources begin speaking in such vague abstractions, try to bring them back to earth by asking for concrete examples. Then, when you write the story, you can ignore the abstractions and focus on something tangible.

Who Says: Attribution

The body of a news story consists of attributed and documented detail which adds up to, and expands upon, the lead's opening statement. Essentially, reporters show the reader fact after fact and where they got them. Because they must present much information on some authority other than personal knowledge, reporters are constantly telling the reader "who says." They attribute the information to its source, either explicitly or by implication. This gives authority for reporting any event which a reporter didn't personally witness, any fact which isn't already accepted as common knowledge or easily verifiable from public records. And opinion always must be attributed. This means that in speech stories and others dealing largely with opinion and unsubstantiated declarations, almost every sentence must contain some version of "he said."

The primary reason for attribution is fair play. Readers are justified in asking where the information came from so that they can judge its value according to their perception of the source's expertise or proven reliability. Like the reporter, the reader considers the source. And for this reason reporters often attribute information to a source with high credibility even when they could present it on their own authority. They know the reader will be more likely to believe the information when it comes from a person in a position to know.

Reporters also attribute much information to persons simply to keep their channels open. The policeman or minor public official who sees his name in the paper will be more likely to cooperate with the reporter than will the person who is ignored. The wise reporter often tells "who says" even when it isn't necessary.

Attribution soon becomes automatic. But to beginners, it's usually a headache. Until they learn to separate fact from hearsay and opinion, and until they develop a richer vocabulary, beginners are likely to (1) attribute too little, (2) attribute too much, (3) put the attribution in an awkward place, either stopping the reader's train of thought or leaving him in doubt about who is speaking, or (4) bore the reader with sentence after sentence that ends with "he said."

An example of overattribution:

> SIOUX FALLS, S.D. (AP)—The Big Sioux River was fast approaching flood stage today, *the U.S. Weather Bureau reported.*

Because of the attribution, a reader might wonder whether there is some doubt about the situation. If any person wandering past can see that the river is high, the reporter needn't attribute that fact. On the other hand, the river's *exact* height definitely should be attributed to the agency that measured it.

If professionals are overly cautious about attribution, beginners more often err in the other direction. Students often attribute the first few sentences of a speech or interview, then forget attribution for the rest of the story. Unless the reporter knows that the source is presenting fact, each sentence must be attributed.

Specifically, what *must* be attributed? Even professionals disagree, so it's impossible to lay down an all-inclusive list, but these guidelines may help:

1. *All direct quotations*—Unlike the fiction writer, the journalist avoids "orphan quotes." He attributes every direct quotation clearly, usually at the first natural pause, so that the reader has no doubt about who is speaking.
2. *All statements of opinion*—This applies whether they are quoted directly or paraphrased.
3. *Any potentially defamatory statement which libel law allows newspapers to publish in the public interest*—This applies primarily to testimony in court or statements made by congressmen or legislators on the floor of their legislative houses.
4. *Anything newsworthy that a public speaker or interviewee says*—There may be an exception to this rule if the speaker is merely recounting background information which either is generally accepted as fact or easily verifiable from other sources.
5. *Anything obtained from another periodical publication*—Newsmen in all media frequently quote *The Congressional Record, Congressional Quarterly, Jane's Fighting Ships,* the *Scientific American,* the *National Geographic,* and many newspapers, especially *The New York Times.* Even when the publication or the individual story isn't copyrighted, professional courtesy requires attribution. If the information is spot news, the reporter should attempt to verify it. If it can't be verified, the reporter still may use information from a reliable publication if it is attributed.

Although reporters tend to think of attribution as a protective device, it is no protection by itself in a libel suit. If a public speaker commits slander (oral defamation), the newspaper commits libel (published defamation) if it quotes him. The speaker, the publisher, and everyone who handles the story is legally liable. As a matter of practice, usually only the publisher is sued for damages. Reporters may lose nothing but their jobs—and the chances of getting another.

WHEN: IN ONE SENSE, ALWAYS IN THE PAST

All stories are based on knowledge of past action, even when they concern future events. This is because nobody can predict the future with any degree of confidence. Astronomers, political scientists, and economists may *try* (always based on their knowledge of the past), but their best calculations could be wiped out at any moment by a nuclear accident. With this pessimistic possibility in mind, journalists seldom attempt to predict the future without considerable qualification.

Reporters know they can't say for certain what will happen tomorrow or even what will be happening at the moment the reader sees a story. Therefore, they write most stories in the past tense or the past participle. Instead of writing that "the President will meet the press Tuesday," they write that "the President *has scheduled* a press conference for Tuesday." The President may change his mind or die of a heart attack, or the press may decide to ignore him. None of these events may be likely, but reporters can't be sure. They play safe by putting the story in the past.

One dependable way of putting the future into past tense is to add attribution. For example, instead of writing only that "Construction of a new crosstown expressway will begin next week," the reporter adds "Highway Director Sam Johnson announced today." If construction *doesn't* start, we can then blame Johnson. We didn't say it *would* start, only that Johnson *said* it would start.

Reporters who do not understand the reasoning behind editors' insistence on the past tense may produce awkward and illogical sentences. Thinking (wrongly) that *every* verb must be past tense, a reporter may write:

> Sampson said he thought the war was immoral.

The meaning more likely is:

> Sampson said he *thinks* the war *is* immoral.

(If, of course, the war continues and Sampson survives until press time.) Most of the time, we can assume that any expression of opinion should be put into present tense. Persons who voice opinions seldom change them overnight.

In practice, the general rule of writing mostly in the past tense is often ignored. But the reporter who is devoted to accuracy will be careful when and how the rule is violated. He or she will tell the reader only what is known for certain—and that is never more than what already has occurred.

When Needn't Be Today

Most stories for afternoon newspapers or broadcast contain "today" near the verb in the first sentence. Similarly, stories for morning newspapers usually contain the day of the week in the same place. The theory is that the lead should tell the reader not only what happened, but also the fact that it's *news*.

Many editors have criticized overuse of the "today" lead, especially among news service reporters. They point out that the overall situation often is more important than the most recent action, and that the writer may weaken the story by playing up a relatively minor development in eagerness to be first with the latest. Instead of straining for a "today" lead, the writer should keep the entire story in its proper perspective. If the early action is more important than the later, then perhaps the lead should focus on something that isn't entirely new. Sometimes this is best accomplished by using present progressive tense ("is threatening") or present perfect ("has developed") instead of the traditional past tense. Present perfect (present tense of the auxiliary plus the past participle) is especially convenient. It allows us to eliminate the day of the week, so that we can build a lead around old action without announcing its age.

Expressing Time

Newspapers have developed several conventions for expressing time. The general rule is to be as specific as possible. This rules out such relative terms as yesterday, tomorrow, last year, and next month. Instead, we write Monday, Wednesday, 1975, and July. And in an announcement, "this evening" becomes "8 p.m. today."

When an event falls within a week of publication, we normally use the day of the week. If the time is more distant, we use the month and date. The conventional method of expressing time is to write hour, day or date, then place, thus:

> The committee will meet at 9 a.m. Thursday at City Hall.

If, however, the meeting is scheduled at a more distant time, it might be more logical to place the date before the hour, thus:

> The committee will meet Sept. 18 at 9 a.m. in City Hall.

Time as Context

Each event occupies a place in space and time (or space-time, if you prefer). This context of where and when, the relation of an event to others in space-time, helps give a story meaning. By giving precise time and place, elapsed time, and sequence of events, we enable the reader to make many mental associations. For example, he can relate the event to his own experience ("Why, I was just two blocks away at the time that happened!") or perhaps to his personal schedule ("I'm booked for a night class, but maybe I'll go to that concert instead.") Or maybe we can help him relate the unexpected ("a 3:48 mile!") to something he already knows.

PRECISE TIME AND PLACE

The exact hour and place is a necessity in every story of a future scheduled event. If we don't supply the hour, the building or address—and sometimes even the room number—the reader who would like to be there won't have the necessary information. The announcement story fails to fulfill its basic function without this specific information.

The exact time also may be important in a story of a past action, especially if it is violent or dramatic. We try to pin down the exact time and place of many such events—fires, disasters, accidents, military attacks, and major crimes. This helps the reader relate the event to his own whereabouts or to other events that were happening elsewhere at the same time. And it often says something important about the event. An armed bank robbery at noon, for example, may be witnessed by hundreds. Many persons may be in physical danger. This makes it a much bigger story than a burglary at 11 P.M. when nobody is around. A trailer truck that jackknifes in a freeway underpass during the evening rush hour creates a bigger story than the truck that jackknifes in the same spot at 3 A.M. or one that jackknifes on a lonely road at any hour.

Many past-action stories, of course, concern routine events or actions that occur over a span of time—sports events, speeches, or interviews, for example. The exact hour is irrelevant in reporting such stories; we can easily settle for "Tuesday night in Mackay Auditorium." Even this much detail may be unimportant after an event; "Wednesday in Omaha" may tell all the reader wants to know.

ELAPSED TIME

Most of us are aware that a three-day brush fire or a five-hour surgical operation is worth attention. Usually prepared speeches which take some time both to prepare and to deliver are more significant (if not necessarily more sincere) than offhand remarks, and deserve greater attention. We also recognize the news value of speed records, whether they happen to concern sports events, reaction time to emergencies, or six-day wars in the Middle East. The amount of time elapsed during any particular action may or may not be an important factor in the story, but it is something the reporter always should note and consider.

Elapsed time has other aspects which journalists occasionally overlook. If, for example, a year passes without an arrest after a mysterious homicide, it may be time to review the case with a new story. And we probably should pay some attention to any scientific report that results from years of research.

SEQUENCE

The order in which events occur often helps the reader understand them better. For example, in interpreting a politician's strongly worded comment, a reporter might ask: Does it come after a rival's attack? Does it come immediately before election day? Does it come after a reporter's question? Or was it volunteered?

The fact that B follows A doesn't necessarily mean that B is caused by A, but often their relation in time has considerable significance. For example, if a policeman hits a suspect over the head, the reader will understand the action better if he is told that first the suspect kicked the policeman in the groin. The objective reporter doesn't say that the first action caused the second. He merely relates them in their proper time sequence and lets the reader decide for himself.

And most readers are quick to read cause and effect into a time sequence. For example, if the reporter writes that the chancellor of the university submitted his resignation three days after his wife filed for divorce, who would not assume, rightly or wrongly, some relationship between the two events? If there is any danger that the implications of the time sequence might misrepresent the facts, the reporter should investigate the matter further—or at least exercise caution in the way he or she reports the sequence of events in order to avoid such misrepresentation.

WHERE: MORE ABOUT CONTEXT

As we observed earlier, place often is expressed in conjunction with time. But in the interest of keeping a lead brief and readable, "where" sometimes may be delayed. This is a frequent practice in speech stories. The lead usually consists of what was said, when, and by whom. The second paragraph then sets the scene by telling where, to whom, under what circumstances. The standard procedure for the third paragraph is to return to the lead's central statement and develop it further. For example:

> The Republican administration is ignoring the problems of cattlemen, Democratic Sen. Irving Saunders said Tuesday.
> Opening his campaign for reelection, Saunders addressed more than 1,000

> members of the Livestock Growers Association in Municipal Auditorium.
> He said Republicans have. . . .

The technique illustrated above is similar to the "action shot" and "establishing shot" used in film production. We get the reader's attention first with action, then we establish setting.

The extent to which we specify "where" depends largely on the reader. A story about an event in Chicago, for example, normally would not include the street address when it is transmitted for use in another city; the exact Chicago address would be irrelevant in Denver. We might, however, include some general identifying terms such as "southside" or "north shore." Chicago newspapers, on the other hand, probably would include the specific address or at least the street.

In writing for local readers, we often identify a location by naming a well-known building (Skirvin Tower, City Hall). But if the building isn't known to nearly all readers, we should also include the address.

Sometimes the only "where" necessary is the name of a city. Major cities (Los Angeles, Minneapolis, Philadelphia, etc.) are merely named, but references to lesser cities include the name of the state (Enid, Okla.; Danbury, Conn.). Still smaller communities are identified by their population, the section of the state in which they lie, or the distance and direction from a better-known town. For example, "Philip, S.D., a prairie town 90 miles east of Rapid City."

HOW: SELECT YOUR VERBS CAREFULLY

Telling readers "how" means describing action well enough so they can visualize it and perhaps even "hear" it. This is seldom attempted in straight news stories. Reporters simply write that something happened without trying to describe how it happened. Sometimes *how* is obvious, sometimes it is irrelevant. Even when it would improve the story, it may require more words than the subject merits.

One problem with telling "how" is that it sometimes requires detailed description that slows the narration. And it may be pointless: why tell how a person crossed the street when we can simply say that "he crossed the street"?

Still, some description of action can be a valuable asset—provided it is accurate, objective, and economical. And much of it can be accomplished by careful selection of verbs. By choosing a specific descriptive verb, we can often eliminate the necessity for adverbs or long phrases of explanation. For example:

> The policeman *moved* down the alley.
> The policeman *moved rapidly* down the alley.
> The policeman *hurried* down the alley.
> or
> The plane came down low over the crowd at high speed.
> The plane *buzzed* the crowd.
> or
> Sitting down in a relaxed fashion with one leg draped over the arm of the chair, he explained. . . .
> *Slumping* down in the chair, he explained. . . .

The goal is to make each verb say as much as possible. Writers should avoid long, qualifying phrases or clauses and even look twice at the simple adverb. Adverbs are especially suspect when they modify adjectives. If writers are tempted to use such vague, intensifying adverbs as "very" or "slightly," they probably have picked a poor adjective.

How Was It Said?

The verb of attribution deserves special consideration. For the sake of liveliness as well as preciseness, often it is tempting to use one of the many specific verbs denoting the manner in which something was said: *exclaimed, shouted, declared, drawled, pronounced, sneered,* etc. Some substitutes for "said" are relatively colorless. These included *added, continued, remarked,* and *suggested.* But most verbs that tell *how* a person said something are loaded with connotations.

Thus any departure from the neutral "said" must be considered cautiously. The story can be slanted drastically—often unconsciously—merely by substituting such verbs as *confessed, admitted, protested, jeered, quipped, noted,* or *pointed out.* "Admitted" implies guilt or error; "pointed out" implies that whatever the speaker said is factual. Even the simple "according to" has a slant: it suggests that the reporter takes no responsibility for what the person has said.

In deciding on a verb of attribution, a reporter must always decide whether the verb he or she has in mind is truly descriptive or merely a personal inference. Whenever there is doubt, the reporter should restrict himself to "said."

How Much and How Many: Be Specific

When editors tell reporters to "be specific," they mean to name and identify everyone and everything, to give the exact hour, the calendar date, exact ages and addresses, even room numbers. Here are only a few examples:

Vague	*Specific*
toddler	3-year-old boy
senior citizen	75-year-old man
late in the summer	on Aug. 30
this evening	7:30 P.M. today
holocaust	fire that left seven dead
on Main Street	at 121 W. Main St.
gale	35-m.p.h. winds gusting to 55
a small crowd	50 persons
traffic pileup	six-car collision
large deficit	$35-billion deficit

A second glance at the list above should make one thing clear: the command to be specific often means to put numbers into your story—ages, dates, addresses, hours, measurements, dollars and cents, exact amounts of anything. Numbers are the most precise form of expression we have.

But don't stop merely with exact numbers. Pay particular attention to numerical change. Whenever possible, compare and contrast. Is the runner's time a record? What was the previous mark? How much time did he shave off it? And this year's $15-million city budget —what is the percentage of increase from last year? (If it's a decrease, you have an even bigger story.) Mere numbers without comparison may be meaningless, so do a little simple arithmetic. Don't make the reader figure it out for himself. To give a story meaning, try to relate the new and unfamiliar to what is already known.

Despite the value of figures, you can't use them as substitutes for words. Your goal is to tell the story clearly, and an overdose of statistics may confuse the meaning instead of clarify it. The reader is slow to absorb numbers, and the radio or television listener often finds it impossible. If numbers can't be spread out readably through a story, then the print reporter should group them into a table. And the television newscaster had better get an artist to prepare a chart. As for radio, the broadcaster can only use round numbers and hope that the ear will absorb them—and distinguish "billion" from "million."

WHY: MOTIVATION, CAUSE, AND CONSEQUENCE

The old United Press posted a sign in each bureau to remind staff members to "Always Ask Why." News reporters today are following this advice more than ever. But beginners should be warned that the answer to "why" is only as good as the person who gives it. Wise reporters automatically ask the question but do not automatically present the answer. They weigh the answer with unusual care.

"Why?" almost always calls for a personal judgment. It asks the target of the question (1) to evaluate human motives—often the person's own, (2) to try to determine a cause-and-effect relationship, or (3) to predict consequences. The source may be totally incapable of doing any of these, but the chances are that he or she will try. Most people try to answer any question put to them, regardless of ability.

Motivation

When "why?" requires people to explain their own motives, they generally can be expected to show their actions in the best possible light, portraying themselves as acting unselfishly in the public interest. They may be correct or they may be lying. In any case, they are unlikely to be objective, which is why the self-report is always suspect—whether the interviewer is a policeman, a psychotherapist, or a news reporter.

When the respondent is a public official, the explanation of motives may be a thinly disguised version of "the end justifies the means" or an attempt to gloss over poor results with honorable motives. A pragmatist would observe that means are ends in themselves and that "good" motives recalled after the event can't change the facts of an action.

If the event in no way involves the source, you have a better chance of getting an objective, disinterested explanation of motives— provided the source has any means of knowing the motivation for an event in which he or she was in no way involved.

Cause-Effect Relationship

There are at least three pitfalls inherent in cause-effect reasoning, with a good deal of overlapping among them:

1. *Oversimplification*—This is assigning a single, simple cause to a complex effect. "Poverty causes crime." "Permissive parents have produced a generation with no respect for authority." (The latter statement not only oversimplifies the cause, but also begs the question since it must first be established that we do, in fact, have a generation with no respect for authority.)

   If a situation is at all complex, it usually has several causes of varying degrees of significance. When your sources appear to be oversimplifying, ask whether they can think of any other factors that may be involved.

2. *Confusing correlation in time or place with causation*—"The Dem-

ocratic Party has been in power at the beginning of every major war of this century. Clearly that party is to blame for the lack of peace in our time." "Sen. Jordan and industrialist George Randall were both vacationing in the Bahamas in January of 1971, a fact which substantiates the recent charges that Jordan has accepted bribes from oil executives."

As these examples indicate, confusing correlation with causation is often a form of oversimplification. The coincidence in time (or some other factor) is used to justify a cause-effect relationship.

3. *Confusing chronological sequence with cause-effect relationship*— Like confusion of correlation with causation, this is the after-that-therefore-because-of-that *(post hoc ergo propter hoc)* fallacy on which a great deal of advertising depends: "She's beautiful. She's engaged. She uses Pond's." It also occurs in many other contexts, sometimes more by implication than direct statement: "After watching three bloody whodunits on television, Smith drew a pistol and shot his wife." The suggestion of a cause-effect relationship in this statement is too strong, unless there is other evidence besides the time sequence to indicate that the television viewing influenced the assault.

Consequences

Closely related to the question of "why?" is the question of "what now?" What will the consequences of this event, action, or situation be? In fact, what promises, or threatens, to result from the action usually is more important than why it happened.

But here again, there is a danger of oversimplification. If a situation is at all complex, it is likely to produce more than one effect. When a speaker asserts that "Recent Supreme Court rulings concerning police techniques only coddle criminals," he or she is overlooking all the effects of these judgments except one. If someone assures us that the election of a particular candidate will mean lower taxes, we must not only ask why, but also what else will result from the election of this candidate.

A request for a prediction of consequences may assume an unlikely degree of clairvoyance. Reporters should consider the respondent's record of reliability before encouraging him to become a prophet. And they should also look for concrete evidence that bears out such predictions. Answering the questions of "what now?" or "what then?" is not an easy matter. But wherever possible reporters and readers should attempt to evaluate an action by its consequences or probable consequences.

BACKGROUNDING: A SUBSTITUTE FOR "WHY"

Every story must be written so that it stands alone; that is, it must be complete in itself. Reporters must supply enough information to explain the action fully, even when this means repeating something that has been published dozens of times. The story should never force the reader to go back to a previous edition in order to understand the latest action. Supplying this information—telling the reader what has transpired before—is known as "backgrounding."

At the lowest level, backgrounding rehashes only enough recent history to make the story meaningful to a stranger who might be passing through town. A typical example is the brief paragraph in a trial story that tells who was killed, when, and where, none of which might have been mentioned in that day's testimony. Another kind of backgrounding is the compare-and-contrast section that might appear in almost any story: comparing last month's living costs with the figures for the same month a year ago, comparing a new union contract with pay increases won last week in another industry. Another recaps an entire week's developments in a given situation.

Whatever the variety, backgrounding is explanatory writing of a special kind. It consists of factual information, not theorizing. The nature and extent of the content is guided by the axiom that the writer should never underestimate readers' intelligence, but never overestimate their information. We can assume an average education but no specific knowledge of the story at hand.

Backgrounding, by itself, doesn't necessarily tell readers "why." But often it accomplishes that goal at least partially by implication. By recounting related events, we place the story in the perspective of time, often giving readers the information they need to draw their own conclusions.

In a continuing story, the professional may supply the necessary minimum of backgrounding from memory. Sometimes, however, a reporter may have lived with the story so long that he or she has lost perspective. The more a reporter knows about the story, the more difficult it may be to put himself in the place of the uninformed reader. Reporters may fall into the trap of assuming that the reader knows everything that they do and inadvertently omit some essential fact. An alert editor usually will spot the omission and throw back the story for an insert. The beginner, often working without an instructor or editor, can test the clarity and completeness of a story on a friend or relative. If the reader doesn't understand, more backgrounding may be required.

Backgrounding in depth means that a reporter must read—reference works, public documents, or at least the back issues of his own newspaper. An explanatory feature may be 90 percent backgrounding obtained by library research, with only the public's current interest as its news peg.

CONCLUSION

Let's look again at your readers. There they sit, newspaper in hand, trying to tune out everything around them for a few minutes while they find out what's going on in the world. Readers may be sitting at the kitchen table, sipping morning coffee, or relaxing in an easy chair after dinner. Your reader may be riding a bus to or from work or hanging onto a strap in a subway car. No matter where readers are, they are engaged in a highly private activity. Even if people are all around them, each reader is essentially alone with you for the moment. Unlike listeners at a public speech, they are not affected by crowd psychology. They may chuckle quietly or whistle with surprise at what you say, but you can hardly expect them to cheer, applaud, or hiss the way you say it. Readers are much more interested in your content than in your style. Slick techniques may hook them and even keep them reading to the end, but if you have nothing to say—or if you fail to say it fully and clearly—they will feel cheated. The reader of news, like the detectives in the old "Dragnet" series on television, wants "just the facts."

This is why we have placed so much emphasis on the Five W's and H. Your basic goal is reader satisfaction, and the only way to achieve that is by answering every question the reader might have. It should help if you realize early how much detail is required—before you begin asking questions and collecting information.

The most important thing is to have something to say. If you have nothing to say, no one will listen. And no one will care.

SUGGESTED ASSIGNMENTS

1. From your own community, choose some person listed in *Who's Who in America* or some other biographical source. Using only published information, write an obituary of this person. You may fictionalize the cause of death. Make certain that you include all the identification that normally appears in an obituary.
2. Interview the person who was the subject of your obituary. Base this story on his opinions regarding some current issue about which he or she has special knowledge. You may use some of the information that appeared in the obituary, but add direct quota-

tion and any physical description that may help the reader see and hear the speaker.

3. Write a story announcing a future scheduled event. Be specific about what is expected to happen, when and where. The story should be attributed, although you may use implied attribution. It need not be long.

CHAPTER FOUR / GETTING THE INFORMATION

The time comes for you to get the story. You know what you're looking for: an interesting event, idea, or situation. At least some element of it must be new—something the reader hasn't yet heard. You know that it requires a lot of factual detail—names, places, numbers—and that you will have to think in terms of identification, attribution, and backgrounding as you collect the information. The problem now is where and how to get it.

Getting information is a problem that confronts the student more often than the professional. Collegiate reporters often return from their campus rounds with glum expressions and the report that "there's no news today." They're almost always wrong. Even the smaller campuses have a multitude of *activities*—sports events, concerts, plays, art exhibits, workshops and seminars, speeches by visiting lecturers, student social and political activities. Curriculum changes, experimental programs, scholarship awards, and faculty honors all provide material for stories. And every campus has its continuing *situations,* including some controversies that seemingly never end. In addition, the numerous theses, dissertations, and research projects in progress on any campus, as well as the current theories of education, are excellent sources for stories dealing with *ideas.* And to the human interest writer, each *person* is a potential subject for a factual novel—or at least one good feature story.

But in a way, the student reporter's complaint is understandable. News seldom comes to student journalists. They have to go out and get it. They must circulate, read bulletin boards, attend events, sit in on lectures, visit administrators, ask questions of fellow students, and listen and keep their eyes open wherever they go. A student reporter must be a one person newsgathering system. It's good training. The student who learns to operate alone will find the job much easier after graduation when he or she has the support of a professional organization.

The first day on the job, beginning professionals may make an unexpected discovery. Much of the news they once had to go after now comes to them. People with something to tell the public bring their information directly to the newspaper or broadcast station. Stories, tips, and suggestions arrive by mail and telephone—or walk through the doorway—and reporters may be so deluged with unsolicited information that they have little time to look for anything else. A new reporter may even begin to think that digging isn't necessary. But that would be seeing only one side of the situation.

In many instances, of course, editors are glad to have such help. They could hardly function without the cooperation of the funeral home that supplies obituaries by telephone, the bride's mother who supplies information for the wedding story, or the brokerage firm that provides special market data. They appreciate the cooperation of the winning high school basketball coach (the loser can't always be trusted to call), and they learn to rely on the integrity of many public relations practitioners.

But no news agency can subsist entirely on news that comes so easily. Indeed, the fact that a story is volunteered sometimes makes it suspect. Why does the source want it published? What individual or organization might benefit from its publication? When a story comes too easily, a cynical editor might observe that the real news is not what the source *wants* you to print, but what the person or group *doesn't* want you to print. According to this rather narrow view, the volunteered story is only publicity. It would be more accurate to say that routine information comes easily, but important news is like milk: the source doesn't give it voluntarily—you have to work to get it.

Editors have developed an efficient system for handling both the easy story and the one that takes some effort. How well the system operates depends on individual initiative, expertise, persistence, organization, and teamwork. And as many small-town editors might observe, its success depends on having enough people to do the job. Let's first examine the way the overall system of getting the news is set up. Then we will take a closer look at the responsibilities and techniques of the individual reporter.

HOW THE SYSTEM WORKS

The logistics of straight news gathering are much the same from one newspaper to another. Naturally the size of the staff, the number of duties, and the degree of specialization vary greatly from *The New York Times* to the *Greenville Gazette*. But the division of labor—the crux of the system—is worked out along similar lines in most newspaper offices. And broadcasting has adopted some features of the newspaper system.

Rewrite

This function exists in every newsroom. The rewrite person's job consists mostly of taking information over the telephone—calls from funeral homes, the weather service, the highway patrol, publicists, and beat reporters. It may also include confirming and rewriting publicity releases that arrive by mail. Sometimes the rewrite person initiates calls, making a series of routine checks of hospitals and police and fire stations just before deadline. In other cases such checks are left to beat reporters, and the rewrite person takes only incoming calls.

A metropolitan newspaper may have several persons on rewrite, some of them highly specialized. Some may write nothing but obituaries, others may take only incoming calls from beat reporters, and still others may work closely with the city editor and handle any kind of story that can be obtained by telephone. And not all of these are dull by any means.

Whatever his specific duties, the full-time rewrite person never leaves the office. Beginning reporters are often broken in on rewrite because it acquaints them with the newsroom's internal procedures. But because they want to see the events they write about, they usually ask for a beat or general assignment as soon as possible. Some editors have tried to make rewrite more attractive to trained reporters by assigning some of the duller routine to clerical help.

Beat Reporting

In the strict sense, a beat consists of a group of offices which are proven sources of information. A beat reporter is assigned to cover a particular beat full-time—to gather, confirm, organize, and write all the news that emanates from that beat. Beats may be distinguished either by subject matter or geography or both. On many newspapers, for example, crime, a particular kind of subject matter, constitutes a beat to which one or more reporters might be assigned. Their job is to cover all crime news regardless of its source: police, courts, FBI, district attorney's office, or prison warden. The city hall reporter, on the other hand, handles a geographic beat. He or she is responsible for all news that originates in that building, whether it involves a new mayor or plans for the summer recreation program. Under strict geographical organization two reporters sometimes get the same information from different sources. A federal criminal investigation, for example, might be reported by both the Federal Bureau of Investigation and the U.S. marshal's office, which often are in different buildings.

Typical beats are city hall, schools, the county building, federal courts, state capitol, police department, and civic clubs. Much of any newspaper's daily fare—but by no means all of it—comes from these areas.

The beat reporters' goal is to know everything that's happening on their beats. This requires regular surveillance. The reporters call at each important office daily, talk to the same people, and read the same routine reports: budgets, accident reports, criminal complaints, marriage license applications, building permits, divorces filed or granted, pleadings in civil suits, engineering studies, etc. They attend the same regular meetings each week or month: the city council, the school board, the county board of commissioners, or the luncheon meetings of civic clubs.

Because a reporter can't be everywhere at once, he or she must develop reliable sources who can be depended upon to phone in with a story at any hour. This is relatively easy for beat reporters because they see their sources daily. They get to know the secretaries as well as their bosses. They listen to the office gossip and share coffee breaks with the staff. Like salespeople, beat reporters cultivate personal contacts. They must work at making themselves welcome wherever they go, yet they try to maintain a friendly independence.

Although the beat system is still the basic method of daily surveillance, it has been widely criticized. An overemphasis on beat reporting may result in a newspaper that slights nongovernmental activities. Further, it may result in one-sided stories that reflect only the establishment view of the news. Reporters who spend too much time on a beat may develop a tendency to see the world the way their sources do.

Reporters' ability to write clearly may also suffer because of the beat system. If journalists adopt the specialized vocabularies of their sources, they may lose the ability to tell a story in words that the general reader understands. Beat reporters must continue to think in plain language and avoid the jargon of lawyers, social workers, and police officers.

Perhaps the best that can be said for the beat system is that it allows the reporter to become something of an expert on a small portion of the world's activities. The person who covers the same beat daily soon learns to write about it with authority.

General Assignment

Each day is different for general assignment reporters. There is no regular routine, either inside the office or out, unless the weekly schedule requires them to substitute for a beat reporter. Instead, they work on special assignments, usually under the direction of the city editor. General assignment reporters may not know what they are expected to do each day until they report for work and pick up an assignment sheet. They cover the unexpected: plane crashes, disasters, celebrity interviews, and the odd and unusual human interest stories. Occasionally they may be assigned to an investigation that requires weeks. About the only thing general assignment reporters can be certain of is variety.

General assignment reporters seldom have time to cultivate sources or to become experts. Success depends on the ability to operate anywhere under any circumstances, without specialized knowledge, getting stories from people they have never met before. They must be adaptable enough to cover a riot, a beauty contest, a plane crash, or a wedding on motorcycles. Initiative and imagination are at least as important in this job as following the city editor's instructions. One of the rules that the reporter learns early is always to carry enough change so that he can telephone the city desk. And if there is competition on a story, the reporter tries to tie up the nearest telephone by hiring someone to hold the line open to the office until he gets the information.

General assignment reporting is active, competitive, and sometimes physically hazardous. It often involves travel and irregular working hours. But it is seldom dull. It appeals especially to young reporters. In order to avoid discouraging talented beginners with an overdose of routine, many editors break them in on general assignment rather than rewrite.

HOW THE INDIVIDUAL WORKS

Regardless of where they fit into the system, all reporters operate in the same general manner. They collect, confirm, record, and interpret information. For all but the rewrite person, this means legwork: moving around, looking and listening, talking with people, attending meetings, asking questions, and taking notes. It also means homework: getting acquainted with subjects and sources by reading about them. Each story, each day on the beat, requires some reading as preparation.

Specifically, reporters have five ways of getting information:

1. Participating in the action
2. Observing the action
3. Asking questions of someone else who participated in the action, observed it, or has special information
4. Reading (reports, documents, reference works)
5. Using scientific research techniques, such as public opinion polling.

The most commonly used methods are observation, interviewing, and reading. But let's examine them all.

Personal Participation: A Rarity

Short of life-or-death situations, reporters try to avoid personal involvement in any activity that is likely to make news. The normal role is that of a disinterested observer, politically and ideologically neutral. The ethic of neutrality often is enforced by company policy that bars a reporter from overt political activity or moonlighting in publicity or advertising.

Although it is an adage of journalism that the reporter is never part of the news, sometimes it can't be avoided. Reporters can't, for example, stand by passively and watch a person die. Like anyone else, they must try to help—and in doing so they become part of a newsworthy action. They then may write about themselves, either in third or first person.

Reporters, however, seldom initiate newsworthy action. More often, if they are directly involved at all, they are the target of it. A reporter becomes a name in the news when he or she is gassed, wounded, taken prisoner, or thrown out of a meeting. It seldom happens, but when it does, the reporter is entitled to write a first-person account. An outstanding example of such reporting was a series of articles written in 1971 by Kate Webb of United Press International. Believed dead, she emerged after 23 days of captivity by the Viet Cong and began writing what she had experienced on the other side of the Vietnamese War. In the words of a UPI editor, Kate Webb's lengthy story was "an extraordinary piece of journalism . . . Even more extraordinary perhaps is the fact that it got written at all."

A more common variety of participation is emotional rather than physical. The reporter is on the scene primarily as an observer, but occasionally the action is such that he or she cannot help being involved emotionally and revealing that involvement in the story. Reporters are, after all, human beings, not robots. When the circumstances justify such treatment and it is handled well, as in the following example, such stories are high points in news reporting:

By CHRISTOPHER WAIN
United Press International
TRANG BANG, South Vietnam—We knew what was going to happen, and there was nothing we could do to stop it from happening. That was the worst part.

South Vietnamese army troops were getting the worst of a firefight Thursday with about 100 North Vietnamese infantry, who were dug into bunkers in the tiny hamlet of Gia Log on Highway 1 on the outskirts of Trang Bang.

At about 11:30 a.m. the heavy monsoon

rains lifted enough for the South Vietnamese to call in an airstrike, but we—a
group of watching newsmen—were sur-
prised when the A1 Skyraiders turned up.
The cloud base was very low at about
600 feet, and the A1s kept disappearing
into the clouds.

A forward air control plane flew in
and, ignoring bursts of gunfire from the
ground, sent in two white marker rockets
to indicate the North Vietnamese positions. The ARVN (South Vietnamese
troops) showed their own lines in the
traditional way with a purple smoke
grenade.

But the white smoke dissipated in the
rain.

It was then that things started going
wrong. An A1 came in and, as we saw
the four high explosives fall from his
wings, we realized they had been released
over the wrong side of the road at least
300 yards from the North Vietnamese
bunkers. The bombs exploded and then
we could see ARVN troops racing across
the road. Their own positions had suddenly become death traps.

Among the olive-green ARVN uni-
forms, I could see white shirts of the vil-
lagers who had been caught in the cross-
fire and were trying to get to safety. I
could see the soldiers waving the civilians
to safety, and I could also see what they
couldn't—another A1 coming in, straight
at them.

I suppose all the pilot could see was
figures running, which was what he would
expect the North Vietnamese to be doing. You cannot identify people when
you are 100 feet up and flying at 300
miles per hour, so he flew in and drop-
ped four canisters of napalm on top of
them. They exploded right on target. I
turned away instinctively.

Out of the dense black smoke caused
by the flaming bombs, a group of figures
eventually emerged. We left our positions and walked forward, slowly, hoping
the A1s would not return.

A little girl, aged about nine, stumbled

forward, barefooted, naked, whimpering. Three boys, who I suppose were her brothers, were with her. The girl's back was in shreds, with the skin hanging off, as if she had suffered a sudden instant case of third-degree sunburn. As she reached me, she stopped. An ARVN soldier asked me if I had any water. I emptied my water-bottle on her back. There's not much you can do for napalm burns, but water does reduce the surface temperature.

The little girl stopped whimpering. Then, still obviously in deep shock, she walked along the highway back toward the refugees cowering beneath their buses and ox-carts.

The other casualties were far, far worse. There was a baby whose skin was hanging off so that it looked like a doll that had been savaged by wild dogs. The mother, next to the child, moaned in a sort of monotone. There were other burn cases. I tried not to look too hard.

An ARVN officer said he had five men dead and several others wounded, some in the fighting and some by the napalm.

It was one of those incidents that has happened countless times before in this war and presumably will happen many more times.

These were South Vietnamese planes dropping napalm on South Vietnamese peasants and troops. I believe the usual Vietnamese phrase is "Xin Loi"—or "Sorry about that."

Observation: Staffing the Event

In the language of editors, a newspaper "staffs" an event when one or more reporters is sent to cover it in person. Some events are staffed as a matter of routine: major criminal trials, college football games, legislative sessions, and meetings of the city council and school board. Others, such as weddings and funerals, are almost never staffed. In between these extremes lies a vast body of news, ranging from speeches to natural disasters, requiring editorial decision. Shall we or shall we not? Staffing is an expensive, time-consuming way to cover the news, and the decision is seldom taken lightly. Is the story truly important? Must we have a reporter present to get the facts straight, or is it the kind of event we can cover just as well with a series of telephone calls? Supposing that it can be covered by phone, do we have a chance of getting a much better story if a reporter is sent to the scene?

Competition, time, and the availability of reporters all must be considered. Space is another factor. There is no point in generating a long story, full of description, if the newspaper has no space. But if there is space, time, and money, staffing usually produces the best story. The eyes and ears of the reporter can put the reader there. Color, atmosphere, and words uttered at the moment can be captured better at the scene.

Given a choice, most reporters would prefer to observe the event in person. They tend to trust their own senses more than the second-hand reports of others. But as you may recall from the exercises at the end of Chapter 1, passive observation is never enough. Reporters still must ask questions, if only to confirm what they think they have seen and heard.

At best, the reporter's observation never approaches that of the scientist. Events and situations aren't inanimate objects. They won't stand still. Reporters can't walk around all their subjects, get beneath them and above them and look at them from all angles. They can't put them under a microscope. Nobody, for example, can observe a war—or even one battle. All we can see is a limited portion of the activity on one side. The reporter who staffs an event should recognize his or her own limitations and always seek other viewpoints, other information.

Most stories that are staffed are *planned* events, scheduled well in advance. As a result, reporters can plan the coverage. They can read about the subject in advance, get to the scene early and ask questions, make arrangements to sit where they can see and hear best, and even estimate how much time they will have to write the story when they get back to the office.

Let's examine some specific methods for covering three kinds of planned events.

SPEECHES

These are the easiest events to cover, yet they still require much more than just being in the right place at the right time. Reporters must prepare for speeches, they must use their eyes as well as their ears, and they must confirm their notes before the speaker leaves the hall.

Preparation at the most basic level consists only of learning enough about the speaker to identify him properly. This information usually can be obtained from clippings of previously published stories, from *Who's Who in America* or some other biographical reference, or from a biography supplied by the speaker's sponsor or publicist. What you want is the speaker's credentials, the information that tells why this person's words merit attention.

If the subject is highly technical, the reporter also should study it before listening to the speech. And if the speaker has a prepared text, the reporter should ask for a copy—then follow the text, underline points of emphasis, note departures, and verify quotations.

Punctuality is important. Granted that the speaker may waste several minutes with anecdotes or other trivia not worth reporting, reporters still must be early in order to get seats where they can see and hear. Near the front but off to the side is usually best for observing both the speaker and the audience. If there is no prepared text, seating becomes especially important. Reporters want to catch each word and be in a position to reach the speaker quickly and confirm their notes immediately after the talk ends.

Normally the speech story will focus on the most important thing the speaker had to say. Since speech stories are highly condensed, with much more paraphrase than direct quotation, reporters needn't try to note every word. They want only the most important points, so they take notes much like those of a student. A word of warning: reporters should never become so enthralled that they forget to take notes.

But the story is more than just the speaker's words. The reporter also must consider:

1. *The speaker himself.* Does he tremble? Shout? Gesture wildly? Grimace? Would physical description help the story or is it irrelevant?
2. *The audience.* Who are the members? Is this a public meeting or a select group? How many are present? (Ask the fire marshal or a policeman or make your own estimate.) Do they applaud? Boo or hiss? Sit on their hands? Interrupt the speaker with a staged demonstration? Do some walk out? Do they give the speaker a standing ovation? Perfunctory reaction is hardly worth reporting, but at least we should recognize that an audience is present—that the speech wasn't delivered to an empty hall.
3. *The total situation.* What is the temperature in the hall? Does it affect the speaker or the audience's reaction? Do competing sounds from the street drown out the speaker's words? And let's not forget the time and space context: how does this speech relate to other events, here or elsewhere, now or previously? Where did the speaker come from? Why is he here? Where is he going next? All this may be irrelevant, but it should be observed and evaluated, even if it isn't reported.

Few speeches are covered as extensively as this. But if an editor considers a speech worth staffing, the reporter at least must bring back something more than merely a digest of the prepared text. It needn't be long, but it should contain some fruit of personal observation.

MEETINGS OF PUBLIC BOARDS

Any general assignment reporter may be called upon to cover a speech, but the staffing of public boards usually is reserved for the beat reporter who knows the issues and personalities. Without such a background of daily coverage, even the best reporter may be baffled by the complexities of staffing the city council or the school board meeting. Here we have not one speaker, but several; not one topic, but a dozen or more. To do the job well, the reporter must know the community's geography, tax structure, and political history. He or she must know the laws and bylaws that govern the board, the role of every official present, and the background of each specific issue.

Where to start? Usually the reporter can study an agenda and a pile of clippings of earlier news stories on particular issues. The clippings probably will be far more helpful; agendas tend to be terse and sometimes incomprehensible to anyone but an expert, and the board may choose to ignore it anyway. But if the agenda is available, it provides an opportunity to get some information before the meeting. The reporter can take it to the town clerk or the secretary of the board and ask for background or explanation of specific items in order to be prepared for at least part of the action.

Elected officials are seldom the best sources of background information. At city hall, the people to know are the clerk, the engineer, and the city attorney. In the school system, they are the superintendent and other administrators. These are trained specialists, often better informed about the board's business than the members themselves.

As in speech coverage, in staffing meetings reporters should arrive early—but not necessarily for the same reasons. They may be required to sit at a press table. If not, they try to sit near the clerk or secretary, the person who keeps the official record, so that they can confirm their notes on each action throughout the meeting.

Another reason for arriving early is to get acquainted (or reacquainted) with the presiding officer and the other members of the board. The novice reporter must get each person clearly identified, first by introducing himself, then by drawing a diagram of the seating arrangement with each person carefully labeled. Then, when someone speaks or votes, the reporter can immediately identify the speaker by consulting the diagram.

Another identification problem arises when persons in the crowd rise to speak. In larger communities, the presiding officer usually will ask such speakers to identify themselves. If this is not the practice, the reporter should make a special request. In small communities, however, the new reporter may be the only stranger present. If you face this predicament, perhaps you can nudge the clerk and ask "Who's that?"

For the reporter's purposes in covering a meeting, official actions are more important than debate. The reader wants to know the outcome—which ordinances were approved, what contracts were awarded to whom for what sum. And usually readers want to know how each person voted if the action was not unanimous. Often the board moves so quickly than an observer can't keep up. The reporter can get only the broad outline of the action at the time and hope to fill in the details later. For this reason, a good reporter will stay for 15 minutes or more after the meeting has ended, comparing notes with the official record. It helps to remain even longer and listen to the board members discussing their action after the public has left and they have shed some of their official reserve. In fact, the best story may develop *after* the meeting.

FOOTBALL GAMES

Why pick on football? Perhaps because no other major sport presents so many problems in observation—and no other sport is so well covered. There are 22 players on the field and a small army of newsmen and statisticians watching them from the press box above. No one observer can see and record everything that happens, so the labor is divided. One statistician watches for yards gained rushing, another for yards gained passing, another for penalties, etc.—and a separate crew watches each team. Sports reporters always rely heavily on official scorekeepers, but perhaps nowhere as much as in football.

Quick identification is another serious problem, particularly for broadcasters. The sportcasters must tell immediately who carried the ball and who made the tackle; they can't wait for the announcer on the public address system. Perhaps a broadcaster knows the numbers of the outstanding players, but he seldom knows them all and has little time to refer to a printed program. To solve the problem, two assistants known as spotters are usually recruited from the opposing teams. Flanking the sportscaster, the spotters watch their respective teams and call out the names of the men involved in each play.

Official statistics are distributed to all news personnel at halftime and again at the end of the game. The newspaper or wire-service reporter who has been keeping a careful play-by-play account can have the story moving by phone or wire within seconds. If the game involves major colleges or professional teams, the nearest metropolitan newspaper may staff it with as many as four reporters and a half dozen photographers. One reporter, stationed in the press box, will write the main story while two others cover the locker rooms at the end of the game. A fourth reporter—perhaps more than one—will concentrate on the "color": spectators, bands, and all the other hoopla associated with college football. Meanwhile, photographers have been shooting from the press box and the sidelines.

Football writers, like the beat reporters who cover city hall, usually know the subject thoroughly. Yet they prepare for the game as any other reporter would do by reading clippings and publicity releases, interviewing coaches and players, and getting a copy of the lineups. They face the same problems of getting identification and exact figures during the action. But they have a more sophisticated method of solving them.

Football offers a particularly good example of saturation coverage through teamwork. Few legislatures are covered as thoroughly as a major football game. Many capitol reporters would be happy to have the help that the sports editor has.

Asking Questions: The Interview

The interview is a highly flexible method of getting information.

It may be conducted face to face or by telephone, television, or mail. It may be highly structured, with the reporter preparing a long list of carefully phrased questions, or it may be little more than an informal conversation. The reporter may be seeking factual information, an expression of opinion, or a combination of both. He or she may be interested in what the interviewee knows, what he thinks, or simply what kind of person he is. We usually think of the interview as a one-to-one encounter between reporter and source, but the number can be multiplied on either side. In the press conference, several reporters interview one source; in the panel interview, one or more reporters interviews a group.

The interview is an excellent method of getting a person's opinion, but often a poor way to get facts. Few interviewees have instant total recall of statistical information. Usually questions involving such data can be answered better by printed sources. But the interview is a helpful way to get an impression of the source's personality. It is particularly effective on television, which permits the viewer to observe the same facial expression, gestures, and visible reactions which the reporter sees.

Although the interview has been described cynically as "two people working together to distort the truth," it is often the only means we have of getting certain information. We can't always observe the event in person. We can't always read about it—if it is truly new, nothing has been written yet. We are forced to ask questions, on the telephone, around the beat, at the speech or meeting, at the scene of the accident. We use a form of interview so often that reporters can be evaluated almost entirely by their skill at interviewing. Do they pick the right source? Do they ask the right questions? Do they ask in a way that gets the answers? Do they *confirm* the information? Successful interviewing requires planning, persuasion, perception, and persistence.

PLANNING

You may approach the interview from either of two routes, the person or the situation. As an example of the first case, you may be assigned to interview a celebrity for a personality profile, with no stipulation about questions to ask. You will have to think of an "angle," a central subject to ask about, and prepare a tentative list of questions. What interests this person? What do we know about him? What will he talk freely about? In the second case when your focus is on a situation, you will have to prepare a list of sources. Do they have the information you want? Can they speak with authority? Will they cooperate? In either situation, you must do your homework by researching both the source and the subject, then preparing a list of specific questions.

If you are interviewing a celebrity, learn as much as possible about his or her background by reading clip files or biographical references. It may help to know, for example, that Ronald Reagan was once a sportscaster in Des Moines or that Anne Baxter is the granddaughter of Frank Lloyd Wright or that Raquel Welch is a Mexican-American. Such knowledge may give you a different angle for the story or at least aid you in getting the source to talk more freely.

Remember as you phrase the questions that you are concerned about activities, situations, and ideas: what the people have been doing or are planning to do, what special information they have, what they think. Your opening question, therefore, will probably be some variant of one of these:

1. What have you been *doing* about . . . ? (or since . . . ?)
2. What are you *planning* to do about . . . ?
3. What do you *know* about (some other person's activities) . . . ?
4. What do you *think* about . . . ?

Obviously, you as the reporter must supply a specific ending to each question. These may be quite broad, merely identifying the general subject that you want to inquire about, or they may be sharply focused. In any case, they should be open-ended questions that require the interviewee to respond at some length, much like the questions professors design for essay quizzes. The goal is to get the person talking about the subject. Once that is accomplished, you can follow up by asking *who, what, when, where, why,* and *how*—questions that arise naturally in the course of the interview. It's wise, too, to keep asking, "How do you spell that?"

Questions about what the interviewee knows or thinks about something could be called probing questions. Use them when you don't know exactly what kind of information you're searching for. They are the exact opposite of the closed question, which calls for a "yes" or "no" answer. Most of the time you will want to avoid questions that can be answered with "yes" or "no." But in some cases ("Are you going to run for President, Senator?"), a simple, definite "yes" or "no" may be the most interesting answer you can get. Then the trick is to get that answer.

Another type of question that can be planned before the interview is the *problem* question, in which you set up a hypothetical situation. "Suppose such and such happens," you ask. "What would you do?"

As you plan questions, remember that a story involves people struggling toward a goal. Think in terms of motivation, consequences, difficulties, and solutions. Why is this action being taken? Who is responsible? What are the benefits? What are the drawbacks? What difficulties were encountered? How were they surmounted? What was the final outcome? Get these answers and you'll have the makings of a story.

Preparation for the interview may also include selection of time and place. Often, reporters have no choice: they must interview the actor at the air terminal, the politician in a busy corridor, the executive in a crowded hotel room, the protest leader in a noisy street. They may even have to jump into a taxi and ask questions rapidly during a ride across town. But whenever possible, they try to avoid such situations. They try to arrange for privacy and more than enough time to ask all their questions.

The easiest place to arrange the interview is the subject's home territory: his office or residence. And usually it's the best. The subject is at ease and privacy can be assured by barring visitors and stopping phone calls. Another workable setting is the special interview room that many metropolitan newspapers have. Some reporters prefer to conduct the interview in a quiet restaurant because the subject can relax while he eats, but the presence of waiters limits privacy. Perhaps the worst place is a noisy, bustling newsroom—unless, of course, the subject is accustomed to this environment.

The amount of time required varies greatly. A spot news interview can be conducted by telephone in less than 5 minutes or face to face in 15. A depth interview, however, will require at least 45 minutes and perhaps as much as 2 hours. At what time of day? If you have a choice, the best times are in the morning when the interviewee is fresh or in the evening when he can relax. Late afternoon is seldom the best time to approach a person who has been working all day.

Another preparatory step is to alert the interviewee to the general subject you want to ask about so that he, too, can be prepared by collecting information.

PERSUASION

Assuming that the source is both informed and reasonably willing to cooperate, successful interviewing depends largely on the reporter himself: his or her personality, appearance, and behavior, the order in which questions are asked, the quality of the questions, the manner in which notes are taken, the reporter's alertness in improvising and reactions throughout the interview.

As a reporter, you must be both an interrogator and an empathic listener. Above all, you must control the situation. You must never let the interviewee reverse roles and become the questioner. Nothing is more frustrating than suddenly to find yourself being interviewed by your source.

If all else is equal, the best interviewer may be a woman. Studies indicate that both men and women would rather talk to a woman. Given the same list of questions in a test of public opinion polling, women received more and longer responses than did men.

Another study shows that the person who gets the most answers is simply the person who asks the most questions. And experience demonstrates that the *quality* of the questions is at least as important as the quantity. A large number of answers is of little value if they are irrelevant to the main topic of interest.

All we know for certain about the choice of reporter is that he or she should not be someone who offends or antagonizes the source from the outset. We do not, for example, pick the office cynic to interview a person he would describe as a "bleeding heart." We don't send the man with the longest hair to interview the Marine general or the hard-hat leader. The reporter at least must be someone the source will speak to.

A reporter's success depends to a large extent on his or her being acceptable to many different sources. To achieve this goal, reporters for generations have cultivated a casual neutrality of dress and manner. They dress like other office workers, though sometimes less formally, trying to blend in easily with any crowd. They try to maintain a friendly neutrality, expressing as few personal opinions as possible in order to avoid antagonizing a source whose opinions may not be known. If they must ask embarrassing questions, they save them until the end of the interview. In most situations, they try to present a "good guy" image.

Exceptions exist, however. When a source is suspected of lying or concealing important information, the friendly newsperson may turn inquisitor. He or she may use the technique of firing tough questions so rapidly that the source panics and blurts out something he didn't intend to say. Or two reporters may work together in the manner of policemen, one appearing sympathetic and the other taking the hard-boiled role.

But these techniques are rare. Most interviews resemble an informal conversation, guided loosely by the reporter's statement of purpose and the specific questions that are asked. Reporters listen more than they talk. The customary technique is to get the source talking and let him talk it out without interruption. If something isn't clear, good reporters put a question mark beside the notation and wait until the source pauses before they ask for clarification. Then they go on to the next question.

While the source talks, the reporter tries to maintain a friendly but noncommital attitude, keep eye contact most of the time to indicate interest, sit or stand in a relaxed posture, and take notes unobtrusively. His or her only movement may be a nod, a smile, and slow, steady notetaking. Reporters try to avoid overreacting to anything the source says, no matter how startling. An exclamation of astonishment, a sudden laugh, or hurried scribbling may alarm the source and curtail the interview before the reporter has enough information.

The most productive attitude has been described as one of *empathy* (understanding), not necessarily sympathy. Reporters who show interest and understanding can draw information from people with whom they may have no sympathy whatever. Empathy is conveyed both by actions—nodding, smiling, taking notes, maintaining eye contact—and by words. You can say, "That's very interesting. Tell me more." Or you can simply say, "Hmmm . . . ."

In some cases, effective persuasion may take the form of suggesting to the source that it's in his own interest to talk. This technique is particularly useful when the person is involved in a controversy: "Gov. Rivers has charged you with what he calls a shocking lack of concern about water pollution, Senator. He cites your voting record as evidence. What are your feelings on this issue?" or "There are rumors linking you to a profitable smuggling operation, Mr. Ambassador. It would be a good idea to get your side of the story in print." If necessary, this approach might be even more blunt: "If you don't care to discuss your part in this affair, I can get the information from. . . ." This remark is a statement of fact not a threat, but the source often rushes to cooperate as if it were a club.

PERCEPTION

In a face-to-face interview of any length, astute reporters come away with some definite impressions about the source's attitudes and feelings, even if these were not made explicit in their dialogue. But however certain they may be of their impressions, they cannot relay them to the reader directly. You cannot write, for example, that "Wilbur Park, principal of South High was shocked and frightened by the rioting of some ten students during the school lunch hour today" (unless, of course, Principal Park has described his reaction in these terms). Nor can you declare that "Sen. Green is clearly jealous of the prominence his younger colleague has achieved." Both of these are inferences, not provable facts.

On the basis of careful perception, however, the reporter sometimes can suggest significant attitudes and reactions by reporting objective behavior. For example, "Wilbur Park, principal of South High, was pale and visibly trembling as he described the rioting in the school lunchroom today," or "Hesitating momentarily and tapping his foot rapidly against the chair, Sen. Green replied he could not approve of his younger colleague's recent actions."

Whatever the event or situation you may be covering, visual perception is important. Probably it is more important in getting the story of an automobile accident than in interviewing a city councilman. Nonetheless, even in interviews, you should make a habit of noting physical details: dress, hair styles, facial expressions, gestures, mannerisms. How much of this material you actually incorporate into a given news story will vary greatly. In some instances, such observations, carefully recorded, may be the most interesting element in the story. In other cases, they will not add anything significant to what your sources have told you. Or they may not reveal anything particularly noteworthy about the person in question. And often the story is not important enough to merit such detail.

Still you will not have wasted your efforts. You may have acquired insights that will prove useful on another occasion. And, through practice, you will have sharpened your powers of observation.

PERSISTENCE

Unlike many students, reporters seldom hesitate to admit they don't understand. Throughout the interview, they ask for clarification, and they are persistent if it isn't forthcoming. You can say, "I don't understand. Can you explain that? Could you give me an example? What does that mean in layman's terms?" If the issue is extremely simple, of course, you may show yourself in a bad light by admitting ignorance. But in most cases, the source will be flattered to take the role of teacher. He or she can demonstrate superiority by telling you something you didn't know.

Persistence may also be necessary to keep the interview under control. The reporter may have to say, "That's all very interesting, but let's go back to . . . ." Or, if the source threatens to become the interviewer, the reporter may have to say, "Look, *I'm* the reporter; I'm here to find out what *you* have to say." This is a blunt tactic, but if accompanied by a laugh, it often works well.

When the source fails to answer the question, either by remaining silent or by talking about something entirely different, the reporter should persist. You can repeat the question or say, "Let me put it a different way," then rephrase it.

Throughout the interview, reporters are constantly confirming what they hear. This may be done simply by repeating what the source has said, turning it into a question, or asking him to repeat it. It also may be accomplished by paraphrase: "You're saying, then, that . . . ." The paraphrase may take the form of a long summary, such as: "So far, you've said that . . . ." Summaries are particularly helpful in that they not only clear up any doubtful points, but they also show the source the direction the story is taking, often inspiring him to add more information that the reporter hasn't asked for. At least one such review is almost mandatory at the end of the interview.

As in any other form of coverage, reporters should make certain that their notes are complete and accurate before closing the interview. It is often advisable, also, to make arrangements to phone the source later if doubt arises when the story is being written.

After the reporter has concluded the interview and thanked the source, it may pay to remain for a few minutes of casual conversation. The best information often comes when the interview is "finished" and the source relaxes.

If the goal of the interview is factual information rather than opinion, reporters must persist still further. They must verify whatever the source has said by checking with what already is known (reference works, clipping files) or by questioning other persons. No matter how many precautions have been taken, the reporter still has only a one-sided story if it came from only one source.

Recording What You Hear

Reporters covering trials, council meetings, or football games have a backstop. If they miss something and have time to wait, they can check the transcript of testimony, the minutes of a meeting, or the official statistics. But when reporters conduct interviews, they have no such support. They themselves keep the only record of what was said. Their notes must be clear, accurate, and complete.

Many reporters use a tape recorder as insurance, but few rely on it completely. Tape can be valuable in verifying a direct quotation, and it is a handy record to have when a source argues that he or she has been misquoted. But it creates as many problems as it solves. The reporter who relies on tape alone finds that the time it take to prepare

the story has doubled because the words must be transcribed into type-
script. Further, tape has an inhibiting effect on many sources. They
become suddenly pompous or overly cautious, and some even refuse
to have their voices recorded.

If the source is agreeable, tape recording can be a valuable tool.
But it is hardly a substitute for written notes, which constitute a far
more concise and logically organized record. Tape is at best a backstop, to be consulted only when you want exact wording.

Historically, reporters' notes have been jotted down almost anywhere—on envelopes, scraps of copy paper, even tablecloths. But most
reporters today use a small stenographic pad and ballpoint pen to
attain a certain degree of permanence. And they *keep* their notes
until they are certain they won't need them again. Usually this means
only a few days after publication, but sometimes notes—and tapes—
may be stored permanently in a safe.

Few reporters take shorthand, nor do they try to outline. Instead,
they write in sentence fragments filled with abbreviations. Although
each reporter has his own variations, the system of abbreviation used
by journalists is relatively uniform, especially among wire service reporters. It is based on short forms used in telegraphy and cable communication and consists mostly of omitting vowels, spelling phonetically, and making sensible substitutions. For example:

today	tdy	words	wds
tomorrow	tmw	story	sty
morning	ayem	paragraph	graf
evening	pm	fullback	flbk
schools	skuls	black or block	blk
legislature	xgr	steady or study	stdy
police	pox		
Supreme Court of		court	ct
the United States	scotus	with	w/
politicians	pols	going	gg
soon as possible	sap or sappest	arrive	arv

Wire service reporters also save time and space by using the
call letters for major bureaus to represent the names of cities—in
Associated Press usage, Wx for Washington, NY for New York, Fx
for San Francisco, Kx for Kansas City, Dx for Denver. And some
reporters incorporate foreign words because they are shorter (for example, ayer for yesterday).

Ideally, a reporter's notes should be clear enough that another
reporter could decipher them in case he or she falls dead before finish-
ing the story. But they seldom are. More likely they will be almost
incoherent to anyone but the person who took them. They will be

filled with stars, circles, boxes, underscores, and question marks—all devices that reporters use to indicate emphasis or doubt. They will be meaningful only at the moment. Even the person who took them may not understand them the next day. For this reason, every reporter tries to get the story on paper as fast as possible, before the notes get cold.

Reading for Information

Every journalist reads much more than the public might suspect.

Print, in fact, is as important a source of news as people. All reporters, especially the rewrite people, read publicity releases. Specialized reporters read trade magazines, scientific or scholarly journals, *Congressional Quarterly,* the *Congressional Record,* and many other publications. The police reporter scans officers' accident reports, the dispatcher's log, and a variety of records. The state editor watches all the smaller newspapers in his territory, and the city editor keeps a close eye on any local competitor.

Reporters begin each day by reading the most recent edition of their own newspaper, and many of their stories are based on new developments in continuing situations. Often a story results from checking last year's files to see what's likely to be happening at the present. And every reporter uses background information from the clipping files or from the encyclopedia, almanacs, directories, atlases, and other reference works that a newspaper library contains.

Let's follow an average reporter's reading through a typical day. Suppose you are beat reporter on an afternoon newspaper. You report for work at 8 A.M. and empty your mailbox of incoming letters and any special assignment from the city editor. The next stop is the office bulletin board, where you look for announcements of any changes in policy or general procedure. Perhaps there is a notice of an office party or a clipping of an hilarious error posted by some editor. At your desk, you open your mail, smile at a congratulatory note from a source, and sort out the usable from the unwanted publicity. You check your desk calendar, make a list of the routine stories you expect to produce today, and assemble the agendas, speech texts, and publicity releases you will use. Next you read the latest edition of the morning paper, searching primarily for developments on your beat. You at least glance at every story on the front page and you probably look at the editorials. In the back of the paper, you survey the legal notices to see if anything pertains to your beat: tax notices, sheriff's sales, official minutes of meetings, calls for bids on public contracts.

If it is a slow day, you read some of the ads, especially the personals and other oddities in the classified section. Perhaps you'll run across an idea for a human interest story. Once this is finished, you consult with the city editor, rewrite any publicity releases that can be handled immediately, then check out of the office shortly after 9 A.M. to make your rounds.

Let's suppose the beat is city hall, with several offices to cover. You inspect each bulletin board and jot down ideas for questions. At the city engineer's office, you read the list of building permits granted. Your paper may publish each permit, or you may search only for a major development. At the planning office, you pick up a copy of a protest petition. At the parks department, you get a copy of a consultant's proposal for two new swimming pools. You may pick up printed materials at every stop, ask questions about each, and return to the office with your pockets full. In less than an hour, you may have collected enough material for a half dozen or more stories. Some will demand immediate attention, and some can be put off until after deadline and written for the next day.

Before you write the major stories, you call the library for the necessary clipping files. Maybe you have all the background information you need in your head, but you'd better make certain. You remember the blunder made by a colleague on rewrite—identifying that fellow arrested in another state only as a "North Centerville man" because he hadn't bothered to pull the clip file. If he had checked it out, he would have discovered that the subject was a fugitive accused of a series of bank robberies. The rewrite man really caught it from the city editor.

After each story is finished, you double-check spelling by consulting your notes again and using the city directory and the dictionary. You can spell better than most people, but some words always baffle you.

Throughout the day, much of the beat reporter's reading is directly connected with the stories at hand. You have little time for continuing education. Maybe you have a chance to skim through *Editor & Publisher, The Quill,* or *New York Magazine,* but you probably won't read anything in detail until after work. However, some specialists— the drama critic, the business editor, the political writer—may spend most of the day inside the office and manage considerable general reading during working hours. The specialist also may have to visit libraries frequently, as will the investigative reporter.

Notice that the reporter reads many things mainly in order to get ideas for stories. When you read newspapers from other cities, you discover situations that could be investigated in your own town. You get even more specific ideas from bulletin boards and the legal notices in your own newspaper. You may even get an idea merely by glancing at the calendar and noticing what holidays are approaching or considering the kind of news that is likely to develop during this particular season.

Scientific Research Methods

Reporters often use the findings of social scientists as the basis for
stories. On occasion, a journalist may also use some of the scientist's methods. Ordinarily, however, the actual research is conducted
by universities, independent marketing research or opinion polling
firms, or a separate research department within the newspaper organization. Few reporters are trained in scientific research, although the
number is growing.

Many newspapers publish syndicated opinion polls regularly. A
few have their own polls, such as the Minnesota Poll published by the
Cowles newspapers of Minneapolis. A growing practice is to use
scientific methods to investigate special problems, such as attitudes of
minority groups in the inner city. This has been done successfully in
some major cities where the findings of researchers were supplemented
by reportorial investigation.

The basic requirement of a scientific poll is that everyone in the
population to be surveyed have an equal chance of being interviewed.
This is accomplished by taking a random sample—getting a list of all
the names in the population and selecting interviewees according to a
table of random numbers. If all members of the population have telephones, a telephone directory can be used as the source of names.

Questions must be prepared carefully. They often must include
filter questions to eliminate persons who are uninformed. Or perhaps
they include questions designed to explain the subject as well as to
get an opinion. Designing questions of this subtlety is too time-
consuming for most reporters. Thus, it is usually better to leave
opinion polling to the behavioral scientists.

Scientific polling should never be confused with the "man on
the street" interviews that some newspapers publish. These may be interesting and often highly entertaining, but they are hardly scientific.
And that fact should be made perfectly clear to the reader who might
confuse a summary of off-the-cuff opinions with the results of a
Gallup survey.

Many Methods, Many Sources

If the facts are simple and noncontroversial, and the source is
known to be reliable, the reporter may use only the informal interview. Similarly, in a routine traffic accident or burglary, the beat
reporter may only read the police report, without talking to anyone.
But if the situation is at all controversial or complex, if the reporter
knows it is a sensitive area, he or she will use more than one personal
source and more than one method to get the information. A thorough
investigative story might require all five: personal participation, observation, talking with witnesses, reading documents, and conducting
a poll.

The five methods have been separated in this chapter for the purpose of analysis. In practice, two or more of them almost always merge, and reporters move easily back and forth from reading to observing to asking questions throughout the day. The only time they are likely to be conscious of the different methods is when they run into difficulty getting a particular bit of information. Then the reporter will look for a different way.

SUGGESTED ASSIGNMENTS

1. An unseasonably early blizzard has stricken your city and several surrounding counties, causing undetermined damage and hardship. You are assigned to write a general roundup. List the questions you must answer, then list as many sources as you can think of for each bit of information. You should have a total of at least 10 sources.
2. Visit city hall or interview your newspaper's city government reporter. What offices are covered regularly for news? Describe the information collected routinely from each office. What regular board meetings are covered?
3. You will attend a presidential news conference this week in Washington. Using current newspapers as source material, list 20 questions you would like to ask the president.

CHAPTER FIVE / PUTTING IT TOGETHER

Any piece of prose, fact or fiction, can be divided into three parts: beginning, middle, and end. The beginning should get the reader's attention and promise interesting information. The middle, by far the longest part, should fulfill that promise with supporting detail. The only absolute requirements of the end are that it be brief and satisfying—requirements usually fulfilled simply by stopping when you run out of relevant information.

If this sounds easy, it's because it is—at least, in the basic approach. You grab the readers, tell them what you have to say, then quit. You need only know your readers and have a clear idea of what you are trying to tell them. The writing itself is the easiest part of the reporter's job—and the quickest. A simple story of a half dozen paragraphs can be written in less than 15 minutes. A fairly thorough story can be written in less than an hour, although you may have spent half a day gathering the facts. And you can write and revise a long investigative series in two days, although you may have spent months collecting the information. The time-consuming part of the job is getting, confirming, sifting, and organizing facts. Once you know the story thoroughly, you merely tell it to your typewriter.

Imagine that a friend is starting a bus trip to a nearby town. The bus is pulling away from the station as you arrive panting with an important message. Your friend leans out the window while you run along beside the bus, waving to get his attention. You have to give him the message fast, before the bus picks up speed. You have to give him the essential facts immediately. You can't waste words on unnecessary preliminaries. You don't think about the finer points of discourse, nor do you think of entertaining your listener or trying to impress him with the extent of your vocabulary. All you think about is the message itself and the fact that your friend needs it *now*, before the bus gets away. So you tell it, in one great rush, starting with the most important fact. You get to the heart of the matter immediately. And you tell it in shirtsleeve English, using words your friend will readily understand.

This is the way a news story is told. And this is why journalistic prose is more often breathless than deathless. Nobody is criticizing your delivery, and it wouldn't matter if someone were. The story is strictly a private matter between you and your reader. It is communication, not literature, and the only goal is to get the message across—clearly, accurately, and quickly. The keys to success are (1) knowing what is most important to your reader, (2) having all the facts he wants, and (3) telling it fast, while the total story is still fresh in your mind.

ANALYZING THE STRUCTURE

Most news stories are told in *logical* order. This means that the most important fact appears in the lead, regardless of its place in the time sequence involved. Thereafter, the facts are arranged more or less in order of descending importance. A few human interest stories are told *chronologically*, the events narrated in the order in which they occurred, but such organization is rare. Editors prefer stories using logical organization because they take fewer words and therefore less space, they take less time and talent to produce, and they are more easily trimmed when space is limited. Further, logical organization best serves the busy reader: it tells what he most wants to know right at the beginning.

Logical organization consists of two main parts: lead and body. They can be compared to a sharp iron spike atop a concrete pillar. The lead makes the point, and the body supports it with solid, factual —indeed concrete—information. Or, using a more dynamic analogy, we can compare the story to a boxer's jab: both writer and boxer must hit the target fast and squarely, then follow through.

To illustrate, let's take the simplest kind of story and compare the way you would tell it orally with the way you would organize it for print. Remember your friend who was leaving on the bus? There he is, leaning out the window, and you're running along beside the bus, shouting at him:

> *"Hey, Joe! There was a fire a few minutes ago in the kitchen at your place. Nobody hurt—just some grease on the stove. Your wife put it out with baking soda. But the wall got scorched up some, and she wants you to call when you get to Midland."*

It's hardly an important event, certainly not worth space in a metropolitan newspaper. But the message is important to Joe, and you've told it quickly and clearly. You've told him what happened (a fire, put out), how (with baking soda), where (in the kitchen at his place), when (a few minutes ago), and by whom (his wife). In addition, you've assured him that nobody was hurt, which is always an important question in an accident story, and you've asked him to call home when he reaches his destination. You've told a surprising amount in a few words.

You did not tell Joe about the fire exactly as you would have written the story, but you did fulfill the major objectives of news-writing. First you got Joe's attention (by calling his name). Then you quickly identified the subject (a fire) and gave him the fact that *he* was most interested in (nobody was hurt). If you were writing it in standard news form, you would also begin with the *subject* and the *outcome,* perhaps like this:

> *LEAD:* A small grease fire was put out with baking soda today at the home of Joseph T. O'Brien, 1139 Maple Ave. Nobody was injured.
>
> *BODY:* The fire began at the kitchen range where Mrs. O'Brien was frying chicken. She quickly smothered it with soda.
> The fire was out before firemen arrived, but they said a wall was slightly damaged by the burning grease.

No two reporters see an event exactly alike, of course, and the fire story could be told in several different ways without departing from logical organization. Here's an example of a different approach:

> *LEAD:* A housewife escaped injury today when blazing grease set fire to her kitchen wall.
>
> *BODY:* She was Mrs. Joseph T. O'Brien, 1139 Maple Ave. While a neighbor called the fire department, Mrs. O'Brien put out the flames with baking soda.

The Inverted Pyramid

Logical organization sometimes is diagrammed as an inverted pyramid because most of the vital information—the base of the story—is placed at the top or beginning. It then dwindles into less and less important detail, so that theoretically the story could be cut from the bottom without sacrificing anything essential. We summarize the major facts, then support and expand.

Here is a story that follows the classic inverted pyramid form:

OLBIA, SARDINIA (UPI)—The director of New York's Metropolitan Opera and two of his daughters died Tuesday when their rented car crashed head-on into a cement truck. His wife and another daughter were seriously injured, police said.

Goeran Gentele, 55, a Stockholm native who lived in New York, was vacationing in the posh Porto Cervo resort and had rented a car to take a drive around Sardinia's northern coast.

He tried to pass a small car ahead of him, and crashed head-on into a cement truck. He died instantly, as did his daughters Beatrice, 15, and Anne, 21, who were sitting in the front seat, police said.

His wife Marie and his third daughter, Jannette, who were in the back were taken to the Olbia hospital.

Spokesmen for the Metropolitan Opera said Gentele and his family had been on a three-week vacation in Sardinia and were due back in New York Monday.

Gentele took over the helm of the Met from Rudolf Bing July 1. He was tapped for the job while he was head of the Stockholm Opera. His appointment was announced a year before so Gentele could come to New York to prepare for the 1972-73 season.

At the announcement of his appointment, Gentele, who had been both an actor and a director, said he would stress the theatrical.

"Opera is theater," he said, "and the theatrical part must be as important as the music."

Born in Stockholm, Gentele was a graduate of Stockholm University and the School of Royal Dramatic Theatre.

Mayor Lindsay termed his death a "devastating tragedy."

The mayor called Gentele a "great artist most certainly headed for further greatness at the Met" and Lindsay added, "we pray for the recovery of his wife Marie and their surviving daughter."

Two characteristics of the inverted pyramid are the summary lead, which presents all the essential information in the first or the first two paragraphs, and the extreme brevity of the paragraphs. This allows the editor to cut the story at any point. In the example above, the first four paragraphs constitute a complete story. Depending on space requirements, the story could be cut there or following any one of the remaining paragraphs, which provide background information on the subject.

The End Is in the Beginning

You may have noted that the visual analogy of the inverted pyramid is almost the opposite of the earlier comparison of a news story to a pillar topped with a spike. But the meaning of the metaphors is very similar. The point, the thrust, the basis, the essence of the story comes at the beginning. Compared to other kinds of writing, the news story is always upside down. It begins at the "end" —the fiction writer's climax or the scholarly writer's conclusion. If, for example, we were to change "Cinderella" into a news story, we would begin with the wedding, thus:

> A former maid-of-all work became the bride of Prince Charming today.

And if we were to convert a master's degree thesis to a news story, we would find the lead somewhere in Part IV, Summary and Conclusion. We would be much more interested in what the scholar discovered and how he assesses that discovery, than in the way he went about his investigation.

Applying this principle to a few common varieties of stories, here is the information with which we would probably build the leads:

Trial—The verdict and the sentence, not the testimony or closing arguments.
Athletic contest—Who won and by what score, not the fact that the teams met.
Congressional action—The final outcome, not the debate or maneuvering leading up to it.
Speech—The most important thing said, not the mere fact that somebody spoke.
Traffic accident—The number of deaths or the extent of injuries, not the fact that two cars collided.

Professionals have the leads "written" in their heads long before they can get to a typewriter. They often begin phrasing it in their minds while still conducting the interview or sitting through the meeting. Before getting back to the office, they probably know what they will say throughout the story and almost the exact wording of the first few paragraphs. From the first, professional reporters visualize the story as a unit. This is a knack which you can begin to develop as soon as you learn to think in terms of leads.

LEAD WITH AN ACE

Broadcast newspeople organize their stories in three parts: (1) Action or climax, (2) Cause, and (3) Effect. Because an entire story for broadcast usually amounts to only what would be the beginning for a newspaper story, this pattern can be helpful in learning to write the lead. You can remember it by the letters A-C-E.

Here is a simple story as it might be written for radio or television:

> A water main burst today in the 800 block of Elm Avenue, closing the street to traffic for nearly a quarter of a mile. (Action and Effect)
>
> Police said the main was ruptured by workers digging a trench for a power cable. (Cause)
>
> Homes in the area are expected to be without water most of the night. (Effect)

This covers the five W's and H in a general way and would be sufficient for broadcast. But newspaper readers would expect more detail. At what hour did the main burst? What was the name of the company laying the cable, and why was it being installed? How are residents reacting to the lack of water? What steps are being taken to restore service? Newspaper readers expect details which broadcasters don't have time to supply.

GETTING ATTENTION, AND WHERE TO GO FROM THERE

Writing becomes easier if you realize that your basic problem is the same as the teacher's or the salesperson's. Before you can tell or sell readers anything, you must first get their attention and arouse their interest. These preliminary steps are basic to all communication. If you don't get the reader's attention—and hold it—his eye will wander to the advertisements or he will turn the page. The television viewer has similar options—changing the channel or going to the refrigerator or bathroom as your story starts.

Because getting attention is the first step, editors put a premium on striking leads. Any device that will make the reader look twice—direct address, a colorful quotation, a question or even a verse—is considered legitimate as long as it doesn't misrepresent the facts, violate the tone, or distort the overall meaning of the story. But flashy techniques are the exception rather than the rule. Usually the best lead is a simple declarative statement which identifies the subject immediately and presents the central action and its effect. If the story is worth telling, its major feature should be sufficient to capture the attention of those who will be interested in it.

Striving for an attention-getting lead, many beginners get off to what seems a good start, then bog down in the second paragraph. They don't know where to go after the first sentence. Sometimes the remedy is simple: if the lead raises a logical question, either directly or implicitly, the second paragraph should at least begin to answer that question. Often a transition from the lead to the body of the story can be accomplished merely by repeating a key word or phrase or by rewording the central idea.

In the following story the writer combines the logical answer to an implied question and a rewording of the central idea as he moves from the lead to the second paragraph of the story:

> Sen. Carl Johnson announced today that he will retire at the end of his present term.
>
> The 80-year-old Milltown Republican *said he would not be a candidate for reelection* (repetition of the central idea) *because of his advanced age and recurring illnesses.* (answering the implicit "why?")

Going back to the Action-Cause-Effect organization, the next section of the story logically would quote officials of both major parties on prospective candidates for the Senate seat. Then the reporter might give Johnson's announcement verbatim and recount his recent illnesses.

The tie-back to the lead—the phrase rewording the central idea—doesn't always appear as early as the second paragraph. A speech story, for example, often follows this formula:

1. What was said, when, by whom.
2. Where, to whom, under what circumstances.
3. Rewording and expansion of what was said.

This formula illustrates another approach to the problem of where to go from the lead. Normally not all of the major components —the five W's and H—will be covered in the first paragraph. And some may be covered only in a general way. Those remaining (presumably the elements of secondary importance for the particular story) will then be mentioned in the second paragraph. At the same time, one or more components might be made more concrete. For example, in the story concerning Goeran Gentele's death, the lead covers who, what, when, and how, but the people involved are identified only by professional position (director of New York's Metropolitan Opera) and relationship (two of his daughters). The second paragraph begins with Gentele's name, gives further identifying facts, and elaborates on where the accident occurred (previously indicated only in the dateline). In the third paragraph, the matter of "how" is made more specific, as are the consequences of the action.

When you have trouble moving from the lead into the body of the story, it may be because you chose the wrong lead. Perhaps you tried too hard to be bright, resulting in a lead that was unnatural to the subject. If you must strain, if the lead doesn't come naturally to mind and if the rest of the story doesn't flow naturally from it, it's probably the wrong choice.

Internal Summaries

Logical organization often requires short summaries throughout the story. These perform the same function as the lead, but with a narrower focus and less important information. They pull several facts together and must be followed by more detailed elaboration. The development of a summary may require several paragraphs, or a summary may be contained within one or two sentences.

Typically, the internal summary is introduced with a transition that identifies a new subject and indicates its relation to what has already been told. The latter may be achieved with no more than the repetition of a key name or circumstance. The body of the story, then, often falls into a repeated pattern of transition, summary, and development. Note how the story concerning the Metropolitan Opera director's death illustrates this general approach. Here is another example. Following a lead giving the basic facts concerning a debate between two senators, the body of the story might be developed as follows:

> On trade with mainland China, the two senators disagreed sharply. Sen Black said. . . . This was challenged by Sen. White who maintained that. . . .
>
> *(This might be followed by several short paragraphs devoted to Black's position, then several paragraphs presenting White's views. But the point is to summarize both positions as succinctly as possible before we give either side in detail.)*
>
> Agreeing several times during the de-

bate, both senators supported the President on strategic arms limitation, national health insurance, and food price strategy.

(Again, this would be developed in detail, if only to remind the reader what the President's position has been on each issue.)

Replaceable and Removable Blocks

Professional reporters build stories that are relatively easy to modify if the facts change. For this purpose they keep paragraphs short and make each one a self-contained unit. For example, in an election roundup, political reporters generally devote a separate paragraph to the returns in each major race. This allows them to revise the figures for any individual contest without changing the rest of the story.

Short paragraphs also make the story easy to cut after it has been set in type. This is one reason why paragraphs are seldom more than three sentences long—and many are only a single sentence. The editor can throw away three or four lines of type without having anything to reset.

Another reason for the short paragraph is its psychological effect. Most newspaper columns are narrow, and the standard paragraph taught in English composition courses (a full development of a single point or idea) would result in several inches of unbroken gray. Readers see all those words and think it must be difficult to read. And they may be right. We try to make the story more inviting to the eye (and mind) by indenting frequently and leaving some white space.

Varying the Form

Although few question the need for logical organization in newswriting, many reporters object to the concept of the inverted pyramid. If the story were perfect, they argue, cutting from the bottom would be impossible. Every sentence and paragraph would be essential to the whole. And they argue rightly that strict adherence to the inverted pyramid form may force the writer into a straitjacket, discouraging imaginative treatment and causing many stories to read alike. A news story, they say, should be approached like any other form of exposition. Writers should be flexible enough to vary their treatment with different subjects. They should, to a certain extent at least, let the content of each story determine its organization. If every incident is unique, why can't the story form reflect its uniqueness?

Actually, few writers follow the inverted pyramid religiously. The day is past when the wise reporter automatically tacked a superfluous paragraph to the end of each story "to give the city editor something to throw away." Reporters today use surprise endings, summary endings, narrative leads, complete narratives, and a combination of logical and chronological treatment. A truly sophisticated news story almost defies analysis and may be as difficult to cut as fiction. Here is an example:

OKLAHOMA CITY (AP)—They laid him to rest in an unmarked grave, the final stop for one of the restless wanderers who dot the highways, seeking a ride to somewhere they haven't been.

There were no mourners. The commitment service was brief and nondenominational, read by a layman.

His parents and relatives weren't there. No friends offered condolences.

There was no marker on his grave because authorities weren't able to discover his name.

It was three weeks ago Monday when the youth was struck by a car and killed at the intersection of Interstate 40 and U.S. 183 near Clinton in western Oklahoma.

He carried no identification and there was nothing to indicate where he had been or where he was going.

Authorities said he had long dark hair and probably was between 15 and 19 years of age.

Intensive efforts to establish his identity have failed. Hundreds of inquiries have been received from across the country, but in each case the result was negative.

For more than two weeks his body lay unclaimed in the morgue.

"We decided it would be better to go ahead and bury him," Dr. A. J. Chapman, state medical examiner, said Monday. "We have the dental charts and description on file with pictures and other information."

He was buried in Resurrection Memorial Cemetery as a welfare case. The cemetery's general manager, Joseph

Levesque, conducted the brief service.

Authorities are still trying to identify the youth. Fingerprints sent to the FBI laboratory in Washington have failed to bring any report. There was no reaction to pictures circulated by the Oklahoma Highway Patrol.

Arthur Larson, FBI special agent in charge here, said the youth could go un-identified for a long time if he were younger than 18.

A rule-conscious editor might observe that the example above violates several taboos. It begins with a pronoun that has no antecedent, it contains a series of negative statements, and it employs the irritating "there are." But rules are broken regularly by writers who know when and how to do it to make a story more effective.

MIXING THE LOGICAL AND THE CHRONOLOGICAL

When the story is mostly physical action (for example, a sports event or a police chase) you may start with several summary paragraphs, then go into a narrative or play-by-play account. This still is logical organization, but obviously not the inverted pyramid, since it can't be cut arbitrarily from the bottom. Once the writer begins the play-by-play, nothing can be eliminated without ruining the story. The editor must use all or nothing.

Chronology in this form is so familiar that no example should be necessary. In sports stories the chronology is easily introduced by a terse, indented phrase: "The play-by-play:"

Writers of general news sometimes have more trouble with the transition from summary to chronology. Occasionally they use a device similar to the sportswriter's: "Police gave this account:" or "Here's how Jones described the crash." Often, however, they attempt a fiction-like flashback and resort to the tired "It all began when . . . ," a device that causes editors and English teachers alike to shudder. A better solution would be something like "Peterson's misadventures began last August when . . . ." Notice how reference to a specific person, situation, and time makes the transition both clear and smooth. Skillful transitions are among the writer's most important devices for keeping the reader reading.

THE ANECDOTE LEAD

The sequence of summary and narration is often reversed, especially at the beginning of the story. One of the more common techniques of feature writing is to begin with an anecdote, a short narrative or case history picked for its attention-getting quality and its ability to humanize the story. The ideal anecdote lead is one that il-

lustrates the general situation. It is a concrete example of everything
the writer plans to treat in the body of the story. From the single, specific instance, the writer moves to the general subject but often returns
to the anecdote in the final paragraph to achieve the journalist's
equivalent of the fiction writer's "satisfactory ending."

Note the transitions in this exaggerated example of an anecdote
lead and the ending which brings the reader back to the beginning:

All day, Johnny Blank crouches wild-
eyed in a corner, as frightened as a
jungle animal.

Tuesday he threw a plate of food at
the attendant. Today he only retreats.

*(Now the writer moves from the spe-
cific case to the general situation.)*

Thousands of other Johnnys crouch in
other corners in mental institutions
throughout the nation, extreme examples
of paranoid schizophrenia. A few years
ago nearly all would have been subjected
to electric shock treatments. Today the
shock treatment is all but abandoned.
Doctors are achieving far better results
with a mixture of chemicals and psychotherapy.

At Central State Hospital. . . .

*(Here the writer makes another transi-
tion to establish the local angle. This is
where the story actually begins. All the
foregoing could have been eliminated—
but the story would have been far less
interesting.)*

*(After describing the treatment and
the local application, the writer returns
to his opening anecdote.)*

Today, only a week after the treatment has begun, Johnny Blank still
shows no response. But next weekend,
when his parents visit him, perhaps there
will be a flicker of recognition. Within a
few more days he should begin talking.
And the odds are good that Johnny will
go home within three months, a living
example of the successful marriage of
chemistry and psychotherapy.

Anecdotes may be used throughout the story, as well as at the
beginning and the end. The entire story may be told chronologically,
of course, and the complete narrative often is used for short "brites"

and even longer human interest stories. But the complete narrative usually is avoided for straight news because it requires more words and skill than the story may be worth. And it is seldom applicable to interpretive or investigative stories, because the sequence of events usually isn't as important or interesting as the outcome.

Approaching Objectivity

Most editors insist that news stories be "objective," as the term is defined in the media. By this, they mean that reporters should look outward at the world, rather than inward into themselves. They should present the facts fully, fairly, and without comment. Editors don't expect miracles. They know that "science is objective but scientists aren't," and that reporters usually are less so than scientists. Few will argue that complete objectivity is possible—except perhaps in compiling box scores, market reports, and the daily temperature readings—and many question whether it is even desirable. But all insist that reporters keep their opinions out of the news. They expect reporters to tell only what *is,* not what should or shouldn't be. Any editorializing must be left to writers who are hired specifically for that purpose.

How can beginners improve their objectivity? Nobody has a sure-fire recipe, and the writings of psychologist Abraham Maslow show how difficult the problem can be. Maslow suggests that the more one concentrates on "the matter at hand," the more he forgets himself and his opinions. It would seem, then, that the first step toward objectivity is total mental—not emotional—involvement in the here and now. But this narrow focus has a built-in handicap; if people concentrate *too much* on the matter at hand, Maslow observes, they may fail to see how the immediate event fits into the overall reality. For example, totally involved reporters may think their own "big" story is the only one of the day that merits attention. The editor, who sees hundreds of stories daily, knows better.

It would appear that the most objective story is one written with total concentration, then set aside to "cool" and later revised when the writer has regained a critical perspective and can return to the subject with some detachment. Unfortunately, reporters seldom have time to revise fast-breaking stories. At one sitting, they must somehow achieve a combination of deep concentration, emotional detachment, a tight focus on the here and now, and the ability to show how the immediate event fits into the total picture.

A combination of objectivity and perspective seldom develops overnight. But the new reporter can begin by following a set of guidelines that governs the professionals:

1. *Never write in the first person,* unless you are a legitimate participant in the action. The prevailing theory is that reporters themselves aren't news.

2. *Never describe a state of mind.* Tell only what is done or said, not what is felt or thought. You can't be certain what people think, either by observing their behavior or by listening to what they say. You can't get inside their minds, nor can you make inferences from outer appearances.

   Instead of writing that "the mayor was angry," write that the mayor's face reddened, and he shouted as he pounded the table." This tells only what anyone present could have seen or heard. Readers can decide for themselves whether the mayor really was angry or whether he was only acting.

3. *Always choose precise, descriptive adjectives.* Instead of calling the winner of a beauty contest "a statuesque beauty"—an impression, not a description—say she is "a 5-foot, 9-inch blonde, 38-24-36." Beauty is a matter of opinion. Measurements and hair color aren't.

   Instead of writing that a speaker is "prominent" or "well known," give his credentials—degrees, experience, positions held. If a person is really prominent, the reader doesn't have to be told. If not, the adjective won't make him so.

4. *Avoid superlatives.* Any superlative *(unique, always, never, for the first time in history, the greatest, the smallest, the youngest, the oldest)* is risky and should be avoided unless you are prepared to prove it.

5. *Always consider the source.* Weigh both your source's motives and his or her reputation for fairness and accuracy. When the story is controversial, always try to get other viewpoints and factual evidence.

6. *Interpret events and situations only when you are certain of their meaning.* Don't try to read significance into an event unless you know all the background. Instead, tell only what happened as clearly and factually as you can, and quote persons who appear qualified to determine the action's significance.

7. *Pinpoint every event in space and time.* Tell when and where it happened. This enables readers to relate the new information to what they already know. They can then fit the isolated event into their own private picture of overall reality.

WRITING THE STORY

Following Copy Form

To reach your readers, you must first get the story past the editor and into print. This means that your product must at least look like a news story—it must be presented in a form the editor recognizes and accepts, a form that is easy to edit and set into type. The form described here is relatively standard in schools of journalism and many newspapers, although specific rules may not apply in newspaper plants using electronic editing or computerized typesetting.

All news stories are typewritten, double- or triple-spaced, on one side of the sheet of paper. Margins are at least an inch wide and ample space is left at the top and bottom of the sheet. This gives the editor (or professor) plenty of space to make corrections or changes.

Unless given other instructions, type your name in the extreme upper left of each sheet. Immediately below your name is a working title or "slug," one or two words that merely identify the story. All except the first page of the story are numbered immediately after the slug.

On the first sheet of paper (sheets are also known as "takes"), leave at least three inches blank below the slug before you begin the story. This allows room for the editor to write instructions to the printer, if necessary. After the first page, however, you need leave only a normal amount of space at the top.

Thus far, copy form may seem little different from the way you would prepare essays in English composition. But many newspapers have two rules you may never have encountered before:

1. A word is never broken between lines; that is, you never hyphenate a word at the end of a line and continue it on the next.
2. A paragraph is never broken between takes. Each page must end at the end of a paragraph.

The reason for both of these rules is to make the typesetter's work easier. (The second rule may not apply at plants with computer technology.) When each page does end with the end of a paragraph, we must have still another rule: the bottom of the page must indicate whether there is more to the story or whether it ends at that point. If there is more, we center MORE at the bottom and circle it so the printer knows not to set it. When you get to the end of the story, center 30 or ### and circle it. These are each recognized universally as a symbol for the end, although some reporters indicate the end by centering their initials, another widely recognized symbol. Newspaper plants with computer technology may have their own codes or systems for ending each take and for ending the story itself.

Write It Fast

Speed is essential. If a story isn't finished by deadline, it doesn't get into print—and the reporter doesn't keep the job long. You should be able to type about 40 words a minute if you expect to reach professional speed.

More important than manual skill, however, is the ability to compose at the typewriter. You must learn to think at the keyboard. Forget about writing in longhand. It's too slow. You can write and revise a story at the typewriter in less time than it would take to try out two or three leads in longhand.

And you should get started as soon as you have the necessary information. Few reporters take such legible and well-organized notes that they can decipher them a day later. It's best to get the story on paper before any essential fact escapes you.

Write it fast. If you write self-consciously, trying to satisfy all the requirements of what you think a news story should be, the result is likely to be wooden and awkward. Try not to edit in your mind. Let the words spill out as they come. The faster you write, the simpler your language will be. You won't have time to think of all those long words and complex sentences. And your story will have more unity. You won't have time to digress. One idea will flow naturally into another, and you will seldom have trouble producing a story that "hangs together." If you make an error, don't stop to edit; XXX it out and keep going. You don't want to lose that momentum. The time to make corrections is after you have finished, not while you are still writing.

Testing the Finished Story

The first draft of your story probably won't be exactly what you want. In your haste to get it on paper, you probably will omit some essential fact. You may also unintentionally let some of your own opinion creep into the story, and you almost certainly will use too many words. So go back over your copy, eliminate the editorializing and the unnecessary words, then compare the story with your notes. Does it meet the test? Do dates, amounts, and the spelling of proper names check out? Does the story answer all the questions? Is the language simple, precise, and concrete?

One way to test the story is to try it out on a friend who knows nothing about the subject. If the reader raises questions, you will have to revise the story to supply the missing information. Another test is to read the story aloud. If you must pause for breath in the middle of a sentence, or if you stumble all over your tongue, you will have to shorten some sentences or simplify the language.

It is also important to check the story's objectivity. Have you made yourself invisible? Have you written only what you could prove in court? If the story involves a controversy, have you presented opposing viewpoints?

Adding Transitions

Mark the points where you need more information and write the necessary paragraphs on a separate sheet of paper. Paste these inserts into the story, then look again at the finished product. The chances are that you'll suffer a shock. The story that once read so smoothly has suddenly become awkward. By trimming and inserting, you disrupted the story's continuity. You lost some of the original unity and even more of the rhythm when you inserted those paragraphs. You may have to rewrite the entire story and supply some new transitions to tie it back together.

What is a transition? It's any word or phrase a writer uses to indicate a change in time, place, subject, speaker, or idea. At the same time, it generally establishes continuity by suggesting the relationship between what has gone before and what is to follow. It can be as simple as the words *and, but, then, another, similarly,* or *nevertheless.* It may indicate a contrast between two facts or ideas *(however, although, on the other hand),* a cause-effect relationship *(since, thus, therefore, because),* or a chronological relationship *(meanwhile, later, earlier).*

Transitional words or phrases are only one of several methods of effecting a smooth transition. Another transitional device is to repeat a key word, phrase, or idea from the preceding sentence, then add another thought. Another is simply using a pronoun that refers to a noun in the preceding sentence ("it," for example). Another is reference to a different time or place ("But in 1968, in Vietnam, he had . . ."). Still another device is to use paraphrase when you introduce a new speaker, to avoid the confusion that would result if you had two direct quotations from different persons with nothing between them. (Before you let anyone else speak, point to him.)

Transitions are simply pointers, advance signals to the reader that "now we're going to talk about something different, but still related." They serve three purposes: (1) to alert the reader to something new, (2) to glue each succeeding thought to the one immediately preceding it, and (3) to establish a rhythm that moves the reader smoothly and quickly through the story.

The transition usually is placed at the beginning of the sentence, although logic or the writer's ear for rhythm sometimes dictates that it be delayed. Experience indicates that transitions come to mind most readily when the writer views the story as a unit and writes it quickly from beginning to end. This is why a completely rewritten story usually is much smoother than one that merely has been patched up with inserts.

Transitions are relatively simple when the story concerns a single event which happens at a specific time and place. But when time, place, or subject matter keeps changing throughout the story, we have to pay particular attention to transitions. This applies especially to roundup stories, of which there are two common types. In Type A, the unifying element is the situation or the action, and the variable element is the place. Familiar examples are a politician's campaign flight which takes him to several cities within a few hours, a war roundup with action on land and in the air at various points, or a national strike with developments in different places around the nation as well as in Washington. In Type B, the unifying element is the setting or agency, and the variable element is the action. Examples are stories rounding up a variety of actions by the city council, the state legislature, or the Supreme Court. The only thing the actions have in common is that they were taken by the same body. In both kinds of roundups the inherent unity is limited, and we must establish and maintain continuity with transitions, constantly reminding the reader of a change in place or subject.

Here is a simple story that illustrates skillful and restrained use of transitions, which we have italicized:

By ERNIE COWAN
Copley News Service
SAN DIEGO, Calif.—There are lots of people here who think President Ford was in San Diego recently.

Some think they even have a picture to prove it.

But the pictures they took were actually of Canadian Robert Smeding, a look-alike of the President.

Smeding, here on vacation from his home in British Columbia, has been the center of much attention.

"I get two reactions from people," says Smeding, 49. "They either panic, thinking I am the President, or they are immediately skeptical."

He said the first words out of most people's mouths are "President Ford?"

Smeding, who is two inches taller and 20 pounds lighter than Ford, said people began to recognize him when Ford became vice president.

"*And* almost everywhere I went, someone would notice, but it's never been as bad as it was here in San Diego the last few days," he said.

While touring places such as the zoo, or nearby Mission Bay Park, Smeding said he sometimes had groups of people following him, and many people who took pictures.

"But now I'm a little worried. I'm very proud to look like Mr. Ford, but I don't want anyone to take a shot at me," he says.

On a short walk with a reporter, Smeding turned many heads as people looked twice to be sure of what they saw.

At a gift shop at the Islandia Motel here, clerk Anna Whittiker was shocked when he walked in.

"It was a shock at first, *but then* I knew it had to be someone who just looked like the President," Mrs. Whittiker said. "If it was the President, someone would have told us ahead of time."

Smeding has the same receding hairline as Ford, the same build and smile. He doesn't smoke a pipe, *however,* and his Dutch Canadian accent quickly gives him away.

Although he enjoys the treatment he gets, Smeding said he never tries to act like the President.

Recently in a restaurant he caused some commotion until they realized he was not the President.

"At first they wanted to know where my escorts were," Smeding said.

Has looking like the President of the United States changed his life?

"No, it hasn't until now, but as Mr. Ford becomes better known, I may have problems," Smeding, an interior decorator, says.

So far, all of the people who have mistaken him for the President have treated him with "great respect."

Although proud of his look-alike image, Smeding wears a Canadian maple leaf on his coat pocket.

"That is so people will know I'm a *Canadian,"* he says.

Writers who have a natural ear for rhythm may use more transitions than they should. You may have to eliminate some of them merely to determine what they have said, and occasionally you may discover that they have said little. A certain kind of writer tends to substitute slick techniques for content. And many others, with excellent content, may bury it beneath wordy transitions. Sometimes, too, a gifted ear tricks a writer into using a ridiculous phrase simply because it sounds right. An example is the obituary transition, "In his long lifetime, he . . ." Whatever he did, it obviously was not after he died.

Transitions are necessary, but they never should be allowed to overshadow the basic content of the story or to bury the most important part of an individual sentence. Like everything else in newswriting, they should be kept short and simple.

Making Attribution Easier

As a beginner, you are almost certain to have a problem with attribution. Never before have you had to attribute so much, and suddenly you become conscious of all those "he saids" and "she saids." You would like to vary it somehow, but the instructor keeps reminding you that "said" is usually the best verb of attribution because of its neutrality. If you can't change the word, what can you do?

One solution is simply to stop struggling so hard for variety. The "he said" that seems so monotonous to the writer may slip past the readers almost unnoticed. It doesn't seem nearly as awkward to them as it does to you. Readers hardly notice attribution unless they are looking for it, as you can determine for yourself by first reading a speech story quickly, then going back through it and underlining all the attribution. Obviously, readers can absorb a lot of monotony without being aware of it.

Still, if you are going to satisfy yourself as well as the readers, you will strive for *some* variety. And your efforts may be as awkward as a baby's first steps. Nothing about this business of attribution seems natural, you may think. And you're at least partly right—it often isn't. Normally we write news in a pseudoconversational manner, trying to make the story sound much the way we would tell it orally. But we depart from conversational style almost every time we use a direct quotation. This is because the use of quotation marks allows us to achieve effects in print that would be impossible orally.

The natural way to attribute a comment orally would be:

> Councilman Thomas T. Jones said he absolutely refused to accept what he called dictation from some bureaucrat in Washington.

Notice that this example requires *two* phrases of attribution. We can't assume that what Jones refuses to accept actually is dictation or that its source can be described properly as a bureaucrat, so the second part of the sentence must be attributed separately. The result would be acceptable for print, but not nearly as strong as we could make it with the use of quotation marks:

> "I absolutely refuse to accept dictation from some bureaucrat in Washington," Councilman Thomas T. Jones declared.

This construction emphasizes what was said, rather than who said it, by placing the stronger thought at the beginning of the sentence. We usually place the attribution *after* the direct quotation if the quote is limited to only one sentence. We could, however, place it at any point where the speaker might normally pause, for example:

> "I absolutely refuse," Councilman Thomas T. Jones said, "to accept dictation from some bureaucrat in Washington."

Reporters generally use far more paraphrase than direct quotation. As professionals, they can convey the newsworthy portions of a speaker's thoughts in far fewer words than he uses—and often much more clearly. They select and summarize what will interest the reader, using direct quotations only when a speaker's exact words get to the heart of his entire message or express an isolated thought more graphically than the reporter could do in an objective summary.

Summary, paraphrase, and indirect quotation also allow the reporter to use a device known as blanket attribution. This is an introductory attribution line which suffices for a long passage to follow, for example:

> Police said Jones told this story:

This clearly identifies whatever follows as second-hand information and relieves the reporter of further attribution as long as he continues to relate the police version of Jones's story.

Enumeration permits still another form of blanket attribution with paraphrase, for example:

> The President outlined an eight-point program for economic recovery:
> 1. Job retraining for thousands of unemployed persons.
> 2. A new effort. . . .

After the eight points are enumerated, of course, the writer must return to normal attribution.

Notice that we usually place the attribution at the beginning of the sentence when we paraphrase. In this construction, no comma separates the name of the speaker from what he says. But if the attribution comes in the middle or at the end of the sentence, it must be set off by commas, for example:

> Jones, according to police, told this story:

or

> All he knew was what he read in the papers, the Oklahoma humorist said.

If you are quoting facts, not opinion, and you have every reason to believe that your source is reliable, you can save words by *implying* attribution. You name the source once or twice and thereby imply that the entire story must be attributed to him. This is the common way of presenting routine traffic accidents. The only "attribution" may be a single sentence at the end that says:

> The accident was investigated by the Highway Patrol.

Writing for Outer Space

Almost all news stories are written so that they would be understandable to "the man from outer space," whether he is from another planet, another nation, another state, or only from a neighboring city. We may assume that the reader is interested in our subject, but we never assume that he is informed about the community. We don't even assume he lives here. Instead, we try to write a story that would be as readable in Canada, England, or Australia as it is in our own town. After all, if the story is accepted by one of the major wire services, it may be published in one of those countries.

This means we can't use the first person plural—we can't write about "our state" or "this country" or "our natural resources," because none of these phrases applies to the man from outer space. We can't, for example, write the way this sentence is written. Everything must be in the third person. We also must be story-conscious. We must emphasize those actions that would interest the greatest number of people everywhere, so that our locally written story will require a minimum of revision when we prepare it for wire distribution.

Once the outer space approach becomes a habit, you can convert any local story into wire copy by cutting it, putting on a dateline, and adding any special background material that may be necessary for distant readers.

The dateline consists of the city of origin, the state if necessary, and the initials of the wire service. It is an economical way of telling the reader *where* and *who says*. It is indented and written as part of the lead, with the city in all capital letters and the state, if used, in caps and lower case:

> YUKON, Okla.—A cow that jumped into a silo was rescued today, thanks to. . . .

The dateline identifies the place where the story was written, not necessarily where the action took place. For example, the arrest of a fugitive in Atlanta may be announced by the FBI in Washington, in which case the Washington bureau of the wire service would get the story first. The announcement would then carry a Washington dateline. Reporters in Atlanta probably would act quickly to get additional details, and the Washington story might be superseded in a matter of minutes by a story carrying an Atlanta dateline. In the above example about the cow, the Yukon dateline implies that the story was written by a reporter at the scene. If the information had been collected by telephone and written in a news service bureau in Oklahoma City, the story might have carried an Oklahoma City dateline.

An old rule, sometimes forgotten, says that you can't use a place name as a dateline unless that place has a post office. This allows you to use the name of a naval vessel (ABOARD THE USS FORRESTAL) because ships have post offices, but it rules out some well-known landmarks, such as Chimney Rock, Neb. Occasionally a wire service bends the rule and we get a dateline like EN ROUTE WITH THE PRESI-DENT. More often, however, stories written from a plane or train use what is called an *undated lead)* The lead has no dateline, but it is preceded by a centered line, caps and lower case:

> By the Associated Press

or

> By United Press International

The wire story usually is much shorter than the local version. Partly this is because the wire story must compete with hundreds of others—first for transmission time and later for space in subscribing newspapers. To get it accepted, we keep it as tight as possible. We make every word count, eliminating any information that would be of no interest outside the city of origin. We may use only the top half dozen paragraphs of a long local story, cutting out the word "here" (the dateline already has told the reader where), street addresses, and anything else that would be meaningless in "outer space." Many details of interest to the local reader will be sacrificed. .

Occasionally, however, the wire story must include some background that we leave out of the local story. For example, a national wire story from Deadwood, S.D., might identify the point of origin as "this historic gold-rush city, now a summer tourist mecca," all of which South Dakotans already know.

Staying Ahead of the Clock

When reporters know what is scheduled to happen they may write a story in past tense and even have it in type before the event takes place. Such a story is called an *advance*. Reporters need only put a "hold for release" on the story, then let it go as soon as they have confirmed that the event followed the script. This is a common practice in reporting a prepared speech, a graduation exercise, a bill-signing ceremony, an award presentation, and many other ordinary activities that seldom deviate in their outcome. The advance may even carry an automatic release at a certain hour, although this is a dangerous practice. On the day that John F. Kennedy was assassinated, many editors were embarrassed to discover they had printed a speech he had never delivered. No advance story ever should be released until reporters have confirmed that the event actually took place—and according to plan. Political speeches are a particular problem because the speaker may discard his script and talk about something entirely different. As a result, wire service advance stories often contain the qualifying phrase, "in a speech *prepared for delivery* tonight."

Sometimes reporters know most of the scenario, but not all. They may then write what they know and turn in the story to the city editor with the warning that it is subject to later revision with insert paragraphs or a new lead. In a metropolitan newspaper, such a story may be held until the action is final, or it may be published in the original version for one or more editions before it is revised. Here is a typical example of a lead for an early afternoon paper:

> FIRST EDITION: Convicted killer James E. Howell was scheduled to be formally sentenced in District Court at 1 p.m. today for the murder of Samuel B. Jackson. A jury has recommended life imprisonment.
>
> FINAL EDITION: Convicted killer James E. Howell was sentenced today to life imprisonment for the murder of Samuel B. Jackson.

The lead for the final edition might be followed by two or three more paragraphs of new information—perhaps a direct quotation from the judge and a description of the defendant's appearance and behavior—but thereafter the story would be exactly the same as in the first edition.

CONCLUSION

If only one talent separates outstanding reporters from the hacks, it is the ability to put themselves in the reader's place. Perhaps unconsciously, the top reporters have become so closely attuned to their readers' interests that they automatically recognize the makings of a good story. And—again because they are so sensitive to the reader—they tell it in the reader's language. They write much as if they were writing a letter to a friend, except that they keep themselves and their opinions out of it. They don't have to guess about what belongs in the story, nor do they often grope for words. Their prose is almost conversational, and if you watch closely, you may even see their lips move as they write. It's not a bad habit. If you talk to the typewriter, your copy will be easier to read. And you need never fear that the typewriter will talk back.

SUGGESTED ASSIGNMENTS

1. From a daily newspaper, clip five stories with action leads which you consider weak. Rewrite them to include causes and effects within the first three sentences.
2. Find a long feature story that begins with a summary lead. Search the body for an anecdote that exemplifies the overall story. Rewrite the story with an anecdote lead. If possible, return to the anecdote for the ending.
3. Clip a major news story of some length and complexity. Type the entire story using double or triple spacing and ample margins. Then go through and identify or label all the parts and techniques you recognize, using such terms as *transition, tie-back to lead, summary, development,* etc. Also mark where information corresponding to the five W's and H occurs. Then write a short analysis of the structure employed in the story.
4. Clip a long local story and underline the transitions. Can any be eliminated? Can any be shortened? Should more be inserted? Rewrite the story and make the desirable changes.
5. Clip four long local stories that might be of interest to readers outside the state. Rewrite them for wire service distribution.

CHAPTER SIX / FIGHTING THE FORMULA STORY

One of the ever present headaches of journalism is the trite story.

This is the piece written to prescription—the story you seem to have read a thousand times before, with only the names changed. It is "fill-in-the-blanks" writing, with a limited number of standard forms for each standard subject. Once the reader recognizes the subject—an engagement announcement, a wedding, a routine death, a traffic fatality, or a high school basketball game—he knows almost exactly what information will be presented and in what order. After all, how many ways can you say that Susan Smith became the bride of Jonathan Jones? Or that Samuel Brown died at 86? With such material, how can you avoid producing a cliché? Is it even worth the effort to try?

Before we answer these questions, let's first try to determine what makes a story trite. Presumably, the problem lies either in the content or in its expression. The prime offender conceivably could be the subject itself, the list of facts about that subject, the overall organization, or the individual words or phrases—any individual element that is dull, commonplace, or worn out by repetition.

Most trite stories, however, are the product of more than one overworked element. A commonplace subject itself is seldom the culprit. Literature amply testifies to the facts that infinite variations can be played upon a familiar theme and works of art can be created out of the most trifling human experience. Nor is the problem simply familiar organization; one can write sonnets or three-act plays for a lifetime without being accused of banality. And although many reporters have a penchant for the hackneyed phrase (a weakness fostered by the pressure of deadlines), few readers are offended by commonplace language. If any one element is more at fault than the others, it is the standard set of facts that we supply for all stories in a given class. But what truly makes the story trite is the total combination—

the use of a familiar form and familiar language to present familiar facts about a familiar subject.

In searching for original combinations, beginners may feel defeated from the start. Day after day they must write about the same subjects—death, taxes, weather, and violence—and they are limited by law, ethics, style, and the policy of the organization as to what they can say in each story. Further, their best efforts toward originality may be frustrated by old-fashioned editors who reject any story that doesn't follow the inverted pyramid form. It is easy to argue that all the words, all the subjects, and all the acceptable combinations already have been used, that journalism is trite by nature. But all this is rationalization. The problem usually is not in the restrictions of journalism; it is in the limitations of the individual reporter's mind, imagination, or methods.

Reporters who continually produce clichés—unless they are observing rigid company policy—are cases of arrested development. They have learned part of their craft, but not enough. And what they have learned has had a tendency to blind them to what they have missed.

THE FUNCTION OF FORMULAS

Consider how we learn to write. We begin with imitation. As children we watch the teacher's hand movements and try to shape our letters exactly the same. We group the letters into words exactly the way the teacher shows us; we arrange words and punctuation marks into sentences according to the teacher's prescription. We innovate only in a limited sense. We create sentences, essays, stories and poems that are original in content but rigidly stereotyped in phrasing and organization. In other words, we write according to teacher-approved formulas.

Sometime in adolescence, experimentation may replace imitation. Talented young writers aspire to "originality." Perhaps they encounter Faulkner or Joyce—in which case experimentation may be only another form of imitation—or perhaps young writers begin to think for themselves, with no such revolutionary models as guides. At any rate, they begin to fret at formulas. They want to rearrange the language, throwing out every trite word or phrase, every restrictive form. If they succeed, they may become so original that nobody understands them. They may end by talking only to themselves.

Writers who expect to be paid regularly soon repress the urge to revolutionize the language. Instead, they use familiar words in their most commonly accepted meanings—aware, of course, that only a fine line separates the familiar from the trite—and organize stories into patterns the reader will recognize and accept. They also treat familiar subjects. The writer gives readers what they want in the form they expect to see it. To do otherwise would be to disappoint the readers, confuse them, and risk losing them.

To be certain of doing the job right, the beginning reporter returns to the school child's practice of imitating forms that already have been proved satisfactory. Faced with an unfamiliar kind of story, he or she searches through back issues of the newspaper to find out how Joe or Sue handled one "just like it" last week. He carefully notes the details that Joe covered and makes certain his own story supplies the same facts. He may even arrange them in the same order that Joe did. This can be an effective way to learn—as long as the model is well written and contains all the necesary details. But it is only a beginning. At best, the result will be an imitation. And the imitator can only hope to conceal the borrowed skeleton by covering it with new flesh.

Competent beginners quickly outgrow the need for models. Paradoxically, however, it is precisely at this stage that they are in the gravest danger of stunting their future development. They are in trouble the moment they think they have learned how to write a "traffic fatality," a "fender-bender," an "obit," or a "weather yarn." The mere fact that they have begun to classify stories in this manner is the giveaway. They have discovered formulas. They have begun to treat people and events as categories, statistics. Name any common subject, and they can tell you exactly what must be told and in what order to tell it. They have discovered a recipe for everything that is served to the public on a regular basis.

The danger is not in the formula itself, but in the reporter's readiness to accept it for every story that seems to fit the category. Used properly, formulas, like recipes, can be helpful. They enable reporters to check their work, to be sure they have put in all the essential ingredients in appropriate order. With the help of a formula, beginners can turn the story out fast, get it past the editor, and tell the reader all he needs to know. And words won't be wasted. Pressed for time or space, beginners may find the solution to all their problems in the formula story.

What beginners probably don't realize, however, is that *the formula story is a minimal story.* The formula specifies only those facts that are absolutely essential, and it spells out nothing more than an acceptable way of telling them. Because it provides no guidelines for anything out of the ordinary, either in content or treatment, the result inevitably will be a cliché. And a formula will never do for any story of consequence. Hence, the writer who never gets beyond formula writing remains forever a mechanic, incapable of handling anything more than simple events.

OUTGROWING THE RECIPE
To become more than a word mechanic, you must:

1. *Change your way of looking at people and events.* Instead of noticing only similarities between one occurrence and another, you also
   must observe differences.
2. *Collect more information.* Often a formula story is the result of
   half-done reporting. The reporter simply quit when the minimum
   requirements were fulfilled. A complete job would have produced
   a different story.
3. *Increase your vocabulary.* As your stock of words grows, so does
   your total knowledge. And the more you understand, the less likely
   you will be to oversimplify a story.

Categories Can Be Blinding
When the beginner thumbed through the back issues for a story
"just like" the one he or she had to write, the motive was better
than the logic. Adoption of a model is a sensible step at an early stage,
but it is a mistake to assume that any two stories are exactly alike.
They may have strong similarities, but each is unique in some respect.

And looking only for similarities in order to fit a story into a category, reporters are often blinded to its uniqueness. They recognize
the obligatory details for each story fall into the category, but they
may fail to notice facts which set the individual story apart from others of its kind. Or perhaps beginning reporters notice the difference,
but underrate its importance. Treating the story as a member of a
class, they may overlook the most noteworthy element, the most newsworthy angle.

One revolutionary remedy would be to quit classifying stories entirely, to approach each event or situation as if nothing quite like it
had ever happened before. Instead of saying, "Ho, hum—here's another just like the last," the reporter might try for a while to adopt a
wide-eyed attitude of a child who finds everything novel and exciting.
But this is neither entirely realistic nor practical, except as a short-
term learning experiment. It would be foolish to go through life with
a "gee whiz" approach to every minor happening. No editor would
tolerate it, for reporters who ignore relationships and similarities are
as immature as reporters who see nothing else.

Although professionals continue to classify stories for conven-
ience, they are constantly alert for any clue that the information may
be more than routine. Automatically, they look for an "angle," a "different slant," for some hint of a significant departure from the norm.
This, after all, is one of the earmarks of a good story—action that is
somehow out of the ordinary. And reporters who can't find something

different, after searching hard, either have only a formula story or no story at all.

Reporting is the Foundation

Many reporters seem able to spot an "angle" almost immediately. They focus quickly on something unique in an otherwise ordinary situation. If you listen to the questions such reporters ask, you can almost visualize the lead that is taking form in their minds. They find the angle first, then shape the opening questions to develop what will be the lead. Last, they fill in any gaps in the obligatory information by asking routine questions. They have become so story-conscious that they ask questions almost in the order that the answers will appear in print.

Reporters who work so quickly and confidently may be geniuses or simply lead-happy hacks. In either case, they are taking a major risk if they fail to explore more than one angle. They are gambling that the angle they so promptly discover is either the only one or the best one. They decide what the story is before they have all the information. They operate more from intuition than from evidence.

Intuition, the celebrated "nose for news," has succeeded so often and so dramatically that it has a permanent position in the folklore of journalism. But it is no substitute for thorough reporting. Reporters who get the most answers are those who ask the most questions. And the more they learn, the more different angles they discover. If they are professional, they pursue each to the point where it ceases to be productive. This takes time, but it is the only way to approach an important story. The story developed in this manner may be less spectacular than the one that quickly follows a flash of intuition, but it usually will be more faithful to reality.

The Value of Vocabulary

One of the best protections against trite thinking, as well as trite writing is a large vocabulary. When students first encounter the objectivity and shirtsleeve English of journalism, they sometimes get the impression that a reporter's vocabulary is drab and limited. They could hardly be more mistaken. At the least, a reporter's language is (or should be) as lively and varied as the subjects he or she writes about. And this is only the language used to address the readers. It seldom represents more than a small fraction of the reporter's total store of words.

Reporters use words to *get* stories as well as to tell them. They must be able to understand the special vocabularies of their sources, then translate these into everyday English for their readers. They must understand legal terms, medical terms, and the professional languages of civil engineering and government finance. They must be able to decipher the double-talk of politicians, the jargon of social scientists, and the slang of street people.

Yet with all their exposure to varied experiences and language, reporters too often resort to the stock phrases with which our language abounds. Journalists, no less than other people, are still guilty of the kind of writing George Orwell indicted some years ago:

> Prose (nowadays) consists less and less of *words* chosen for the sake of their meaning, and more and more of *phrases* tacked together like sections of a prefabricated henhouse. . . . There is a huge dump of wornout metaphors which have lost all evocative power and are merely used because they save people the trouble of inventing phrases for themselves. . . . Modern writing at its worst . . . consists of gumming together long strips of words which have already been set in order by someone else.

Today's clichés are often yesterday's flashes of genius. Their very originality or aptness resulted in overuse—and hence in the yawns with which we greet them now. Many such phrases, as Orwell suggests, are metaphoric:

shot in the dark	shadow of doubt
calm before the storm	fresh as summer's day
rears its ugly head	bitter end
sober as a judge	acid test
budding genius	beat a hasty retreat
grass roots support	more smoke than fire
see the light of day	to coin a phrase
greener pastures	

Some are grade school personifications that pop into the hurried writer's mind but fail to make much impression on the reader's:

Jack Frost	at death's door
Old Man Winter	Father Time
the fickle finger of fate	Mother Nature

Still others are handy labels, more timeworn than time-honored:

gala affair	the Golden West
blushing bride	the rock-ribbed coast
proud parents	the great outdoors
political pundits	the good old summertime
solemn occasion	the almighty dollar

And most distressing of all perhaps the the weary, wordy transitional phrases:

first and foremost	in the final analysis
in the long run	along these lines
last but not least	in the offing

An ample stockpile of words at your command is your best defense against the cliché. Sometimes you will hit on a fresh word or phrase that expresses your point with color and verve. By trying to see people and things for yourself rather than through the fog of formulas, by trying to find relationships other than those provided by stale metaphors, you may come up with a striking new way of saying something (you may even invent a cliché). But more often you will have to settle for simplicity and precision, qualities of which any writer can be proud.

WORDS AND KNOWLEDGE

A large vocabulary, however, means much more than just a stock of synonyms that help us say the same old things in different ways. Words do not just enable us to say things differently; they also enable us to see things differently and to understand things more fully. A small child's perception and understanding of the world is extremely limited by a lack of words and concepts with which to interpret what he or she sees, hears, and touches. Similarly, adults' perception and understanding of the much larger world they live in is directly related to their mastery of language.

In learning a new word, we acquire a new grasp, however small, on the complex worlds that exist both inside and outside of our individual beings. As a student you have learned that each new field you study—psychology, philosophy, anthropology, chemistry, astronomy, music—significantly increases your vocabulary. You cannot understand the concepts on which the discipline is built without understanding the terminology in which they are couched. Vocabulary, then, represents knowledge itself.

For the adult, as for the young child, vocabulary also functions as a tool for developing understanding. When you know the language of psychology, for example, you begin to perceive everyday human behavior in more complex ways. A word helps us recognize the thing it stands for; and that recognition reinforces and extends our understanding of the word, and perhaps of other words as well. The more familiar you are with the myriad shades and nuances of meaning contained in our language, the better you can perceive the subtle nuances of reality. Words, like mathematical symbols, are tools which allow us to differentiate and integrate, to analyze and evaluate.

A SECOND LANGUAGE: NEW INSIGHTS AND NEW "SIGHT"

Knowing a second language can be of great value to the writer for several reasons. First, reporters are more likely than many of their countrymen to encounter people who speak other languages. Even if they speak English as well, a reporter can make them feel more comfortable and make a better impression by talking informally in their language. And, obviously, if you are interested in working abroad, knowledge of another language can help you get the job. Just the ability to read a foreign language can be a great advantage to the journalist interested in international affairs.

But even if you never use the language you study in school, you probably will benefit much more than you realize just from exposure. Most of us learn the grammar and syntax of English through imitation; we may have little real comprehension of why we say and write things the way we do. Only by studying another language do we begin to grasp the structure of our own and to see how language works. So regardless of whether you become bilingual, acquaintance with a second language can give you valuable insights into your medium.

Finally, people who become bilingual, or very nearly so, begin to understand how language molds our view of the world. Thus they begin to broaden their appreciation of the differences among countries and cultures. Many words and phrases cannot be translated accurately from one language to another because there are no corresponding forms. Language has been compared to a pair of eyeglasses with a specific lens prescription through which their owner perceives his surroundings. No matter how carefully "sight" is nurtured, the owner is always limited by the particular shape and size of the lenses.

The Germanic and Romantic languages we most commonly study differ little from English in their basic structure or in the mode of perception they engender. But they differ enough in details to help us grasp how other languages (oriental, African, or Indian) can be radically different and hence produce (as they were produced by) radically different outlooks, values, and cultures.

On the surface, then, words may appear to be only arbitrary symbols which the writer consciously manipulates. Arbitrary symbols they are, but they exert powerful influences on our conscious and unconscious minds. They determine our mode of vision, breadth of knowledge, and depth of understanding. Most reporters will probably never come close to using all the words they know in the stories they write. But the larger their vocabulary, the broader and sharper their perspectives will be. The more sensitive they are to language, the more sensitive they will be to people, places, and events. The greater their understanding of the medium, the clearer, smoother, and more exact their work will be. Their stories may seldom contain words that a 14-year-old wouldn't be familiar with, but the work they do will be richer for what goes on unconsciously in their minds.

SOME FORMULAS CAN BE JUSTIFIED

Now that we have examined some of the ways that you can outgrow the recipe, let's return to the final question posed at the beginning of this chapter: Is it always worth the effort?

The answer is no, not always, for several practical reasons. First, the formula is fast. We can get a minimal story into print while the reporter groping for a different angle is still trying to collect more information. And many subjects deserve no more than minimal treatment. They are worth reporting, but they amount to little more than statistics. Time spent trying to avoid the stereotype could be spent better on more deserving subject matter.

Second—and this may be the more important reason—the formula story is democratic; it is a way of treating all stories of a certain class equally. If we treat virtually all obituaries, all weddings, and all engagements alike, nobody will be slighted. And we avoid time-wasting arguments with disgruntled families of persons who figure in such stories. We can answer complaints simply by pointing out the equality of treatment and observing that "this is our policy."

Formula treatment of weddings and obituaries has become accepted practice on most American newspapers. These stories not only follow standard forms, but they are written *from* standard forms: information blanks designed to make certain that the newspaper has all the necessary data. Obituary blanks go to funeral homes; wedding blanks go to prospective brides. And when the required information is supplied, either by telephone or mail, the story can be produced in a matter of minutes.

Although policy stipulates that most weddings and obituaries shall be treated equally, common sense requires many exceptions. A White House wedding, for example, gets something more than the usual treatment. So does the death of a head of state or even that of a prominent local business leader or politician. The reporter dealing with what normally is a subject for a formula story still must be alert to circumstances that lift it out of the ordinary.

PATTERNS, PRACTICES, AND PROBLEMS

Weddings and obituaries are extreme examples. No other stories, with the possible exception of engagement announcements, follow such rigid formulas. Yet reporters have developed less restrictive patterns for many other types of stories. There is, in fact, a formula approach to almost any kind of straight news story and to much feature material as well. And there is no doubt that beginners can learn a lot by observing similarities and becoming familiar with standard procedures. They learn what the required information for a particular type of a story is, master an acceptable way of presenting it, and become aware of the special problems encountered in stories of that category. Then, of course, they should begin to develop their own ways of varying the common formulas.

So now we are going to do exactly what we have warned against. We are going to categorize stories for the sake of analysis. But we will do it a bit differently than working reporters do. We will make most of our categories as broad as possible. This will allow us to generalize as well as to look at some types of stories in detail without, we hope, encouraging the student to adopt trite formulas. The categories we will examine are:

1. *Notices*—all announcements of future events.
2. *Athletic contests*—the major meets that are covered in some detail.
3. *Contests of greater significance*—political, legislative, and judicial.
4. *Single-source opinion stories*—the speech, the opinion interview, and the political news release.
5. *Meetings*—those that result in agreed-upon action by a governing body.
6. *Controversies*—balanced presentation of opposing sides, with the reporter neutral.
7. *Violent actions*—accidents, assault, homicide, and natural disaster.
8. *Outright form stories*—weddings, engagements, obituaries, and high school basketball games.

Like any system of classification, this is arbitrary and incomplete. Some stories may easily fall into two or three categories at once. Meetings, for example, often involve contests and controversies, and sometimes violent action. A notice, too, may require backgrounding concerning a controversy or a brief review of past meetings. And stories of violence, coverage of a riot for instance, often must summarize the controversy that led to the action.

Obviously, not all stories that fall into any one category can be treated alike. A controversy over the propriety of having *Little Black Sambo* in public school libraries is quite different from a controversy over the ethics of bombing another country. Nor do we handle a flood in quite the way we would handle a single-car accident. But the point to observe is that all stories within each broad category have similar requirements and similar problems.

Notices

All notices tell the reader that a certain action is scheduled at a specific hour, date, and place. Notices include impending tax deadlines, city council agendas, pregame stories, concert programs—any expected or scheduled action. They range from the single paragraph announcing a club meeting to the long interpretive story announcing an important public hearing. What binds them together is the emphasis on time and place. The notice tells readers where to mail their tax returns and by what hour. It tells them where the game will be played and what time it starts, what time the polls open and close and where they are. It gives them information that is immediately useful.

Despite the emphasis on time and place, the lead seldom begins with either of these elements. Instead, the lead usually centers on what is expected or scheduled to happen, and the only reference to time may be the day. Specific details often appear later in the story, as in this example:

> Citizens will have a chance to register their views on proposed school spending Tuesday evening at the Board of Education's annual budget hearing.
>
> The hearing is scheduled to begin at 7:30 p.m. in the Public School Administration Building, 720 S. 22nd St.
>
> Unless the board changes the budget when it meets Tuesday morning to take final action, the total will be $30,588,471, compared with this year's $28,600,025. Most of the increase will be borne by local taxpayers.
>
> The mill levy is expected to increase from 54.95 to 57.09.

In some cases, of course, time and place are important enough to work into the lead:

> Antelope hunters wanting a license this year should make sure their applications arrive at Game Commission offices between June 1 and 15.

One variation of the notice story that writers sometimes find awkward might be called the "reminder." This is the story that must appear immediately before an event which may have been announced months earlier. The fact that the event has been scheduled is no longer news; all our faithful readers know about it. This means that the reporter must find a "second-day" angle. The story must have some element that is new, or it must say in a new way something that has been said before. This is a particularly difficult problem for sports writers, who treat events scheduled years in advance and publicized for months. Here is a somewhat labored example, illustrating how one writer solved this kind of problem:

> The sugar-and-spice set will put its sweet-swinging golfers on display today at the Omaha Country Club.
>
> It's time to start the Trans-Mississippi Golf Championship—and the 42nd fairway frolic has brought 144 girls to Omaha from coast to coast and from over the sea.
>
> Qualifying rounds of 18 holes make up today's program, with the tournament moving into match play Tuesday. The 32 low scorers in the trials will make up the championship flight, which will wind up with the champion in Saturday's 36 holes.
>
> The first qualifying group is scheduled off the tee at 7 this morning, with. . . .

What does this golf story contain that is really new? Perhaps only the number of entrants, or perhaps nothing except the way the writer put the facts together. And it might be argued that he attempted to make something out of nothing. On the other hand, several details of the schedule—although available for weeks—may have been withheld from publication earlier in order to give the reporter fresh information for his final pretournament story. Writers who must produce several stories before an event soon learn not to tell all they know in the first story. This strategy is easily defended; nobody wants to read all the details, including tee-off time, a month or more before the event. Reporters do the reader as well as themselves a favor by holding back such information until it is needed.

Athletic Contests

When a football coach loses a game, he may try to forget the score by talking about character-building. After all, he may remind you, the important thing is not whether you won or lost, but how you played the game.

Don't believe it. What the fans want to know first is who won and by what score. Next they want to know how this affects the standings. They are interested in how the game was played, of course, but first they want to settle their bets. To serve these interests, you must write a lead that names the winner and gives the final score. But you need not limit it to that.

Because the leads of all contest stories must supply the same basic minimum information, trite beginnings may seem especially difficult to avoid. You can find story after story that begins like this:

> Minnesota's Golden Gophers defeated Notre Dame 16-14 Saturday before a crowd of 60,000 chilled fans.

This lead focuses entirely on the score—the immediate result—with no mention of how it was achieved or what it signifies. Except for giving the size of the crowd and the fact that it was chilly (hardly a newsworthy observation if the game was played in Minnesota), it tells the readers nothing they couldn't learn just as quickly from a list of scores. The writer seems to have been in such a hurry to get the story out *now* that he hasn't stopped to think how the lead will look two hours or more later when the reader finally gets the newspaper. We can easily improve it, however, by starting the lead with *how,* thus:

> A last-minute field goal by. . .

or *so what:*

> Minnesota emerged Saturday as the only unbeaten Big Ten football team after a last-minute field goal gave the Gophers a 16-14 victory over Notre Dame.

Perhaps the first step toward avoiding a trite lead on a game story is to realize that the reader already may have heard the bare score on radio or television. You can't omit this obligatory information, but you are forced to take something of a second-day approach. You must try to give the reader something beyond what he already has heard. The trick is to do this without crowding the lead and making it unreadable.

One problem in sports writing is that the reporter may have difficulty concealing personal bias. A classic example is this football lead that appeared in a Texas newspaper in 1949 after Southern Methodist University tied previously unbeaten and untied Notre Dame:

> SMU proved Saturday that Notre
> Dame was just another team which would
> win some weeks and lose others in the
> Southwest Conference.

In writing sports, reporters face another problem that seldom crops up in any other kind of story. They must identify the game, either by name or implication. They must make it clear whether they are writing about football, basketball, baseball, or track. In a story of normal length, this usually can be accomplished by mentioning "touchdowns" or "home runs" or "hitters" or "linemen" early in the story. But it is surprising how often a beginner produces a one- or two-paragraph "story" that leaves the reader wondering what kind of game was played.

Contests of Greater Significance
In an athletic contest, the only items normally at stake are fans' and players' egos, a few million dollars in bets, and perhaps the coaches' jobs. Win or lose, when the game is over, most people can grin, shrug, and go home and forget about it. The outcome may have no lasting effect on anyone.

Beyond the world of sports, however, are many adversary contests which may yield historic consequences for an entire society. These contests are decided in polling booths, legislative chambers, and court-rooms. They are "played" according to rigid rules, and they end—at least ostensibly—in victory for one side and defeat for another. The margin between winning and losing may even be expressed by a "score." But they are not games, nor can they be treated honestly as such, despite their superficial resemblance to sports. They cannot be reported realistically by using the simplistic, melodramatic style of sports writing. Despite the athletic metaphors that politicians themselves are so fond of, it is a disservice to the reader to treat a political campaign as a kind of verbal boxing match.

In political, legislative, and judicial contests, the ostensible winners and losers may be mere figureheads. Who really wins when a certain bill becomes law? The political party that supported it? The legislator who introduced it? Or is the winner some pressure group which shuns the public spotlight? Or perhaps society itself? Proper reporting of such contests requires much more than merely the ability to determine who carried the ball. Even the "victory" or "defeat" may be only a beginning. To report the outcome in perspective, we must look backward into the past and forward into the future as well as behind the scenes of the present.

Few socially significant contests are conducted entirely in public. Legislators may vote in public, but the real struggle over any bill usually takes place offstage in committee meetings, corridors, and telephone conversations. Even a presidential campaign, which is often reported as if it were a Roman circus, involves much more than meets the eye or ear. And the most important "battles" may be waged mostly on paper by lawyers arguing before the Supreme Court. The reporter who sees only what happens on the surface misses the full story.

Even seasoned reporters sometimes have trouble assessing the consequences of some contests. An example is provided in this story from the summer of 1972:

WASHINGTON (AP)—The Supreme Court held 5-4 Thursday that the death penalty, as it is now used in the United States, violates the Constitution and cannot be imposed.

Although the decision leaves the door open for legislatures to reinstate capital punishment in some circumstances, one of the opinions issued by the court said the immediate result is to remove the death sentences from the 600 condemned inmates across the land.

The nine justices divided so sharply that they issued nine opinions while reversing specifically two death sentences in Georgia and a third in Texas.

The somewhat ambiguous pileup of views evidently leaves the door slightly open for legislatures to reinstate capital punishment in special circumstances.

The five-man majority comprised Justices William O. Douglas, William J. Brennan Jr., Thurgood Marshall and, with some reservations, Potter Stewart and Byron R. White.

The four Nixon appointees stood as a bloc in favor of the death penalty.

Chief Justice Warren Burger stressed in his dissent that the court, while setting aside the death penalty, also gave state legislatures "the opportunity and indeed unavoidable responsiblity to make a thorough re-evaluation of the entire subject of capital punishment."

The other dissenters were Justices Harry A. Blackmun, Lewis F. Powell Jr. and William H. Rehnquist.

The decision evidently serves to maintain a moratorium on executions in the

United States. There are now 600 death-
row inmates in 31 states. There hasn't
been an execution in the United States in
five years.

The central question before the court
was whether capital punishment violates
the Eighth Amendment's prohibition
against "cruel and unusual punishments."

On the surface, the "losers" of this contest were the states of Georgia
and Texas, which were defending the death penalty. But it would be
difficult to determine to the satisfaction of everyone precisely what was
lost and who lost it. Thus, in dealing with this "contest," the reporter
focused more on the division of opinion, the ambiguity of the outcome, and its apparent immediate consequences rather than on any
question of victory or defeat.

Single-Source Opinion Stories

The single-source opinion story is one of the most familiar fixtures
in American journalism. We can find it on nearly every page,
especially in presidential election years. It may be a speech, an interview, or only a political candidate's ghost written handout. In whatever form we see it, it is basically a one-sided story, sometimes filled
with accusations and undocumented assertions of so-called fact. It can
be either a legitimate news story or an insidious vehicle for propaganda.

What characterizes all these stories is that the reporter presents
the source's opinion at face value, carefully attributing it, but taking
no responsibility for its validity. Indeed, there may be no way of
determining validity at the moment. It is only an opinion, with no
"right" or "wrong." Depending on one's viewpoint, this practice can
be defended as "objectivity" or "presenting a forum for all points of
view," or it can be denounced as an abdication of responsibility.

The publication of this kind of story is seldom as irresponsible as
critics charge, however. Long aware of the dangers of the one-sided
story, thoughtful editors are highly selective about those they publish.
They do not staff every speech that is presented, nor do they accept
every news release that is submitted. And they certainly do not waste
staff members' valuable time in interviewing every self-proclaimed
spokesman for a cause. They try to restrict coverage to those persons
whose opinions appear worthy of publication.

Editors face many other considerations before they accept an
opinion story. The first, of course, is whether the subject itself is of
general interest. Second, is the speaker qualified to comment on this

particular issue? Is it related to his field of expertise? (We don't normally quote a football expert on agricultural economics.) Third, is he saying anything new? Or has he or some other person said the same thing a dozen times before? Fourth, did he say this to a large crowd at a public speech, or was he talking only to his typewriter? Rightly or not, we tend to evaluate a speaker's opinions by the number of persons who share them or at least listen to them. Fifth, is the story fair and nonlibelous? If the speaker makes accusations, it would be better to withhold the one-sided story and try for a balanced presentation that allows the accused person to reply in the same story. Finally— and perhaps most important—what does the speaker have to gain?

Given their choice, many editors would permit only one kind of opinion story: the interview. The reason for this is that only the interview allows the journalist a significant degree of control over the substance of the story. In the interview, it is the reporter who determines which subjects are newsworthy and what questions shall be asked. Further, he or she can force the source to amend untruths, qualify exaggerations, and supply concrete explanations of vague generalities. By contrast, in covering a speech or rewriting a news release, the reporter is largely at the mercy of the source, with little to work with other than the words the source *wants* published. This is why editors staff only the most important speeches and always insist that the reporter try to question the speaker afterward. It is also why some editors refuse to permit "typewriter campaigns" by politicians. They want their own story, not the source's.

Regardless of how they are obtained, most opinion stories follow the same pattern. They begin with the most important thing the source said, followed by where and under what circumstances, then they develop the lead with a mixture of paraphrase and direct quotation. The formula is so widely applied that if the reporter fails to tell where and under what circumstances, readers have no way of determining how the story was obtained; they can't distinguish a speech or interview from a prepared news release. Here is an example:

> Democratic congressional nominee Darrel Berg said Thursday that the pension system needs to be overhauled to protect the pension rights of American workers.
>
> "More than one-third of all workers who are participating in pension plans now will not get a nickel back when they retire," Berg said.
>
> "Workers are losing their pension rights every day when their companies go bankrupt, merge with other companies or

> simply go out of business. In addition, many workers lose their pensions when they transfer jobs.
>
> "As a result, only a fraction of the 30 million workers now covered by pension plans will ever receive any benefits."
>
> In addition to pension reform, Berg said, Social Security benefits should be improved.

The omission of time, place, and audience leads us to believe that this was a news release. But how can the untrained reader know? The ethical practice is to *tell* him—to make the attribution line in the second paragraph read: "Berg said in a prepared statement" or "Berg said in a news release."

The example above deviates from the normal form in still another respect. It contains somewhat more direct quotation than usual. This, and its overall brevity, are further signs that the story did not result from a reporter's efforts. If the candidate had been interviewed, the story almost certainly would have been longer and more specific. And it would have contained more paraphrase.

Opinion stories generally are easy to write. You seldom have to search for the lead. When dealing with a press release, you can often base your lead on the one provided by the source. And in covering a speech, you can identify the speaker's central point by the clues that he gives you just before reaching it. Speakers will use such phrases as "above all," "most importantly," "to summarize the situation," or "I especially want to stress." Similar clues will be provided by the person who is being interviewed.

The problem, of course, is that the opinion story is too easy. You can turn out a formula version almost without thinking. You need only write a lead that summarizes the source's principal point, then develop it with his own words, using a combination of paraphrase and direct quotation. The only difficult part of writing such a story is in making attribution clear but unobtrusive.

But before you take the easy course and opt for a formula story, ask yourself a few questions. Is this one individual's opinion the entire story? Or is it only part of a larger story? Try to look at the story in a broader context. The real news often is not in the isolated statement, but in the way it relates to something else: what another person has said or done, what this person said or did earlier, or what happened only an hour ago in a labor dispute or on the floor of Congress. Wise reporters will hesitate before they decide that all they have is a simple opinion story. Indeed, what they have is often only the beginning of something much more complex. The work may have only begun.

Meetings

Organizing the report of a governing body's actions often is as difficult as getting all the information. As we observed in Chapter 4, even the meeting of a small-town city council may result in a dozen or more newsworthy actions. Should we round up all of these in a single story? Or should we treat each action as a separate story with its own headline?

Much depends on the perceptions of reporters. If they are source oriented, they see all these actions as part of a city council story. If they are action or issue oriented, they see little relationship between the firing of the police chief, the announcement of a new paving project, and the imposition of a city sales tax. They see each as a separate story in which the action is more important than the body responsible for it. Instead of viewing the goal as a "city council' story, these reporters see it as a "sales tax" story or a "police firing" story.

Still, the reporter must deal with reader expectations and the custom of the newspaper. If readers have come to expect meeting roundups, any departure may confuse them. Where can they find all those minor newspaper-of-record actions, if not in the weekly meeting roundup? Must they go looking all through the paper to find out what happened?

Most editors in smaller cities prefer to make the news easy to find by using the roundup. To write the roundup the reporter must (1) base the lead on the single most important action, subordinating everything else, or (2) summarize the three or four more newsworthy actions in the first sentence, or (3) try to write a lead that summarizes the entire meeting, without focusing on anything specific. Each option has its disadvantages. The single-action lead may distort the news by giving the chosen subject more status than it deserves. The multiple-action lead may be more honest, but so crowded that it is barely readable. And the overall summary may bury newsworthy specifics and read like a grocery list.

The favored formula beginning for most roundups probably is the lead that specifies the three or four more outstanding actions, as in this hypothetical example:

> The Centerville City Council fired Police Chief Jackson O'Brien Monday night, imposed a 2 percent sales tax and announced plans for a northeast bypass highway.

The next two paragraphs logically would develop the firing of the police chief, then a paragraph would be devoted to each of the other two lead items. This superficial development probably would be followed by enumeration, thus:

> In other action the council:
> 1. Rejected a bid by. . . .
> 2. Approved a proposal for. . . .
> 3. Endorsed School Board plans for. . . .

After the enumeration, the story might then return to more expanded treatment of the three actions chosen for the lead.

Actions of such significance and magnitude as we have shown above seldom occur all at the same meeting. More often, reporters have to cudgel their brains to find something worth elevating into the lead. When all the action seems relatively routine, reporters may be tempted to use a beginning like this one:

> For the first time in history, the Durango City Council adjourned before 10 p.m. last night.

Only an established local humorist, however, can get away with such a lead. Most editors will insist that the lead focus on one or more specific actions. If the generalized approach is accepted, it at least must take a relatively serious tone, as in this example from the *Kansas City Star:*

> The Jackson County Board of Equalization set what members regarded as a record Thursday for the number of cases heard in one day, running through 610 tax appeals in 14 hours.
>
> The board heard businessmen appeal assessment increases on furnishing and equipment as well as on commercial real estate.
>
> "I'm sure it's the most cases the board ever heard in one day," Chairman Harry Wiggins said near the end. "Some of the people who started the day with us are back in New York or California."
>
> The board began at 8 a.m. and sat through the day, eating lunch on the bench of the county courtroom in Kansas City and passing up dinner.
>
> By law, the board must adjourn Saturday.
>
> A Kansas City Star Company appeal of a $100,000 increase in valuation of furn-

ishings and equipment (business personal property) was rejected by the board. A rise from $3,343,960 to $3,442,100 assessed valuation, at 30 per cent of true value, was approved.

A business personal valuation for R. H. Macy and Co., 1034 Main, was raised from $307,740 to $364,060.

Other business appeals heard Thursday included. . . .

The weakness of the generalized approach is that it doesn't immediately tell what specific action was taken. In the example from the *Kansas City Star,* policy may have been involved; the *Star's* management may not have wanted to call particular attention to its own tax appeal, which happened to be the biggest single item. Besides, the story seems to be more in the large number of appeals than in any single action. But the same approach would hardly work for a lesser story. The beginner who tries it too often comes up with something like this:

The City Council took action Monday on several controversial issues.

What action? What issues? This is as weak as the speech lead that says "Congressional candidate Durward Jones outlined his stand on campaign issues Tuesday." What stand? What issues? Leads this vague could have been written before the meeting or speech took place.

The reporter who gets the outcome into the lead still may miss the story. Is the news only what was said and done at the meeting? Or is the real news the *effect* of that action? Reporters who think that all they have is a "meeting story" may be blinding themselves.

Controversies

When a dispute involves points of ascertainable facts, the reporter can and should tell the reader what the facts are. Unfortunately, facts are often difficult to determine, and the only ethical way to serve the reader may be to print the opinions of both sides. Occasionally this is weak journalism, but more often it isn't. In many controversies, fact is not really the issue; there is no "right" or "wrong," only differing interpretations of "good," "bad," or "just." In such cases, the only ethical course is to present all sides as fairly and fully as possible.

In organizing such a story, writers should make it clear at the beginning that there are at least two sides to the argument. They must try to summarize the dispute, rather than present either side first in a way that might imply that this is the *only* version of the situation.

Often this summary approach can be accomplished simply by using the word "controversy," as in this example:

A controversy has arisen over equal radio time to discuss the two special issues in Thursday's city election.

Paul F. Prussman said he walked out of a recording session Friday when he discovered he was to be the only one to speak on behalf of the two issues, while four city commissioners appeared to speak against them.

Robert Reimers, an owner and manager of radio station KBRK; Mayor Orrin F. Juel, and Sid Bostic, a city commissioner, said Prussman was invited to bring other members of his committee. However, he was the only one to show up.

The special election was called after petitions were filed asking to have voters decide if two ordinances are to be kept on the books. One ordinance would eliminate much of the boulevard parking now permitted, and the second would change the present form of city government from five commissioners to three.

Prussman was active in an organization circulating the referendum petitions.

Prussman said he would have taken part in the program, called Forum KBRK, but he wanted the commissioners to talk for half of the program and then he would have used the other half.

Reimers said Prussman was offered half the air time. He said Prussman declined an offer to have the commissioners speak for alternating periods of five minutes each during their 20 minutes of air time. Prussman said he is filing a complaint with the Federal Communications Commission.

Notice that after the initial statement of the nature of the controversy, first one side and then the other is summarized. Two paragraphs providing background on the issue follow, and then two more paragraphs present further details on each side of the controversy. The story ends by announcing action to be taken later.

Editors differ considerably in their policies on coverage of controversy. At one extreme are a few who refuse to publish anything controversial until it either lands in court or reaches a legislative body. At the other are a few who think the newspaper thrives on any difference of opinion. To most, the goal is to keep it in perspective. These editors try to judge each controversy on its merits. They ignore or minimize minor squabbles, discourage disputants from trying the case in the newspaper, and try to avoid portraying a simple difference of opinion as a confrontation. But they never shy away from a controversy of consequence. They try to treat the major issues fully but dispassionately, always aware that a controversy may lead to open conflict.

Violent Actions

Whether we are writing about an automobile accident, a riot, or a natural disaster, the most important element in any story of violence usually is human death or injury. As a result, the formula approach is to begin all such stories with the death toll. This has been criticized by many editors as treating human beings too much like statistics, yet the practice persists because the first question the reader is likely to ask is "How many died?" And the next questions usually are "Who?" and "How?"

Notice the formula approach in these examples:

VICTOR, Colo.—Two Canon City, Colo., men died Wednesday in the crash of a light plane near here.

The single-engine Cessna 172 was piloted by William Leithold, 65, who was manager of the Fremont County Airport. It crashed in rugged terrain about seven miles southeast of Victor. The other victim was Jerry Ballard, 26.

Sheriff Gus Carlson of Teller County said the crash was discovered after a land developer reported about 10:30 A.M. that he had seen smoke in the area.

Carlson said the fire destroyed all except the wings and tail section of the plane.

Leithold and Ballard were on their way to Greeley when the accident occurred, he said.

ABERDEEN, S.D. (AP)—One of five persons involved in a car-truck collision late Thursday morning in northern Brown County died of her injuries.

She was Mrs. Ernest Iverson, 59, Mitchell. Mrs. Iverson was a passenger in a car driven by John Mike Novachich, 67, Ethan.

Other passengers in the car driven by Novachich were Mrs. Iverson's husband, 66, who was taken to Dakota Midland Hospital, and Mrs. Novachich, 48. The Novachichs were taken to St. Luke's Hospital.

The driver of the truck was Brian DeVries, 19, Aberdeen. He was hospitalized at Dakota Midland.

The collision occurred at the junction of State 10 and Brown County 14 southeast of Frederick.

In the collision story, the reporter is careful not to place blame on either driver. He does not say that one vehicle struck the other, only that the two collided. This is standard practice; the reporter never says that anyone was at fault unless a judge or jury so rules. If, of course, a driver is charged with a violation of law, the reporter may report the fact that he was charged.

In outlawry or warfare, the prohibition against placing blame hardly applies. However, questionable statements about guilt must be carefully attributed. Examine these heavily edited versions of two Associated Press stories, noting especially the use of attribution in the first example:

MUNICH (AP)—A day that began with murder and terror by Arab commandos ended in a bloodbath at a military airport 20 miles from Munich. Eleven members of the Israeli Olympic contingent were reported killed, at the hands of the terrorists, plunging the Olympics into sorrow.

A band of Arab guerrillas invaded the Israeli team's quarters at the Olympic grounds before dawn Tuesday and shot down two Israelis. They held nine others hostage through a day of tense negotiations that ended when the captors and hostages were taken by helicopter to the airport and a plane that was to fly them to Cairo.

Police sharpshooters opened fire on the Arabs when the helicopters landed, but missed some because of the darkness. The guerrillas who escaped the first shots turned their guns on the helicopters with the helpless Israelis inside, authorities reported.

Four of the Palestinian commandos were killed, three were captured and one was unaccounted for, police said. One policeman was reported killed, and a helicopter pilot was seriously wounded.

Bavarian Interior Minister Bruno Merck said the Israeli hostages had agreed to go with the Arabs to Cairo. But the German authorities felt "this would have been a certain death sentence for them. . . . We had to take a chance and attempt to free the hostages."

BELFAST (AP)—Gunmen killed two more men in Belfast Tuesday night, but the level of fighting in Northern Ireland eased to scattered skirmishes.

One of those killed during the night was a British soldier, the 100th to die in Ulster's three years of religious warfare. A sniper cut him down at an army post in a Catholic area.

The other man to die was a factory watchman found riddled by bullets. The two deaths raised the toll in Northern Ireland to at least 466 since August 1969, and at least 238 this year.

Terrorists attacked an army post in a lumber yard early today with gasoline bombs under cover of sniper fire. The soldiers fought the fire, the snipers shot at the soldiers and the flames spread to nearby Catholic homes. Then the guerrillas intercepted two fire engines racing to the blaze and held the firemen hostage until the government agreed to rehouse the Catholic families who were burned out.

Priests and housing officials found quarters for the displaced families, but the gunmen kept on shooting at the troops and fire fighters. However, no casualties were reported.

Although the Belfast story is presented without attribution, the writer is careful not to impute guilt to any particular faction. One might infer that the "guerrillas" belong to some branch of the Irish Republican Army, but the writer never identifies them as such. He reports only what he could prove.

A simple plane crash or automobile accident story may be obtained from a single source. Even a story as violent as that from Munich may require only personal observation and quick interviews with three or four persons. None of these examples approaches the difficulty of covering a natural disaster, which often involves dozens or even hundreds of sources. Coverage of this breadth is hardly a one-person operation. Usually a few reporters tour the scene, many more man the telephones, and each develops portions of the story. The fragments they write are then given to a rewrite person who puts it all together. The magnitude of the job may be understood if the student lists all the individual sources of information identified in this example:

RAPID CITY, S.D. (AP)—The death toll passed 200 Sunday as people in the scenic Black Hills of South Dakota began identifying their dead and cleaning away the debris from savage flooding that left hundreds still missing and damage in the millions of dollars.

Civil Defense officials said the death count had reached 208, but feared the toll would go higher. Relatives reported 500 persons still unaccounted for in the area.

Rapid City, a city of 43,000, bore the brunt of the wall of water created when extraordinarily heavy rains forced the earthen Canyon Lake Dam to give way and Rapid Creek to overflow its banks.

National Guardsmen and volunteers joined in the search for more bodies in the flood-stricken southwestern portion of the state, declared a national disaster area by President Nixon. The designation made the area eligible for immediate federal aid.

The U.S. Army Corps of Engineers predicted damage would reach $100 million. Homes were splintered, cars and mobile homes scattered about like toys by the flood waters.

Persons of all ages were cleaning debris and hauling it away with every available truck Sunday. Meanwhile, they also combed through the wreckage for more bodies. Many of the workers were standing in water to their knees.

The Pennington County Health Department administered typhoid and tetanus shots to the survivors.

Gov. Richard Kneip, who toured the flood-ravaged area Saturday and Sunday, said the final death toll may not be known for a week. He called the flooding the "worst disaster to strike this state."

Sen. George McGovern left the presidential campaign trail to fly to his home state to survey damages in Rapid City and surrounding areas. He called the scene "incredible destruction and desolation . . it goes beyond what anyone can comprehend."

The Rapid City water system remained inoperable Sunday. Drinking water was brought to designated places in the city from nearby Ellsworth Air Force Base.

Long distance telephone communications remained difficult and natural gas service was virtually nonexistent.

Police said some instances of looting were reported after flooding Friday night and early Saturday. Mayor Donald Barnett did not declare martial law but ordered the arrest of sightseers. He later asked for 1,500 military policemen to assist local officers early Sunday afternoon. His office said no word had yet been received on the request.

Civil Defense officials said hundreds of low-lying flooded areas still had not been covered by the 2,000 National Guardsmen and a like number of volunteers taking part in search efforts.

"I expect many bodies to be recovered in the lower areas of the city where the waters have remained high," Sheriff Glenn Best said.

Eight bodies were recovered at Keystone, a community near Mt. Rushmore and its famed presidential sculptures. Civil Defense officials said additional tourists camping in the foothills near Keystone may have been trapped by the floodwaters.

Bodies were taken to three mortuaries in Rapid City, where survivors still searched for friends and relatives.

Patrick Dixon, a Civil Defense volunteer, said he saw a preliminary list of the dead that contained mostly Rapid City residents.

Phil Gaddis, a spokesman for the Red Cross, said only 100 to 200 persons needed overnight shelter in five centers set up in the area.

Some seven inches of rain late Friday night and early Saturday turned normally placid streams into roaring rivers, sweeping hundreds of homes, cars and trees in their paths. When the deluge overburdened Canyon Lake, the earthen dam gave way.

The flooding and loss of life seemed to be concentrated in the Rapid City area and the community of Keystone. Other areas in the Black Hills reported damage, but no loss of life.

Authorities cautioned ranchers along the Cheyenne River southeast of Rapid City to watch the river for emerging bodies. Flood-torn Rapid Creek empties into the river.

Civil Defense officials said supplies such as clothing, food and bedding were contributed by communities across South Dakota, Iowa, Wyoming and Nebraska.

Much of the damage came after landslides ruptured gas lines, causing fires and explosions during the predawn hours Saturday.

A spokesman for the National Forest Service in the Black Hills said Sunday that all campers in the National Forest campgrounds around Custer, about 35 miles southwest of Rapid City, apparently were safe, as were occupants of isolated summer homes and ranches.

Cameron Ferweda, public information officer for the Forest Service, said aerial and ground surveillance teams said 275,000 acres of watershed in the Black Hills area received some damage.

In the Rapid City story, as in that from Munich, questionable statements of fact are attributed to responsible sources.

Outright Form Stories

Without being cynical, we can observe that death and marriage have a great deal in common. Each is an end and a beginning. Each is the subject for a story about people as individuals; thus names are among the most important ingredients. Each is a scrapbook story: it will be clipped from the paper and placed in the family album. Therefore, you had better make certain that all the names are spelled right.

The emphasis on names makes wedding stories and obituaries two of the few exceptions to a common rule. Ordinarily, beginning reporters are advised not to start a lead with an unfamiliar name. But in weddings and obituaries, this advice is reversed. We begin the wedding story with the name of the bride, the obituary with the name of the person who died.

WEDDINGS

The formula lead for a wedding tells who was married, when, and where. This is followed by the names of the couple's parents, then the names of the attendants. Some newspapers go into detail about the bride's costume; others omit it. The story normally ends with the reception, the wedding trip, and where the couple will live. Here is a tightly written example:

Miss Margaret Ellen Alexander and William Polk McRee Jr., both of Birmingham, were married at 2 p.m. Sunday at Siberton Baptist Church.

Parents of the couple are Mr. and Mrs. John L. Alexander and Mr. and Mrs. W. P. McRee of Birmingham.

Mrs. Patsy French was honor attendant and Kerry French was flower girl. Lannie Gardner was best man. Stanley French ushered.

Mr. Alexander gave his daughter in marriage. Her gown of taffeta and lace was accented with a velvet ribbon and tatting. A tiara held her veil. She carried spring flowers.

A reception at the home of Mr. and Mrs. Stanley French followed. The couple will live in Birmingham after a Florida wedding trip.

Beginners often must be warned against using flowery description or terms they don't understand. We try to avoid saying that the bride's gown "fell to the floor" or that the vows "were consummated at the altar."

OBITUARIES

The standard obituary begins with who died, when and where, at what age. If the cause of death is available, it is usually included in the opening sentence. The middle of the story lists the members of the dead person's immediate family and may also give the number of grandchildren and great-grandchildren. Funeral and burial details usually are placed at the end. To conserve space, many newspapers write the routine obituary as a single paragraph and set it in type smaller than that used for other stories. Here is an example:

> Frank Samples, 59, of 5666 Edith, Kansas City, Kansas, died last night at Providence Hospital. He was a lifelong Kansas City area resident. Mr. Samples was a switchman for the Union Pacific Railroad for 31 years. He was an Army veteran of World War II. He leaves his wife, Mrs. Leone G. Samples of the home; a daughter, Mrs. Karen Newell, 5535 N. 95th, Wyandotte County; a sister, Mrs. Vera Jones, Gladstone; and a grandson. Services will be at 2 p.m. Saturday in the Fulton-Nickel Chapel, with burial in Chapel Hill Cemetery. Friends may call after 5 p.m. today at the chapel.

The obituary, like the wedding story, has no flowery language. Nor does it employ euphemisms. We say that the person died, not that he passed away. And he will be buried, not interred.

Some newspapers publish only one obituary immediately after the person dies. Others will publish a second story if the funeral arrangements have not been determined in time for the original obituary. If such a follow-up is necessary, the lead should begin with the time of services—the new information—rather than the fact of death. Here is a "second-day" obituary:

> Funeral services for Father Edward J. Jaworowski, 62, pastor of St. Joseph Catholic Church at Superior and Sacred Heart Church at Nelson, will be at 11 a.m. Friday at the Superior church. Burial will be in Osceola.

> Father Jaworowski, who had been pastor at Superior the last two years, died Monday after a heart attack.
>
> He was ordained a priest in 1936 at St. Mary Cathedral in Lincoln. Later he served as assistant pastor of St. Mary Church at David City and then as pastor of Catholic churches at Osceola, Bellwood, Minden, Sutton, Palmyra and Douglas.

HIGH SCHOOL BASKETBALL

Basketball stories are not form stories in quite the same sense as weddings and obituaries, yet there is a similarity in the way they are obtained and written. A sports editor who must cover several high schools usually hires a part-time telephone crew whose job is largely to take down incoming box scores in duplicate. The original is sent to the composing room to be set in type immediately. The duplicate, perhaps with some extra notes, is set aside for the benefit of the person who must write the story—who may or may not be the same person who took the call. The story, seldom more than three paragraphs and often only one, is written from the box score and any extra information that happens to be available. Because of the limited information, the lead seldom contains more than the bare score, the score at the half, and the points made by the leading players on each team—all of which is contained in the box that follows it.

USING YOUR JUDGMENT

Every situation, every event, every newsworthy item is different from every other for the same reason that a person never steps twice into the same stream. Sometimes these differences are important and should determine the approach you take to the story. Sometimes you do not have enough information to distinguish a given story from many others like it. Sometimes the story is too minor to merit more than routine formula presentation, but stressing a unique detail can inflate a trivial matter beyond its proper proportions. In short, sticking to formulas can be dull and misleading, but departing from them can be difficult, undemocratic—and also misleading.

The solution to this daily dilemma lies in experience and judgment. If reporters are to fight the formula story reasonably and effectively, they must learn how to do three things: they must be able to see or dig out the distinctive elements in every situation they encounter; they must be able to evaluate these distinctions and decide how much attention, if any, they merit; and they must be able to vary the formula story accordingly—sometimes only slightly, sometimes moderately, sometimes dramatically. Developing these three abilities takes time, effort, and experience. But what they add up to is skillful reporting and skillful writing.

SUGGESTED ASSIGNMENTS

1. Clip three different kinds of formula stories that seem to offer some potential for more original treatment. Write a brief analysis of the formula used in each story. Then write another version of each one that departs to some extent from the formula.
2. Attend a meeting of a campus governing body or committee. Write a story on the meeting.
3. Take one of the issues discussed at the meeting and explore it in greater depth. Get all the facts and opinions you can find on the subject. Then write a story about it.

CHAPTER SEVEN / WRITING LIVELY LEADS

The girls in Pierson Hall offer something more.

Jonathan Mitnick didn't know who grabbed him, but he felt the needle-sharp point of the knife in his back and he was "too frightened to give it much thought."

Who could prompt 120 teachers to do the hokey-pokey and the bunny hop and make human choo-choo trains and merry-go-rounds?
Dr. John L. Schultz could—and did.

"When you enter the unknown, you feel a particular excitement," said Dr. Christiaan Barnard.
For him, the unknown was to cut out a man's still beating heart and replace it with a new human heart.

HOLLYWOOD (HTNS)—There are certain inexorable laws of nature. Dogs chase cats, Irishmen drink, lions eat Christians, the New York Mets lose, and Miss Doris Day spreads sunshine.

Do the examples above get your attention? Do they make you want to read more? If the answer to both questions is yes, they probably should be considered successful leads. Yet each, to a strict constructionist, violates a time-honored rule of lead writing. The rules, in the same order as the apparent transgressions, are:

1. *The lead must be honest.* If we had included the second paragraph, you would have discovered that the "something more" offered by the girls in Pierson Hall was only a color television set which young men could watch while waiting for their dates. The excuse for writing the story was that it was the first color TV set in any resident hall lounge. But is the lead really dishonest? Or were you only tricked by your own mind?

The rule of honesty means that the lead must reflect the tone as well as the facts of the story. If an automobile accident results in serious injury to people or property, we must resist the temptation to lead with an hilarious description of the car protruding from someone's dining room window. On the other hand, a good reporter will avoid a sober lead when reporting the results of the annual pancake-eating contest. And if we were to announce with solemnity the presence of a new color TV set in a dormitory—a matter hardly worth noting at all—the lead would mislead by attributing more significance to the fact than it merits.

2. *Don't use an unfamiliar name in the first paragraph.* This is good advice. Ordinarily you will convey more meaning by first identifying a person by position, occupation, or role in the news. But as we already have observed, wedding stories and obituaries violate this rule regularly.

As for Jonathan Mitnick, what can we say? He could have been anyone. He just happened to be a young fellow who had come downtown one day to keep a dental appointment—only to find himself the temporary hostage of an escaped convict. The sight of the police closing in with drawn guns, he said, alarmed him almost as much as did the prodding knife in his back. The lead clearly establishes his role in the story, and in this particular instance, beginning with an unfamiliar name (rather than "a young man") seems to enhance the drama inherent in the situation.

3. *Avoid the lead that asks a question.* Since many reporters formulate their stories by asking questions (who? what? when? so what? etc.), beginners are often tempted to lead with a question. Normally, this technique is a poor choice. Your goal is to inform readers, not to interrogate them. If readers want to play guessing games, they can turn to the crossword puzzle. One of the worst possible question leads begins "Have you ever wondered (how to bake better brownies, or what became of Sally, or . . .)?" If readers can answer, "No, I really never cared," then you have lost them.

But if the subject is offbeat and the question will arouse interest, go ahead and use it. Make certain, however, that the question is provocative and that you at least begin to answer it in the next sentence. If the strange behavior of a group of teachers arouses your interest, for example, then the question is sufficiently provocative. What were they doing? In the sentence completing the unconventional lead, we find that they were merely trying to learn how kindergarten pupils might feel during the games they play in school.

Speaking of questions, generally you should avoid telling about the questions you have asked—as well as asking them—in the story. The most common offender is the phrase "when asked about" in the body of the story. The reader assumes the reporter asks questions because that's his job. But this rule, too, has exceptions. Sometimes the reporter must make it clear that the information had to be dragged out of the source, that it wasn't volunteered.

4. *Avoid the direct quote.* This is another rule honored almost as much in violation as in observance. The primary reason for the warning is that a direct quotation lifted out of context can distort the entire story. Any person can be made to look like either a wit or a fool if you select the appropriate quotation. And if the quote doesn't mislead, chances are it will at least confuse the reader.

If, however, the quotation gets to the heart of the speaker's meaning and expresses it better or more colorfully than the reporter could do in an objective paraphrase, it is legitimate material for the lead.

In the story about Dr. Barnard, one might argue that the quotation was weak or even confusing. But the subject of the story was the surgeon's assessment of his own emotional reaction after he had performed the first successful heart transplant. Based on an interview several days after the operation, this was not a spot news story. Dr. Barnard's name and his accomplishment already had made the headlines. Thus, this story demanded something other than routine treatment.

The chief merit of the quotation in this case lies in two attention-getting words, "unknown" and "excitement," both of which imply adventure. But the real strength of the lead is in the second paragraph. Compare the image-evoking power of "to cut out a man's still beating heart" with the more predictable "to transplant a human heart." The short, descriptive verbs leap out at you. Anything less would be pedestrian and thus out of keeping with the extraordinary subject.

5. *Limit the first paragraph to a single declarative sentence of not more than 25 words. If the lead has more than three commas in it, turn it into two sentences, each a separate paragraph.* Mechanical advice of this sort is derived from the readability research of Rudolf Flesch. It is directed mostly to the beginner who has yet to develop

an ear for language, but it can be helpful to any writer struggling to streamline an awkward sentence. It should not, however, be invoked to discourage an imaginative approach.

The lead about Doris Day undoubtedly violates the mechanical standards, but it would be difficult to argue that it is unreadable. And nobody can fault the writer for lack of imagination. He has found an original way of solving a common problem, that of trying to say something new about a familiar subject.

NO SINGLE RIGHT APPROACH

We have stacked the deck, of course, in writing the lead to this chapter. We have deliberately avoided spot news and interpretive stories dealing with conventional subjects. Instead, we selected examples high in human interest to illustrate exceptions to some of the so-called rules. This doesn't mean that the rules are entirely useless. Quite the contrary; they will be helpful for most of the stories you write. But they are only guidelines, not rigid specifications. None should be interpreted as meaning "always" or "never."

The guidelines are relatively few. Those quoted most often are qualified "don'ts." They seldom tell the writer what he *should* do, simply because the range of options is virtually endless. As long as the lead is accurate, honest, and readable, reporters can use almost any device they choose. They are limited only by the facts, the ability to put them together imaginatively, the laws of libel, and the standards of good taste.

Although the purposes of journalism and literature—and hence their techniques—generally are not the same, journalists sometimes use literary techniques with good effect. Here are a few examples:

Alliteration

> Plants are killed by pests. Pests are killed by pesticides. And pesticides may cause pollution.
>
> Saving plants by eliminating pests, pesticides and pollution is the purpose of the International Biological Program. The new program resulted from a $6.2 million increase in U.S. Department of Agriculture funds for pest control research.

Rhyme and Literary Allusion

> "Officer Krupke, we're down on our knees,
> Cuz no one wants a fella with a social disease."

That refrain, sung by a gang of New York teen-age hoodlums in West Side Story, probably evoked chuckles from every audience which saw the musical.

But venereal disease, especially gonorrhea, is no longer a laughing matter, according to health authorities. Many officials say the disease has reached epidemic proportions.

Metaphor

KANSAS CITY (AP)—What began two decades ago as a shotgun marriage between Kansas City and Trans World Airlines will be culminated Oct. 21-23 in dedication of the quarter-billion dollar Kansas City International Airport.

The birth pangs of KCI began in the early 50s when Kansas City bought 5,000 acres of rolling Platte County prairie to provide TWA with its overhaul base. City fathers said the move was necessary to keep TWA, the city's largest employer, from leaving to seek greener pastures.

L. P. Cookingham, then city manager and the mastermind behind the airport, foresaw a project that would keep TWA in Kansas City and also augment existing air service. Little did he realize his dream in those initial stages would grow to the giant the airport became.

Narration

A group of 10 Lincoln residents approached the City Council Monday and charged that the proposed Northeast Radial Highway is "unnecessary and a waste of the taxpayers' money."

Council members listened to the complaints, then voted for the fifth consecutive year to appropriate $500,000 for the highway, with no construction date in sight.

Two other literary techniques, irony and satire, normally are off limits in straight news and even dangerous in editorial columns. The reason was well illustrated in the 1960s when humor columnist

Art Buchwald announced in print that J. Edgar Hoover was a ficti-
tious character. Thousands of readers flooded newspapers with letters
declaring that they knew him to be wrong because they had met the
FBI director. Hyperbole also must be ruled out in most instances; but
if you reexamine the lead about Doris Day at the beginning of this
chapter, you may decide even this restriction has legitimate exceptions.

There is no rule, then, that can't be broken—when reporters are
absolutely sure they know what they're doing. For some beginners,
the freedom we have illustrated is a heady incentive that must be
tempered with restraint. The imaginative writer may have to be ad-
monished occasionally against using nuclear artillery to swat a fly.
But for many others, perhaps the majority, the lack of positive guidelines is like being lost in a wilderness without a map. The existing
rules may help beginners repair weak leads once they have something
on paper, but rules accomplish little toward getting him started in
the right direction.

Obviously there is no *one* right direction. Given an identical list
of facts, no two reporters should be expected to produce identical
leads. If this is what we want, we can turn the job over to a computer. But even the computer's choices would reflect the judgment
of the people who programmed it.

Writers' output is influenced by their *total* input—everything
they have studied, observed, read, or experienced which they may
relate, consciously or unconsciously, to the story at hand. Whatever
strikes their senses at a given moment may function as triggering
stimuli that set the brain to operating along highly private channels,
calling up old memories, making new connections, and coloring perception at that moment. Naturally the more aware writers are of
these psychological processes, the better they will be able to control
them and to place new information and experience in appropriate
perspectives.

But no matter how objectively we try to approach the facts, writing is a subjective process. This is more apparent in the lead than in
any other part of the story, for writers make subjective decisions when
they select the facts on which to base the lead. Objective or not, the
lead to some extent reflects the person who writes it. We should
therefore expect the most striking leads to come from writers who
have had the most varied education and experience. This isn't always
true for beginners, however. Before cub reporters can expect to write
polished leads, they must understand what constitutes a lead, what
its goals are, and the two general ways these goals can be approached.

DEFINING THE LEAD

Editors often spell "lead" as "lede" or "leed" to avoid confusion
with the thin piece of metal—also spelled "lead" but pronounced

"led"—which hot-metal printers used to insert between lines of type to space out a column. When applied to writing, "lead" has at least as many meanings as it has spellings. In its most restricted sense, it refers to the first paragraph of a story, which usually consists of only a single sentence. In the broadest usage, it means an entire story. A "night lead," for example, is an updated version of a story that was first produced during the day, now revised for use the next morning. Between these extremes lies the "new lead," which supersedes part or all of an earlier version of a developing story.

Throughout this book, we use "lead" to mean simply the introduction, regardless of its length. It ends at the point where the subject is clearly established and the reader can see where the story is going. For example, the standard summary ends when the writer ceases to introduce new information and begins to elaborate on what has already been presented in broad outline.

Few straight news leads amount to more than three paragraphs, and many consist of only the first sentence. At the other extreme, a narrative lead for a long feature article may require several typewritten pages.

The lead unifies the entire story. It pulls together, whether by summary or some other device, everything that follows. It also establishes the tone—matter-of-fact, somber, light-hearted—that will characterize the rest of the story. It either presents interesting facts immediately or promises to present them later.

The lead's function is to get readers' attention and lure them into the story. At the minimum, it constitutes the "Hey, you!" of a famous four-part formula described by Walter S. Campbell, director of professional writing courses at the University of Oklahoma. Campbell held that any piece of writing, fact or fiction, follows this pattern:

> HEY! (Get the reader's attention)
> YOU! (Relate the subject to his interests)
> SEE? (Show him what you have to sell)
> SO . . . (Leave him with an idea, a feeling, or
> a suggested course of action).

Campbell, who wrote history and fiction under the name of Stanley Vestal, proved that his formula worked. So have countless students. Based explicitly on learning theory, it was hardly a revolutionary idea. Campbell's chief contribution was in stating it so simply that any beginner may use it, whether he is writing news stories, drama, history—or instructions on a label for patent medicine.

To apply the formula to objective newswriting, we must make one important modification. We must delete the "suggested course of action" at the end. Reporters never tell readers to attend a meeting, to get out and vote, or to do anything else. They don't even hint at such a suggestion. Advocacy is the role of the editorial writer, not the reporter. An ordinary news story doesn't necessarily leave readers with an idea or a feeling, either. It may merely add to their store of information.

If the formula has a weakness, it lies in the implication that the four parts are separate, distinct steps to be taken one at a time. In most writing they tend to flow together, with no visible demarcation. Occasionally you may detect a slow, step-by-step approach to the formula in fiction and magazine articles, but this is too leisurely for most newspaper work. Reporters must get readers' attention immediately, relate the subject to their interests as quickly as possible, show them what the story is all about, and, if possible, give them an idea or feeling at the same time. The journalist often telescopes all four parts of Campbell's formula into the first sentence.

Why try to do so much in so few words? One reason is that space is always a factor. We try to tell the story as briefly as possible—without sacrificing thoroughness or clarity—in order to squeeze all the more important stories into the newspaper. Another reason is competition for the reader's eye. The newswriter, unlike the fiction writer, doesn't have the reader's undivided attention at the beginning. When a person picks up a novel, he is prepared to shut out everything else for a while. But when he picks up a newspaper, a dozen or more stories may compete for his attention on a single page. Newspaper readers are like shoppers in a supermarket as they gaze from product to product. To sell them a particular story, you must immediately offer something they consider of value.

TWO GENERAL METHODS

The lead, then, is a reporter's way of selling the story. Like grocers, reporters can merchandise their product in one of two ways: (1) they can package it in a transparent wrapper, so that the buyer can see the contents at a glance, or (2) they can conceal the contents and try to sell the product with an attractive container that bears a promise of something worthwhile inside. To be successful, either approach must be based on a subject of interest. One reveals it immediately; the other takes a little longer. But both fulfill the same structural purpose: they tie the story together and point toward the details that follow.

The Transparent Wrapper

The transparent wrapper is used for most stories. Writers as salespeople identify their subject immediately and in effect tell the reader, "Here it is; take it or leave it." A glance at the first few pages of a newspaper will verify the dominance of this kind of lead and probably indicate why it is standard procedure. It is honest, direct, and brief. Most stories are so routine that they offer little opportunity for anything but routine leads. If reporters strain for something more imaginative, either the tone or the significance of the story doubtless will be misrepresented. If they try to suspend interest, they may end up making a mystery of nothing. And in many of the stories that do deal with out-of-the-ordinary events—a plane crash, a six-figure ransom payment, results of peace negotiations, a Supreme Court appointment—the gravity of the matter rules out anything but a straightforward lead announcing the most important fact first.

Often it is the story that contains an unusual element, but nonetheless is of only moderate significance, that invites an unconventional lead. But here, too, the reporter must be wary. Most news readers want facts, not fancy. Selling your story is one thing; conning readers into buying something they don't want is another. The transparent wrapper serves readers by conserving time and letting them know immediately whether the story is of interest to them.

A typical example of the transparent wrapper is this summary lead:

> A knife-wielding State Prison Farm trusty was shot and captured Monday in downtown Hartford, an hour after he reportedly assaulted the warden's daughter and escaped in her car.
>
> Arthur "Jo Jo" DeLorenzo, 34, will be arraigned today in circuit court on charges that could put him behind bars for the rest of his days. The Bridgeport convict has been in trouble with the law most of his adult life.
>
> His dash for freedom ended on the sidewalk at Church and Trumbull Streets as police closed in despite his menaces with a homemade knife. He dropped the knife when Policeman Richard Killfeather put a bullet through his wrist.

The transparent wrapper need not be a summary lead. The only requirement is that it identify the subject immediately. This may be accomplished in only a few words, as in this example:

> Burning at the city dump will soon be stopped.
>
> Today the city received a cease-and-desist order from the State Department of Health, requiring that the burning end by June 1.

The Opaque Wrapper

The opaque package with the blurb outside usually is restricted to human interest stories and magazine-style articles. In this approach, the writer arouses interest by promising information before he reveals it. To achieve this end, the writer may use anecdote, questions, narrative, or any technique that delays identifying the subject and whets the reader's interest. All such techniques fall into the category of suspended-interest leads. Here is a typical example:

> Who rides circus elephants in her fifth month of pregnancy and gets bitten by an albino turkey at Thanksgiving?
> Only Miss Linda of television's Romper Room, of course.

Another simple form of suspended interest is the use of a pronoun without an antecedent, as in this example:

> He started out as a night jailer 43 years ago when, he said, policemen were hired more for brawn than brain. He worked his way up in law enforcement.
> Today Joseph T. Carroll, 62, is chief of police. He heads a force of 192 officers.

The most extreme example of suspended interest is the complete narrative that conceals the outcome until the final sentence. The lead for this kind of story can be said to end at the point where the reader clearly understands the action and can see the direction it is taking—though it may not always be easy to determine precisely where that point is. The following example begins with a literary allusion and metaphor, continues with narration, direct quotation, a question, and an anecdote. About halfway through, the reporter begins to explain the curious facts, but not until the last two paragraphs do we learn the outcome, which is really the point of the story.

> MOSCOW (UPI)—The Communist Party newspaper Pravda discovered something rotten in the Soviet Republic of Georgia and some party brass got tarnished.
> It started last month when a Pravda reporter started looking into the affairs of a man named Montselidze, director of a Georgia pipeline factory. The reporter said he got an eyeful.
> "They are building dachas (villas) and

crystal palaces whose architectural values and high cost a computer couldn't describe," Pravada's man wrote.

"Montselidze built a house like in a fairy tale," he added. "He surrounded it with a wall as high as a tower. He built a courtyard decorated with marble and seized 350 square yards of forest."

How did Montselidze get that much money?

According to Pravda, he tried an oldie in explaining it—that he inherited it.

Then someone else put it down to luck. He said a magician multiplied his savings so he could build a dacha. Pravda did not say who gave that reason but insiders speculated it was D. G. Abutidze, deputy minister of Georgian local industry, who also was cited in Pravda's article.

Things stayed that way until the Georgian Ruling Central Committee read the Pravda piece.

Then this weekend, came an explanation.

The key was land set aside for gardening societies—groups of factory workers given communal property where they can grow vegetables in their spare time.

"Certain dishonest persons" used this opportunity to join these societies and build private dachas and homes, said the Georgia newspaper Zarea Vostocka (Dawn of the East).

The officials usually used construction materials, machinery and even manpower from the local communes. They first surrounded the land with high fences, forbidden by commune law, then began the "illegitimate construction" behind them.

"Strange persons and relatives who had nothing to do with the collective gardening society were included," Zarea Vostocka said. "Instead of including workers, only top officials were included."

In one commune of 32 members, none was a worker. Of the 49 members of Montselidze's pipe factory commune, only six were workers.

As in all Soviet tales of corruption, the moral shines through—the worker will triumph. Montselidze was fired and Abutidze lost his deputy minister post.

The "crystal palaces"? They are being turned into rest homes for the district's working people.

CHOOSING THE OPENING WORDS

The opening phrase, perhaps the first word, may determine whether you grab the reader or lose him. Therefore the first sentence should begin with an attention-getting word. This means that normally you will subordinate attribution, identification, and time and place. Such necessary but routine elements will be placed in the middle of the sentence or at the end, or perhaps be delayed entirely until the second or third sentence. For example:

A bomb killed two British soldiers Monday near the border between Northern Ireland and the Irish Republic.

A new charity, the National Library of Talking Books for the Handicapped, has been established in Britain. It has set up a national library of tape-recorded books, its chairman, Maj. Frank Clarke, said.

The emphasis on the first few words often is misinterpreted. Many overzealous reporters approach the reader as if he were the proverbial mule, who must be hit over the head before the trainer can tell him anything. Operating on this theory, they strain for "shocker" leads that hit the reader over the head, kick him in the teeth, do anything necessary to get his attention. And the result often resembles reality about as closely as the opening scene of a television melodrama. If the reporter must strain for a lead, if it doesn't come to mind naturally, it is probably the wrong choice.

Getting the reader's attention is not that difficult. Indeed, anyone can write an effective transparent wrapper lead by following a simple, two-step formula. It may not lead to great literature, but it will get the reader's attention every time. The formula: (1) *Reduce the subject of the story to a single word,* and (2) *begin the lead with that word.*

Because they refer to subjects of universal interest, some words attract immediate attention. Here's a good example:

> Obscenity is a mirror of the times, a group of English teachers was told Thursday morning.
>
> The speaker was Mrs. Kathryn Spelts of Rapid City, who led a roundtable discussion of pornography at the South Dakota Education Association convention.

The word need not be shocking. As long as it identifies a subject of universal interest, the lead will be successful. The list of such words is virtually endless. War. Fighting. Peace. Love. Murder. Cancer. Sex. Assassination. Revolution. Discovery. Invention. Mystery. Adventure. Death. Destruction. Depression. Any of these may be the subject of a news story. And the formula lead would be any simple declarative sentence that begins with the key word. A few examples:

> Fighting broke out again today along the Israeli-Syrian border.

> Cancer can be detected before a person knows he is sick, a British medical scientist said today.

> Love found a way today for Bill Jones and Mary Smith.

It is not necessary, of course, that the subject be of such widespread interest. You can write an effective lead for a routine story by using the same formula, identifying the subject immediately and then letting readers decide for themselves whether the story contains anything for them. For example:

> Foreign students may be forced to go home during the summer because of rising unemployment and the threat of new labor restrictions.
>
> They already are finding it harder to get summer jobs, part-time work and employment for practical training. And Dean R. Y. Chapman, foreign student adviser, said the federal government is considering tighter restrictions on the jobs they can hold.

Obviously, readers who aren't foreign students or aren't interested in their problems can skip the story. And the writer has made it possible for them to make that decision after reading only two words.

Starting with Action

When the story involves strong, dramatic action, you should try to place the predicate—or some phrase that implies action—near the beginning of the sentence, as in these examples:

> SAIGON (UPI)—Rockets crashed into airports at two of South Vietnam's major cities today and Communist infantry stormed into three more hamlets within 25 miles of Saigon.

> BELFAST—Rocks and firebombs flew today as mobs battled British troops.

> Blizzard-stricken midwestern states began digging out today after the decade's heaviest snowfall.

> A 3-year-old boy who suffered permanent brain damage after a series of beatings by his mother's boyfriend has won a $600,000 trust fund which will provide him lifelong care.

The writer usually can get all the action necessary near the beginning of the sentence by using a legitimate noun or one derived from a verb—or by placing the predicate immediately after the subject. Occasionally reporters may use a participial phrase, although editors usually discourage this construction. One such lead that was particularly effective began thus:

> Sobbing and gasping for breath, a key witness. . . .

Even the most conservative editor could hardly quarrel with such an active beginning.

Featuring the Effect

Alert reporters never become so engrossed in the action that they lose sight of its effect. Some of the best leads may consist of a statement of a situation followed by the phrase "as a result of (whatever the action of the moment may be)." Although the phrase may not actually appear, it is at least implied, as in this example:

> The public's right to know is being drowned in a sea of information, according to Secretary of State Allen J. Beermann.

His office has been inundated by reports from candidates on campaign contribution and spending, in compliance with law.

Presidential campaign committees, in particular, have contributed to a flood of incoming paper which Beermann said has jammed the files and kept one staff member busy fulltime just logging reports.

"The reports just can't be meaningful to anyone because of the tremendous volume," Beermann said. "The law has lost a lot of its purpose."

When Names Make News

A newsroom axiom holds that what happened is more important than who did it. Following this rule, we customarily write the leads such as "A federal district judge today ordered picketing halted at Framistan Steel," We delay naming the judge until the second paragraph because most of our readers wouldn't recognize his name.

Sometimes, however, a name may catch the reader's attention more quickly than would the action. The name may identify a member of a prominent family, such as Roosevelt, Kennedy, or Rockefeller, or a powerful agency of government, such as Congress, the United Nations, the Supreme Court, the Central Intelligence Agency, or the FBI. A story may begin with the name of a country, state, city, or region, if the particular place has been much in the news and will immediately indicate the subject of the story to follow. An opening name may even identify a familiar program or concept: social security, woman's liberation, negative income tax, birth control, ecumenism. A story that begins with any of these nouns is certain to attract readers, regardless of the importance of the action involved.

Whether a story should start with a person's name depends not only on the person, but also on the size and homogeneity of the audience to which the story is directed. In a village of 300 persons, where everyone knows everyone else, it would be pompous of the editor to identify most local residents in any manner other than by name at the beginning of a story. A university newspaper probably will identify a well-known professor or administrator or a student leader by name immediately, but the city paper in the same town is likely to begin its story with "A history professor . . . ," "The dean of Northwestern's College of Arts and Sciences said today . . . ," or "NU student body president. . . ." To some extent, the same rule applies to "personal mention" columns in trade magazines. If we were writing for *Editor & Publisher,* we would have no reservations about beginning a story with a name such as Lee Hills, Paul Miller, or Allen

H. Neuharth, although we still would have to identify them later by their positions with the Knight and Gannett newspapers.

When the audience is larger and more diversified, the name must be more widely known before it can be considered usable in the lead. A clue to which names are newsworthy in themselves can be found in a booklet which the *Hartford Courant* distributes to copy editors. The booklet cautions editors to avoid using a name in a headline unless the name is especially familiar, "as, for example, the President or the secretary of state." Mere congressmen, unless they represent Connecticut, seldom qualify. Although reporters usually are not bound by rules as strict as those governing headline writers, the *Courant*'s policy still is worth considering. If the name isn't well known, it won't get enough attention to deserve a place in the lead.

Addressing the Reader

We can't write about each reader individually, nor can we always write about people we know. But often we write about events that will affect each reader. When this situation exists, occasionally we can use direct address, starting a story with "You." A good example is the how-to-do-it story, which tells how to prepare *your* income tax, how to get *your* car ready for winter, or how to save money on *your* grocery bill. The writer relates the story immediately to the reader's interests by using the second person pronoun.

Direct address, however, should be used sparingly. Few stories apply to all readers. And of those that do, only a few can be told easily in the second person. The third person is better for most stories. Applied to the wrong material, the "you" lead may seem patronizing. And if it must be continued throughout the story for consistency, the second person can become monotonous.

If direct address is to be used at any point in the story, it first must be established in the lead. The same rule governs the use of first person. You can't drag either the reader or the writer into the story in the final paragraph without some warning at the start.

WIDE ANGLE VS. CLOSE-UP

In choosing the opening words, and indeed in deciding on the general approach you are going to use, you often must consider another factor—the *scope* of the lead. Should you focus on the overall situation or scene? Or should you limit the lead to a single fact or action? This can pose a dilemma: if you try for the big picture, you may submerge a significant detail; if you choose the close-up, you may lose the context that is necessary to give it meaning.

To illustrate, let's suppose that an Air Force transport crashes, killing all 26 persons aboard. One victim is the commanding general of the North American Air Defense Command. Should the lead begin with "Twenty-six Air Force officers"? Or should it begin with "The commanding general"? Most reporters will choose the latter, playing up the significant difference between this crash and any other. The total number of dead can be brought in at the end of the first sentence, and the result still will be a summary lead.

The problem becomes more difficult when the story concerns the results of a city council meeting. A complete summary may be too vague to draw the reader into the story. And even a partial listing of the major actions may move so fast that the only impression left in the reader's mind is that of a blur. On the other hand, the lead that focuses clearly on a single action may give that action more status than it deserves.

A descriptive, suspended interest approach can present a similar problem. If we try to set the overall scene, we may bore the reader and lose him before we get to the action. On the other hand, the reader may be lost if we begin with unexplained action taken out of the context of its surroundings. He won't know where he is. Richard Harding Davis's famous lead that describes "one unbroken steel-gray column . . . twenty-four hours later is still coming . . . not men marching, but a force of nature like a tidal wave, an avalanche" makes no sense unless we know that he was describing the German invasion of Belgium during World War I.

The solution to the problem of focus often lies not in what you do first, but in what you do *next*. If you begin with a summary, move quickly to specifics; if you begin by describing a single action, establish the setting or context in the next instant. Remember that writing is dynamic, not static. It is more like a motion picture than a still photograph. You can move back and forth between panorama and close-up as quickly as necessary to get all the required facts across. And it makes no difference whether you are trying to describe a scene vividly or trying to convey statistical facts. The process of alternately tightening and expanding the scope is the same.

REPAIRING THE WOODEN LEAD

A lead that properly unifies the story still may fail to entice the reader beyond the first paragraph. Maybe the reporter had the right idea but slipped up in the execution. The potential is there; the product simply doesn't grab anyone. A busy editor may let such a lead get into print, perhaps defending it as "adequate." Privately, however, he may remark that it "lacks punch" or is "wooden."

If the basic idea is correct, the remedy often is relatively mechanical: a simple editing job of substituting words, rearranging the order of those already present, or perhaps deleting a few. If, however, the lead is so crowded and awkward that extensive streamlining is necessary, or if it is so superficial and vague that more substance is called for, a little imagination may be required to repair it.

Strengthen the Verbs

Suppose you see a dog lying in the street. How do you know whether it is alive? The obvious test is to nudge it gently with your toe. If the dog jumps up and bites you, it certainly must be alive. If it doesn't move at all, you probably will decide that it is dead.

The same kind of test can be applied to a lead. Does it move? Or does it only lie there? It isn't necessary, of course, that every lead jump up and bite the reader, but it at least should quiver enough to prove it is alive.

The part of speech that shows action or movement is the verb. Verbals, which are verbs (often in the -ing form) used as nouns or adjectives, usually produce the same effect. Therefore, verbs and verbals should be examined first when the lead fails to move. Any form of "to be," which indicates only existence, will weaken the lead. If possible, change "is," "was," "were," or "will be" to an action verb:

> *BEFORE:* An organization coordinating the distribution of food baskets, Christmas trees, toys and clothing *is* the County Welfare Office.
>
> *AFTER:* County welfare officials *have ironed out* some of Santa's seasonal confusion by *coordinating* the distribution of toys, clothing, food baskets and Christmas trees to needy families.

> *BEFORE:* There *will be* no Christmas lighting contest in Omaha this year.
>
> *AFTER:* Omaha *has called off* its annual Christmas lighting contest.

> *BEFORE:* The president-elect of the American Chemical Society (ACS) *will be the featured speaker* Friday evening at a regional ACS meeting in Fort Collins.
>
> *AFTER:* The president-elect of the American Chemical Society (ACS) *will speak on professionalism* Friday evening at a regional ACS meeting in Fort Collins.

> *BEFORE:* Occupancy in campus residence halls *is slightly higher* than at this time last year, the assistant housing director said Monday.

> *AFTER:* More students *have moved* into campus residence halls, the assistant housing director said Monday.

If the verb already shows action, consider the possibility of finding a stronger substitute. One sign of a weak verb is the amount of help it needs from adverbs or descriptive phrases; try to find a verb strong enough to stand alone.

Compare the verbs in these examples:

> *BEFORE:* An 18-year-old service station attendant was critically injured Thursday when a truck tire explosion *caused* the rim to *hit* him on the head.
>
> *AFTER:* An 18-year-old service station attendant was critically injured Thursday when a truck tire *exploded, slamming* its heavy rim against his head.

> *BEFORE:* A resolution supporting the St. Petersburg dam was *tabled* Wednesday night by the County Planning Commission.
>
> *AFTER:* A resolution supporting the St. Petersburg dam was *killed* Wednesday night. . . .

> *BEFORE:* President Nixon *won* re-election Tuesday night, *defeating* Democratic challenger George McGovern in one of history's greatest landslides.
>
> *AFTER:* President Nixon *swept* to re-election Tuesday night, *burying* Democratic challenger George McGovern. . . .

In searching for strong verbs, considerable caution should be exercised. Avoid verbs you wouldn't use in conversation—leave "rap," "blast," "flay," and "slay" to the few remaining tabloid headline writers who need them. The same applies to "purchase," "stated," and all the other pompous verbs favored by businessmen and public officials. Above all, avoid any verb that exaggerates the nature of the action.

Use Descriptive Identification

Some leads come to life only after we substitute descriptive phrases for vague nouns, as in these examples:

> *BEFORE:* Meet Gary Jackson. He's a *person* who gets his kicks from jumping out of an airplane and reaching speeds up to 200 miles an hour before he touches the ground.

> *AFTER:* Meet Gary Jackson. He's a *250-pound bartender* who. . . .

> *BEFORE: A neighborhood dog* was credited today with saving 9-month-old Tommy Smith from drowning.
> *AFTER: A German Shepherd named Sam* was credited today. . . .

A newsroom proverb holds that every dog has a name. And another declares that it is quicker to *say* "Dachshund" than it is to *describe* one. The use of a common breed name creates an immediate image in the reader's mind.

Delay the Details

No matter how lively the verb, a lead may fail to move if it is weighted down with too much information. You can suspect that the lead is overcrowded if the first sentence is more than three typewritten lines long or if it contains more than three commas. The solution is to break the one sentence into two or three, each restricted to a single thought. Leave the reader with one simple fact before you go on to the next. Here are some examples:

> *BEFORE:* Kurt Weise, 21, a vacationing college student from Cedar Rapids, Iowa, was killed at 10 p.m. Monday when his car went out of control and overturned on Interstate 90 at Black Hawk, near Rapid City.
> *AFTER:* An Iowa college student was killed Monday night when his car overturned on Interstate 90 near Rapid City.
> The victim was identified as Kurt Weise, 21, of Cedar Rapids. His car went out of control about 10 p.m. at Black Hawk.

> *BEFORE:* An effervescent teen-ager, Melissa Galbraith, 16, daughter of Mr. and Mrs. James Galbraith of Clarion, competing with six other teen-agers, has been named Miss Teen-Age Pennsylvania.
> *AFTER:* Clarion's effervescent Melissa Galbraith has been named Miss Teen-Age Pennsylvania.
> Melissa, 16, was one of seven contestants. She is the daughter of Mr. and Mrs. James Galbraith.

In revising each of the stories above, we have removed everything that stood between subject and predicate and gotten rid of all the commas in the opening sentence as well. We have taken out everything that might slow the reader down before he gets into the body of the story.

Tack a New Lead on Top

A lead that is only slightly crowded often can be remedied by making it the *second* paragraph, instead of the first. The wording needn't be changed at all. We simply shove the present lead down and write a shorter summary above it. Here's how it can be done:

> *BEFORE:* Havelock Bank President T. E. (Ted) Dewey was named Tuesday to the Board of Education, filling a vacancy created by the resignation of Robert Magee early in September.
>
> *AFTER:* A banker has joined the school board. Havelock Bank President. . . .

Say a Little More

Although an overcrowded lead is the more common offender, occasionally a lead falls slightly flat because it doesn't say quite enough. A single word may make a vast improvement, as in this example:

> *BEFORE:* In one hour Sunday night, three traffic accidents killed five persons in downtown Omaha.
>
> *AFTER:* In one *deadly* hour. . . .

Sometimes, of course, in order to add life to your lead, to say a little more, you will need to use another angle altogether—shift from a wide-angle approach to a close-up, try featuring effect instead of action, or perhaps substitute a surefire transparent wrapper lead for a sluggish opaque opener.

LEAD-WRITING WITHOUT LEISURE

The beginner soon learns that a well-chosen lead impresses the editor (or professor). It also makes writing the rest of the story easier, because the entire piece hangs from the lead. With both these considerations in mind, beginners are under a great deal of pressure to produce leads that sing or sparkle. And with a textbook or two handy and plenty of time to ponder and play with words, they can probably do so.

Ordinarily, however, leads are not written under such circumstances. Reporters work in a room filled with clacking typewriters and unmuffled shouts—and often the ticking of the clock toward deadline is the loudest noise of all. They have no time to consult texts for lists of do's and don't's and all their exceptions or summaries of several types and all their variations. New reporters probably won't even have time to consult their memories for whatever portions of newswriting manuals might remain there. The student who must turn out a story in class before the bell rings is not much better off. Sometimes the pressure is so great that you simply freeze at the typewriter, unable to write anything for fear of being wrong.

There is, of course, no real "wrong," just as there is no definite "right." And there are at least a couple of solutions to the problem of freezing. First, spend a lot of time on your own, at least in the beginning, writing leads in your leisure. Play with words and ideas. Try writing the same lead ten different ways. Study rules, exceptions, and examples. Practice lead writing until most of the major principles and techniques become more or less automatic.

Then, when the pressure is on, forget about "right" or "wrong." Begin the story anywhere and tell it naturally as it comes to you. If you get a better idea for the lead halfway through the story, make a mental note of it and keep writing. You can always go back and polish the lead after the story is finished.

SUGGESTED ASSIGNMENTS

1. Clip five stories from a newspaper and rewrite the leads so that the first sentence of each begins with the subject of the story.
2. Clip five "transparent wrapper" stories and rewrite them to provide one example of each of these techniques: (a) a narrative lead, (b) a provocative question, (c) direct address, (d) a colorful quotation, and (e) a verse, alliteration, metaphor, or literary allusion.
3. Clip five overcrowded leads and rewrite them to limit each beginning sentence to a single idea. Eliminate anything that stands between subject and predicate in the first sentence.

CHAPTER EIGHT / THE MESSAGE'S MOLECULES

Editors sometimes say that good journalistic writing is no different from any other good prose. After all, the message's molecules—words, sentences, and punctuation marks—are merely standard English. Newswriters follow the same rules of spelling, grammar, syntax, and (with minor exceptions) punctuation that govern other writers. They have the same interest in coherence, unity, euphony, and emphasis. And the clichés so often labeled journalese are no more welcome in newsrooms than in English composition classes.

Yet the language of journalism *is* different, if only to a degree. It is livelier and easier to understand than most other factual prose. Sentences are leaner and cleaner. They contain fewer adjectives, fewer adverbs, fewer modifying phrases and clauses. Except in lists of names with addresses, the semicolon seldom appears; the simple sentence doesn't need it. The result is a series of clear, precise statements linked together with a crackling rhythm that carries the reader quickly and easily through the story.

Attempts to characterize journalistic prose usually focus on the qualities of *objectivity, clarity, brevity, precision,* and *vitality.* But these only begin to describe it. A closer analysis will show that the language of news also is characterized by some strange contradictions. It is both emphatic and cautious. It projects both barely suppressed excitement and cool emotional detachment. It is informal to the point of being pseudo-conversational, yet it is governed by rigid rules of word usage, capitalization, abbreviation, and numerical expression. In short, good journalistic prose is easier to read than it is to write.

Beginners' first efforts to write news can be frustrating. For years they have been encouraged to use increasingly larger words and more complex sentences to express increasingly complex thoughts. Suddenly words and sentences must be shorter and stronger. Students are told to tighten everything, to get to the point immediately, and to get it done fast. Then, when they have accomplished all this, most likely they will be told that they have done something wrong, that "you can't say that." Beginners are almost certain to have violated some rule that is either nonexistent outside journalism or seldom enforced. The advice to write conversational prose hasn't prepared them for the emphasis on precision.

We have good reasons for all this fussiness about language. You must write simply so that all members of your audience, including the least educated, will understand the message. Beginners sometimes are told to write for someone like themselves or for "the average reader." But this advice is slightly misleading. The fact is that you are writing for experts as well as laymen, for the well informed as well as the uninformed, for the educated as well as the uneducated. Your stories will be read by persons who witnessed the event, by those who know a great deal about the subject, and by those who know a great deal about language—and law. They will be read by engineers, financial experts, scientists, physicians, and teachers of English.

No matter how simple and clear your impression, if it is inaccurate or inexact, you're in trouble. If you misuse a technical term, someone will notice it. If you misspell a name, the phone will ring. And if you commit grammatical errors or rely on clichés, some English teacher will use your story as an example of journalese. Somehow you must satisfy all the people as much of the time as possible. No set of rules can save you from occasional error and embarrassment. But luckily you can look to a large body of do's and don'ts for guidance.

CHOOSING THE BEST WORD

Rules which give the novice particular trouble are those which limit the use of certain words to their most commonly accepted meaning. These can be extremely conservative. Some editors, for example, still insist that "electrocution" be limited to its original meaning, execution in the electric chair. And most refuse to accept "over" to mean "more than," although recent dictionaries cite this as common usage. Webster's Third International, copyrighted in 1961, is far too liberal for most newspaper journalists.

A few rules probably could be characterized as nit-picking or hair-splitting. But the editors who enforce them have good reasons: (1) they want to use words that will get the message across clearly to the greatest number of readers, and (2) they want to avoid any phrase that might be construed as defamatory or inflammatory. They do not want to be misunderstood by anyone—especially if it might lead to a libel suit or violence.

The words that convey the most meaning to the greatest number of readers are those we learn earliest: "mama," "daddy," "water," and "eat." We can't, of course, tell much of a story with a vocabulary so limited. But it is a relatively short jump from the child's vocabulary to the journalist's, which is shaped by a set of simple guidelines found in almost all handbooks of English usage:

> Prefer the familiar to the far-fetched.
> Prefer the concrete word to the abstract.
> Prefer the single word to the circumlocution.
> Prefer the short word to the long.
> Prefer the Saxon word to the Romance.

We don't write down to our readers, but we try to avoid sending them to the dictionary unnecessarily. If we must use an unfamiliar word, we either put it in a self-explanatory context or we stop and define it. And if abstractions are necessary, we supply a concrete example. We avoid the artist's French, the lawyer's Latin, and the public servant's gobbledegook. We cut out the fat and tell it in plain English, with no euphemisms. Here is an example:

> *BEFORE:* He stated that he desired to journey to the tavern and purchase his favorite malt beverage because his tongue was parched.
> *AFTER:* He said he wanted to go to the tavern and buy a beer because he was dry.

The general rule is to avoid words you wouldn't use in ordinary conversation. We reserve "stated" for something more formal and enduring than everyday remarks; we never "journey" anywhere ("journey" is a noun); we never "purchase" anything that we could as easily buy—and nobody answers a call with "Did you desire me?"

Avoiding Double Meanings

Stamping out pomposity is only the starting point. Even more important is avoiding any ambiguity. The reason should be evident from these examples:

> *Miss Smith was fatally injured when she was thrown from the car driven by her boyfriend.* Who threw her? Are we libeling the boyfriend by innuendo?

> *Jones slammed Mrs. Jenkins in the rear.* You meant that their cars collided, didn't you?

Careless use of pronouns is a major cause of ambiguity. In determining what noun a pronoun refers to, the reader should have only one option—not two, as in these examples:

> *The governor is two months younger than Sen. White, his Democratic opponent. He celebrated his 60th birthday this week.* Who ate birthday cake this week?

> *Judge Bowman showed the defendant a copy of the book which he wrote.* Who is the author—the judge or the defendant?

Editorial dread of double meanings is behind many of the more restrictive rules of word usage, even when there is little likelihood of a libel suit or a bawdy interpretation. This is clearly illustrated by some of the rules that govern headlines. Because headline writers don't have the luxury of space to explain in detail, each word must be instantly clear. They must reject or carefully limit the use of any word or abbreviation that has more than one common meaning, for example:

Fall—Use autumn or plunge.
FHA—Avoid. Do you mean Federal Housing Administration, Farm
    Home Administration, or Future Homemakers of America?
Groom—a groom cares for horses. A bridegroom is newly married.
Head—Avoid. Aboard ship, it's a toilet.
Hike—Never use to mean increase.
May—Use only to refer to the month. Never speculate in headlines.
REA—Avoid. Do you mean the Rural Electrification Administration
    or the express agency?
Set—Never use to mean scheduled.
Sub—Use substitute or submarine.
Vet—Use veteran or veterinarian.

Improving Odds against Error

Small words cause some of the biggest problems. "Not" and "now" are particularly dangerous because the typesetter can so easily convert one to the other—or lose the little qualifier entirely. If anything at all happens to "not," the entire meaning is reversed.

To guard against the possibility of a libelous disaster if "not" were omitted, it is virtually a universal practice to substitute "innocent" for the legally proper "not guilty." Another protection is the general practice of stating everything positively if at all possible. This reduces the total "nots" and eliminates the objectionable "not unlike" so common in academic writing.

It is even easier to eliminate "now." With the present-tense verb ("is now"), it is redundant. Sometimes the added emphasis is helpful, but more often "now" adds nothing but the hazard of becoming "not."

Eliminating the Overused and Meaningless

A few words are avoided to prevent overuse. One is "new" and another is "report." Everything in a newspaper, after all, is presumed new and indisputably a report, so the words usually are redundant.

Other words on the editor's hate list are "facility" and "incident," two nouns that do little more than take up space. "Facility" can refer to anything from a washroom to a coliseum, so it is best omitted. Say "factory," "theater," "gymnasium," or "warehouse," and leave "facility" to those who thrive on vague generalities. Take the same approach to "incident," which may be applied to anything from a pratfall to a small war. Whenever you encounter a "stabbing incident" or a "shooting incident," ignore the incident and go with the stabbing or shooting.

Another usage generally outlawed is "freak accident." Even if we concede that "freak" can be used legitimately as an adjective—which many editors won't—the phrase is banned to prevent vagueness and monotony. A newspaper may report dozens of accidents daily, and any of these might be described from someone's point of view as "freak."

Several vague qualifiers also fall into the overused-and-meaningless category: "very" (the worst offender), "slightly," "pretty" (as in "pretty fouled up"), "little," and "rather." How slight is slightly? How much is very much? How little is little? Such intensifiers add nothing. Indeed, they may subtract from the emphasis you achieve with a short sentence.

Finally, and perhaps most difficult to deal with, are the everyday abstractions bandied about wherever foggy thinking flourishes. Just as beauty is in the eye of the beholder, the meanings of "justice," "freedom," "democracy," and "progress" presumably are in the mind of the writer or speaker. But, unless the context is unusually specific, we have no assurance that the reader or listener will share the sender's meaning.

Does "free" mean free to or free from—and free to what or free from what? How much and what kind of change constitutes "progress"? What are the standards by which "success" is measured? Is a successful man similar to a successful boondoggle? Where do you draw the lines that cut the "middle class" off from whatever is above and below it? Will your reader automatically draw the same lines?

Avoiding vague terms is difficult. But awareness of the problem is the first step toward solving it.

Coping with the Misused, Confused, or Abused

Words associated with crime, violence, and government cause trouble because they occur so often and precision is so essential. Words used casually, even interchangeably, by the layman ("burglar" and "robber," for example) have specific legal definitions that must be adhered to in print. The following list of problem words is intended primarily for the beginner on rewrite, the police beat, or the city hall run:

Abrasions, contusions, and *lacerations*—Translate to cuts and bruises.

Abutment—The portion of a bridge that supports its weight. If a patrolman tells you the car hit an abutment, ask for a more complete explanation. He may mean that it hit the railing.

Adventure—Don't use to mean merely an exciting experience. An adventure involves danger, risk, or the unknown.

Affect—A transitive verb meaning to influence.

Effect is usually a noun that describes the result you get when you affect something. Used as a verb, *Effect* means to bring about: "He finally effected a change in the procedures."

Altar—The place where couples *alter* their future.

Amateur—A nonprofessional. Don't confuse with a novice, who is inexperienced.

Around—A preposition referring to spatial relationships. Don't use as a synonym for *about* or *approximately.* And "center around" is an impossibility.

Autopsy—A surgical operation to determine the cause of death. Don't confuse with *inquest,* which is a coroner's inquiry. An autopsy may be ordered by a coroner, but it is performed by a pathologist.

Bid—An offer; in public affairs, an offer to supply materials or perform a service for a stated price. Don't confuse with *contract.* Bids are advertised, invited, opened, and tabulated. Contracts are drafted, awarded, or let. "Bid letting" is illiterate.

Bill—A draft of a proposed law. Passed and signed, it becomes a statute or act. It is no longer a bill.

Blizzard—Snow isn't enough. Winds must be at least 35 miles an hour and the temperature not above 20 degrees. Don't call it a blizzard unless the National Weather Service does.

Boat—A boat may be carried aboard a ship. Don't describe a freighter, tanker, or ocean liner as a boat.

Burglary—Breaking and entering at night with intent to commit theft. Change "daytime burglary" to "break-in." Burglary, which need not involve theft, is a crime against habitation. Don't confuse with *robbery*, which is a crime against the person.

Capitol—Only the building; the city and money are *capital*.

Citizen—Don't use as a synonym for resident.

Collision—A violent meeting of moving objects. Don't use as a synonym for crash; a car can't collide with a bridge or a parked vehicle.

Confession—A written statement of guilt becomes a confession only when a judge admits it as evidence. Until then, it is only a statement.

Continuance—A delay of a trial or hearing.

Convince—Don't use as a synonym for persuade. You convince a person of a fact, but persuade him to act.

Comprise—The whole comprises (embraces or includes) the parts. For example, this nation comprises 50 states. Don't say "is comprised of."

Council—A meeting or a governing body. *Counsel* is a verb meaning to advise or a noun that means adviser or attorney.

Critical—When you refer to a patient, make it critical condition.

Dam—The water is a pond or lake; the dam is what holds it back. It is impossible, therefore, to drown in a stock dam—although one conceivably might suffocate.

Demolished, destroyed—Each describes total ruin. Anything less should be reported as damaged. "Completely destroyed" is redundant.

Died—"Died suddenly" and "died of heart failure" are meaningless; everyone does both. "Died of an apparent heart attack" also should be avoided; the heart is seldom apparent. Change it to "died apparently of a heart attack."

Farther—refers to distance; *further* refers to number or degree. For example, "He said further that he would like to go farther."

Flaunt—To display prominently. Don't confuse with *flout*, which means to defy.

Following—Use only as a verb or adjective. The preposition is *after*.

Gutted—Best applied to a butchered animal. Don't use it to describe a burned-out building.

Had—"Had his neck broken" or "had his leg cut off" is nonsense. Only a lunatic would *have* such a thing done.

Hanged—People are hanged; clothes and draperies are hung.

Healthy, Healthful—A healthy person may attribute his condition to healthful food, healthful living, or a healthful climate. "Healthy" applies to the condition of living things—except in the colloquial usage meaning sizable or vigorous, as in "a healthy portion" or "a healthy yell."

Knot—A measurement of speed; one nautical mile per hour. "Knots per hour" is redundant.

Lady—A member of British nobility. "Lady Jane" identifies a woman who was born into the peerage; "Lady Astor" identifies one who arrived by marriage. All other women are women.

Midair—Try *in flight;* nobody knows where midair is.

Murder—Premeditated homicide. A person may be charged with murder, but the act itself can't be called murder until he is convicted. The jury may decide it is manslaughter.

Narcotic—A sleep-inducing drug. Don't use it to describe a stimulant or as a generic term for legally controlled substances.

Principal—Workable synonyms are "chief" and "major"—the chief instructor of a school or the major amount of a loan. Don't confuse with *principle,* which means a general truth or a rule of personal conduct.

Ordinance—A city law. Don't confuse with *ordnance,* which refers to armament.

Refute—To disprove. Don't use to mean contradict or dispute.

Rolled—Don't say the car rolled when you mean that it overturned. Cars are designed to roll.

Strangle—To choke to death. "Strangle to death" is redundant.

Suicide—Don't use the word unless the coroner or medical examiner does. Call it "death by what officials said was a self-inflicted wound" or "death from an overdose of sleeping pills." Let the insurance company try to prove that it was suicide.

Sustained—Don't say "died of injuries sustained in the accident." If they had been sustained, the person would still be alive.

Unique—The only one of its kind; don't use as a synonym for unusual. "Most unique" is wrong; uniqueness has no degree.

Whether—Implies an alternative. It rarely needs to be followed by "or not."

Wreck—Don't use as a synonym for crash. Wreck is either a noun, identifying what remains after the crash, or a verb that requires an object.

IMPROVING YOUR SPELLING

The most common complaint about beginning reporters is that they can't spell. Editors usually attack the problem by sending the offender to the dictionary, the city directory, the atlas, and other reference works. This is no help, however, to the graduate who fails to get a job at the *Herald* because his letter was addressed to the "Harold." The time to remedy this problem is while you are still living in a "dormatory" and working on a "batchlor's" degree.

The importance of correct spelling can hardly be overstated. Suppose you identify a well-known columnist as a well-known communist.

Result: a libel suit. Or a correspondent becomes a corespondent. Trouble again—the latter term usually refers to a person accused of adultery with the defendant in a divorce suit. Or maybe you write that a person is fined for wreckless driving. No trouble this time, because wreckless is the best kind. But you look silly.

If you are a poor speller, it may be some consolation to learn that you have lots of company in journalism schools. This is partially because most would-be writers read a lot—and read rapidly. And the faster you read, the less you notice individual letters. Almost every writing student must learn to read much more slowly, especially when correcting copy.

Spelling rules are little help once you are past elementary school. You almost certainly know the two that are most important: (1) Place *i* before *e* except after *c* or when the sound is *a*, as in "neighbor" and "weigh"; and (2) to form the plural of a word ending in *y*, change the *y* to *i* and add *es*. And you probably have discovered exceptions to each of these. All other rules are so complicated that you can find the word in the dictionary before you can recite the rule.

The best way to teach yourself to spell is to develop the dictionary habit. Always use the same dictionary and make a check besides each word you misspell. When you find three check marks beside a word, go back to the grade school practice of writing it 10 times—or 50, if necessary. But don't just settle for memorization. Learn what the word means and where it came from. This will often help solve a spelling problem. "Dormitory," for example, is easier to spell if you know that it comes from the French "dormir," meaning to sleep.

Other ways to attack the problem are to:

1. *Pronounce words correctly.* Many are misspelled because a syllable is slurred or omitted in normal speech. Examples include bachelor, Niagara, interest, and Venezuela.
2. *Pronounce difficult words phonetically.* Think of Sioux as SIGH-ox, Duquesne as Doo-KEZ-nee, and missile as MISS-aisle.
3. *Compose memory devices for troublesome letters.* Some examples:

> Se*par*ation is *par* for the course.
> He played *on* an accordi*on*.
> A *leo*pard is in j*eo*pardy.
> There is *no ice* in n*iece*.
> Bad gram*mar mar*s writing.

Recognize the Troublemakers

The exercises and tricks suggested above are simply ways of recognizing and coping with troublesome words. And English has a plethora. Some of the toughest problems involve words with (a) one or more doubled consonants, (b) a vowel normally pronounced "uh," which gives no clue to its identity, and (c) spellings which seem to defy all logic, such as "fiery" and "seize."

THE DOUBLED CONSONANT

To master the following words, copy them and underline the doubled consonants. You may also want to underline those single consonants that you have a habit of doubling incorrectly. Merely copying them by typewriter will be a big help.

accelerate	guerrilla
accommodate	harass
arraign	hemorrhage
baccalaureate	legionnaire
Caribbean	misspell
chauffeur	occasion
Cincinnati	occurrence
dilemma	Philippines
disseminate	questionnaire
embarrass	sheriff
suppress	

THE VOWEL PRONOUNCED "UH"

Underline the vowels to master these words. In some cases, correct pronunciation may help.

accordion	dormitory
bachelor	Gibraltar
calendar	grammar
category	homicide
cellar	impostor
cemetery	incredible
defendant	Niagara
definite	nickel
dependent	resistance
dignitary	separation
dominant	villain

OTHERS OFTEN MISPELLED

Review these words from time to time until you can spell them correctly.

arctic	mustache
barbecue	ninety
bouillon	paraphernalia

buoy	parallel
Colombia (the nation)	pavilion
consensus	Pittsburgh (Pennsylvania)
crescent	plaque
deceit	prairie
diphtheria	precede
etiquette	proceed
excel	psychiatry
exemplary	query
extension	restaurant
fiery	seize
fluorescent	siege
forty	sergeant
hilarious	silhouette
inert	souvenir
innovate	strychnine
inoculate	supersede
jeopardy	Venezuela
lambaste	

BUILDING ORDERLY SENTENCES

Webster defines a sentence as a group of words that contains a subject and a predicate. For newswriters, a better definition would be "a group of words that represents a complete thought and conveys it clearly to the reader." This makes the person on the receiving end the final judge of whether a collection of words truly amounts to a sentence. Perhaps this is an extreme position. It will certainly eliminate much that passes for writing. But it is the position to which we are committed. To qualify as a sentence, a group of words must make sense to the reader.

Anyone can write sensible sentences by following five simple rules:

1. *Make sure that the group of words contains a verb.* The shortest sentence consists of only an imperative verb ("Halt!") with the subject (you) understood. The next shortest consists of subject and intransitive verb ("Time flies."). Short or long, every sentence must have a verb.

2. *Arrange the elements in the order in which the reader is accustomed to seeing them.* This means placing the subject before the predicate. It also means avoiding such constructions as "Throw the cow over the fence some hay." Don't write in a way that might prompt the old indictment of *Time* magazine: "Backward ran the sentences till reeled the mind."

3. *Keep related elements together.* This, of course, follows from Rule 2. It means only that modifiers should be placed next to the

words they modify—which is not always as easy as it sounds. The adverb requires special attention: Does it modify the verb? Or does it modify an adjective? Or perhaps another adverb?

4. *Make the parts agree.* Singular subjects require singular verbs. Plural pronouns must refer to plural nouns. Be consistent.

Every*one,* any*one,* no *one, nothing, and* n*one,* are all singular. They are followed by singular verbs and referred to by singular pronouns. For example:

> Every*one* on the committee *is* to submit *his* report next week.
> N*one* of the senators *is* willing to give up *his* special privileges.

Singular subjects immediately followed by phrases containing a plural noun (or vice versa) also create difficulties:

> A staggering *number* of letters *has* been received.

If this sounds too awkward, change the sentence so that it has a plural noun:

> Huge *quantities* of letters *have* been received.

5. *When you complete the thought, stop.* The period is your best friend. Use it often. If the entire sentence is a question, of course, it should end with a question mark. The only other way to end a sentence is with an exclamation point; editors call this the "shout mark" and usually ban it except in direct quotations.

The Prevailing Pattern

The most common English sentence consists of actor, action, and object of the action in that order. Translated into grammatical terms, this means subject, transitive verb, and object of the verb. The frequency of this pattern indicates that it is the order that makes the most sense to the greatest number of readers. It makes no difference whether the sentence is simple, complex, compound, or compound-complex. The pattern still prevails.

> *SIMPLE:* John fired the ball to second base.
> *COMPLEX:* The runner who was rounding third easily stole home.
> *COMPOUND-COMPLEX:* John fired the ball to second base, and the runner who was rounding third easily stole home.

Because of the emphasis on brevity and clarity, most news sentences are simple (one clause) or complex (one principal clause qualified by one or more subordinate clauses). The compound sentence, which comprises two independent clauses, is seldom used unless it is extremely short, such as "Bill went to town, and Mary stayed home." And the compound-complex sentence is still more rare.

Common as it is, the subject-verb-object pattern can't do everything. Some expressions require other forms. And if every sentence began with the subject, our copy would be dull, choppy, and difficult to understand. Varied beginnings, especially those that constitute transitions, are necessary to keep the reader awake and maintain continuity of thought. But when a passage becomes muddy or the entire piece bogs down, reexamine the syntax and consider whether you should revert to the order the reader understands best.

Several Common Problems

Many syntactical errors stem from efforts to vary the beginning of the sentence. These include backward organization, the dangling participle, the nonsense transition ("In his lifetime, he . . ."), and at least one redundancy so familiar that few readers notice it.

Other problems involve non sequiturs—phrases or clauses that may apply to the same subject but are illogically related in the given sentence structure. Sometimes, because the writer knows what he *means,* he fails to detect the fallacy in his manner of saying it. The result may be ridiculous, hilarious, or disastrous.

Here are a few guidelines to help you avoid these and other common pitfalls:

1. *Place the subject before the predicate.*
> *BEFORE:* Meeting him at the plane was the President.
> *AFTER:* The President met him at the plane.

> *BEFORE:* Missing and presumed dead were 20 officers and
> five enlisted men.
> *AFTER:* Twenty officers and five enlisted men were missing
> and presumed dead.

> *BEFORE:* "That was a swifty," said Tom.
> *AFTER:* "That was a swifty," Tom said.

2. *Be sure an opening modifier is followed by the word it modifies.*
> *BEFORE:* At the age of 6, his parents sent him to a board-
> ing school.
> *AFTER:* When he was 6, his parents sent him. . . .

BEFORE: Strolling along the street, a car struck him.
AFTER: Strolling along the street, he was struck by a car.

BEFORE: In wandering through the immense building, the intricate detail of the murals in almost every passageway particularly impressed her.
AFTER: In wandering through the immense building, she was particularly impressed by. . . .

3. *Avoid "Speaking, he said." It's redundant.*

BEFORE: Speaking to a crowd of 500 students, Anderson said. . . .
AFTER: Appearing before a crowd. . . .

4. *Place the time element near the verb it modifies.*

BEFORE: The housewives plan to march on City Hall and protest the new tax on Monday.
AFTER: The housewives plan to march Monday on City Hall and protest the new tax.

5. *Take special care with the placement of adverbs.*

BEFORE: He said he was only thinking of his wife.
AFTER: He said he was thinking only of his wife.

BEFORE: He nearly ran a mile.
AFTER: He ran nearly a mile.

BEFORE: He almost won 100 matches.
AFTER: He won almost 100 matches.

6. *Use a singular pronoun to refer to a singular noun.*

BEFORE: Notre Dame was on their 20-yard line.
AFTER: Notre Dame was on its 20-yard line.
OR: The Irish were on their 20-yard line.

7. *Use a singular verb when the subject is a collective noun.*

BEFORE: The Board of Regents were meeting in a closed session.
AFTER: The Board of Regents was meeting. . . .

8. *Avoid long compound subjects that bury the verb.*

BEFORE: James Torgerson, Michael Guffey, Susan Pratt, Stanley Schafer, Arthur Weinberg, Morton Johnson, Jess Paulsen and Philip George were elected to the board.
AFTER: Those elected to the board were. . . .

9. *Avoid non sequiturs.*

> *BEFORE:* A graduate of Harvard, he was born in 1922.
> *AFTER:* He was born in 1922. After graduating from Harvard, he spent two years in military intelligence overseas.

> *BEFORE:* He was charged with murder in District Court.
> *AFTER:* In a District Court arraignment, he was charged with murder.

> *BEFORE:* His political career got started by being elected to the City Council.
> *AFTER:* His political career got started when he was elected. . . .

> *BEFORE:* The reason he cited for his resignation was because of poor health.
> *AFTER:* The reason he cited for his resignation was poor health.
> *OR:* He said he resigned because of poor health.

SAYING IT BRIEFLY

Tight writing is a fine art. Like other arts, it is based on a philosophy, a sense of mission, insight, and mastery of technique. In journalism, it is a necessity.

The underlying philosophy is that the greatest art is produced with the fewest strokes, the fewest notes, the fewest words. Perhaps this is only rationalization, because necessity gives us no choice. But many painters, sculptors, composers, and poets agree that economy has esthetic as well as functional virtue.

The reporter's mission, of course, is to bring the reader as much news as possible in the available space while it is still news. To accomplish this, insight is indispensable. Unless the reporter understands what the reader wants and needs, what is germane and what is irrelevant, he is lost from the start. Tight writing begins with judgment in the selection of facts—the ability to identify information of consequence and the determination to limit each story to only what is necessary and interesting.

Insight also must include an understanding of what the reader already knows or will assume. The writer must recognize which words and phrases can be omitted and which can be eliminated once the subject is clearly established. He must know, for example, that if he writes "John Jones died Wednesday at 72," the reader will understand that he means *last* Wednesday and that 72 is Jones's age measured in years. And if he writes "The City Planning Board has scheduled a Monday hearing," the reader will understand *this* city and *next* Monday. The same rule applies to "state" or "national" or mention of a month without specifying the year. It applies also to street addresses presented without the name of the city. The reader always will assume here and now (or those things closest to here and now) unless we tell him otherwise. Recognition of this fact can save many words.

Determining the point at which a subject is clearly established may be more difficult. The simplest illustration is the standard method of identifying an adult male who is the principal subject of a story. Once we have given his full name and whatever other identification is necessary, we use only his last name. Usually we repeat the last name at least twice, then drop to the pronoun "he." If no other person is named in the story, we may use only "he" thereafter. But if the story is long, we may need to repeat his last name or some other identifying tag occasionally for clarity or variety.

The same kind of economy is possible with an organization. After it is clearly identified, we often can refer to it as "the board," "the club," "the council," or "the group." We can save still more words by judicious use of "it" to refer to an action, a proposal, a concept, or any common noun.

Editors' Streamlining Techniques

Few reporters manage to combine thoroughness with brevity until they have served time on a copydesk, where they are exposed to (1) wire service copy, the tightest kind in print journalism; (2) the loose writing of their fellow reporters, which often cries out for tightening, and (3) the techniques that editors use to "bleed" stories to minimum wordage.

Many stories, of course, are arbitrarily chopped from the bottom. Editors also have a habit of skimming through a story and eliminating entire paragraphs of background information which they consider unnecessary. But editors are at their best only when they go through the story word by word, substituting short words for long ones, turning clauses into phrases, and phrases into single words, eliminating redundancies and circumlocutions, or shortening sentences and tying them together.

The easiest part of the editors' job is word substitution. They automatically change intoxicated to drunk, contemplate to study or mull, indigent to poor, inundate to flood, conflagration to fire, alleviate to ease, apprehend to arrest, and incarcerate to jail.

A larger saving is possible by reducing clauses and prepositional phrases to short modifiers that can be placed before the words they modify. Here are some examples:

> *BEFORE:* Attacks from the air. . . .
> *AFTER:* Air attacks. . . .

> *BEFORE:* Lars Sorenson, who own a ranch near Cheyenne,
> . . .
> *AFTER:* Cheyenne rancher Lars Sorenson. . .

> *BEFORE:* The committee, named at a meeting which was
> held recently, reported that. . . .
> *AFTER:* The recently named committee reported that. . . .

This technique is so common that its use almost brands the writer as a journalist. It can, of course, be overdone. We can tighten a sentence in this manner to a point where it becomes virtually unreadable. Too many modifiers before the noun can bury the sense of the phrase.

Another common target for tightening is overpredication, the use of more verb forms than the sentence requires. This form of verbosity often involves the words "held" or "made" or some form of "there are." Here are some examples:

> *BEFORE:* He made an announcement that . . .
> *AFTER:* He announced that . . .

> *BEFORE:* The council will hold a meeting Tuesday.
> *AFTER:* The council will meet Tuesday.

> *BEFORE:* There are four carriers patrolling the Caribbean.
> *AFTER:* Four carriers patrol the Caribbean.

> *BEFORE:* The regents will be visiting the campus Monday.
> *AFTER:* The regents will visit the campus Monday.

> *BEFORE:* There will be four members elected.
> *AFTER:* Four members will be elected.

> *BEFORE:* They staged an exhibit of. . .
> *AFTER:* They exhibited (or displayed or showed). . .

One peculiar form of verbosity tells the reader something that should be obvious. An exaggerated example:

> *BEFORE:* He was born in the city of Chicago in the state
> of Illinois in the month of January in the
> year 1934.
> *AFTER:* He was born in Chicago in January of 1934.

If readers don't know that Chicago is a city in Illinois, that January is a month, and that 1934 identifies a year, there is little hope for them.

Other phrases that can be shortened:

BEFORE	AFTER
for the purpose of	for
for a period of	for (or during)
in the area of	in
in the field of	in
in order to	to
in the near future	soon
due to the fact that	because

One small economy consists of eliminating unnecessary articles, especially before plural nouns. This saves little space but makes the sentence more readable, for example:

> *BEFORE:* The cabinet members went before the Congress.
> *AFTER:* Cabinet members went before Congress.

The effect is more obvious when several techniques are combined, as in this example:

> *BEFORE:* The members of the committee reported the results of the survey at the meeting held Tuesday.
> *AFTER:* Committee members reported the survey results at Tuesday's meeting.

Editors take special pains to eliminate redundancies. Here are a few of the more common offenders:

tiny 2-year-old girl	Jewish rabbi
past experience	past history
future plans	planned project
widow woman	few in number
triangular in shape	colored red
bone-chilling 30 below	violent hurricane
consensus of opinion	general consensus
continue on	true facts
8 P.M. tonight	noon luncheon
fatal homicide	former veteran
present incumbent	young teen-ager

accused defendant	projected plans
winning knockout	all-time record
religious prelate	incumbent office-holder
dead body, lifeless corpse	newlywed bride
refer back	

To produce tight copy, you reduce clauses to phrases, phrases to single modifiers—then throw away the modifiers. You write mostly with nouns and verbs.

PUNCTUATION

Punctuation has been called visual inflection. It is a method of indicating in print some of the nuances of meaning which a trained speaker conveys by pausing, raising or lowering his pitch, running words together, breaking off suddenly, or shouting. It can't do everything the voice can (for example, it can't sneer), but it accomplishes much the voice can't. For example, punctuation can indicate the difference between a possessive, a plural, and a contraction.

Punctuation is essential for clarity. And it is completely dependable because it is standardized. We may misinterpret a speaker's inflection, but we never doubt what a punctuation mark means—assuming that the writer has used it correctly.

Sometimes you may get clues to proper punctuation by listening to your voice. These are merely clues, however; vocalized inflection and written inflection are not synonymous. But let's try it. Where you pause briefly, then continue with no perceptible change in voice pitch, place a comma. Where you lower the pitch and pause only briefly, use a semicolon. Where you lower the pitch still further and pause longer, use a period. Where you raise the pitch sharply before pausing, use a question mark. Where you break off abruptly, then quickly resume at the same pitch, use a dash. Where you run two words together rapidly, use a hyphen.

The trust-your-ear approach can go only so far before it breaks down. Does the voice really tell us how to punctuate? Or would it be better to say that correct punctuation tells us how to read? The ear can tell us clearly when to use the question mark or the exclamation point, but it is far less reliable for the hyphen, the dash, or the fine distinction between the semicolon and the period. And it is no help at all with the apostrophe.

The only way to understand punctuation is to recognize that it is a logical system of symbols peculiar to *written* language. It serves readers, not listeners. And it serves them mainly by indicating separation of thoughts or omission of letters. The major exception, the hyphen, joins words that are treated grammatically as a single word. In a sense, the apostrophe unites words when it is used to form contractions, but the apostrophe also shows separation and elision.

The following sections, which omit the seldom-used parentheses and brackets, concentrate on punctuation problems that give beginners the most trouble. Notice the emphasis on separation.

The Period

The period is used after a declarative or imperative sentence:

> The club reelected Simon Moody as president.
> Turn right at the first traffic light.

Although it is used for most abbreviations, it is omitted in acronyms (VISTA, NOVA, SAC) and most all-capital abbreviations.

Common diminutives are not treated as abbreviations and require no periods. Examples are phys ed, Psych 102, gym, ag students. But these are colloquial and should be avoided except in direct quotations.

The Comma

The comma separates:

1. An introductory phrase from the body of the sentence:

> In the middle of the day, the bombardment tapered off.

2. Two independent clauses joined by a conjunction:

> He arrived early, but the bus already had departed.

3. A separable—nonrestrictive—clause or phrase from the principal clause:

> Dr. Jones, who had been coughing for weeks, gave up smoking.

> This water, polluted by industrial waste, is unfit to drink.

> John Barton, chairman of the board, announced that. . . .

Notice that the nonrestrictive element requires a comma at each end. A common error is omission of the second comma.

4. Like elements—dates from years, cities from states:

> He was born Aug. 10, 1947, in Red Wing,
> Minn.

5. Elements in a simple series:

> He flew to Paris, Rome, Athens, Karachi
> and Moscow.

Notice that the comma is omitted before "and" at the end of a series. This is standard newspaper practice, although other publications may require the comma.

6. Ages and addresses from names:

> John Anderson, 21, Birmingham, was
> charged with larceny.

7. A direct or paraphrased quotation from attribution that appears either in the middle or at the end of the sentence:

> "We won't work," he declared, "and
> neither will they."

*The comma is omitted when attribution appears at the beginning of the sentence*s

> He said peace is near.
> He declared his men won't work "and
> neither will they."
> Peace is near, he said.

The Semicolon
The semicolon separates:

1. Phrases containing commas in order to avoid confusion:

> The group consisted of Arthur Johnson;
> Ann Casey, his secretary; Mrs. Johnson; Melanie Soames, her cousin, and
> two drivers.

Note that a comma rather than semicolon precedes "and."

2. Independent clauses too closely related to be treated as separate sentences:

> The semicolon is seldom used; the simple
> sentence doesn't need it.

The Apostrophe
The apostrophe indicates:

1. The possessive case of nouns:

> John's ball
> women's wear
> the Joneses' car
> this year's best stories

2. The plural of single letters:

> His grades included A's, B's and C's.

3. Omission of figures in dates:

> He was a member of the class of '22.

4. Omission of letters in a contraction:

> I've, isn't, don't, it's (it is)

The apostrophe is never used to form the possessive pronoun: his, her, hers, their, theirs, whose, or its. Be sure you observe the difference between it's *and* its.

The Colon
The colon takes the place of an implied "for instance" or "as follows," which is the way we have been using it throughout this section. The most common usage, however, is to introduce a long listing:

> States and funds allotted were: Alabama $6,000; Arizona $4,000. . . .

When the list is brief (a half dozen elements in a simple series), newspaper practice is to omit the colon.

The colon also precedes a final clause or phrase summarizing prior matter:

> Journalism has only three rules: accuracy, accuracy and accuracy.

The Exclamation Point

The exclamation point is used to indicate surprise, incredulity, or some other strong emotion. Think of it as the "shout mark" and use it only in a direct quotation:

> "Gad!" Day cried.
> "You don't mean it!" he said.

The Question Mark

The question mark indicates the end of a question, regardless of whether the entire sentence ends at that point. It is used—and misused—most often in direct quotation:

> *WRONG:* "When are we leaving," he asked?
> *RIGHT:* "When are we leaving?" he asked.

Quotation Marks

Quotation marks enclose direct quotations. They also are used around nicknames and the titles of books, plays, poems, songs, movies, and TV programs. All punctuation marks belonging strictly to the words quoted must be placed within the quotation marks, as shown in the sections on the exclamation point and the question mark. If the end of the quotation coincides with the end of the sentence, the period is placed before the closing quotation mark. A comma is the usual punctuation at the end of a quotation which is followed by attribution:

> "Wait a minute," he pleaded.

Notice that the comma is placed before the closing quotation mark.

The most common error in the use of quotation marks involves a passage of speech which continues for more than one paragraph. Each paragraph must *begin* with a quotation mark, but no closing quote mark is used until the person stops speaking—except for those necessary to set off attribution. Here is an example of proper punctuation of a long quote:

> "We never thought this would happen,"
> Samuels said. "But when you live in this
> district nowadays, I suppose you have to
> expect violence.
> "Years ago, holdup men wouldn't bother with a store this size. But nowadays
> they'll pull a gun on you for half a dollar.
> I don't know what the world is coming
> to."

For a quotation within a quote, use single quote marks:

> "I was reading 'Paradise Lost' when this
> fellow broke in and yelled, 'Stick up your
> hands!' "

The Dash

The dash is often used to indicate an abrupt break in the thought or construction of a sentence—a break too abrupt for commas, but not abrupt enough to demand parentheses. The dash serves to emphasize the phrase it sets off, whereas the parentheses de-emphasize an idea inserted into the sentence. For example:

> Weston was expected today—not tomorrow—but the schedule was rearranged
> to accommodate a later arrival.
> Weston was expected today (Feb. 7),
> but the conference proceeded without
> him.

The dash should be used sparingly. Frequent use creates a sense of excitement which may be unwarranted.

The Hyphen

The most common use of the hyphen is to unite into compounds words that are treated grammatically as a single unit. Most of these are compound adjectives, and the overwhelming majority involves the use of numbers. Sports and farm stories, for example, abound in hyphens:

> The 6-foot, 215-pound challenger ran
> a 15-mile grind daily. But he had never
> run a 4-minute mile, nor could he com-
> pete in the 100-yard dash.

He got an 80-bushel yield per acre from
the 160-acre field.
The duty-free car brought an above-
retail price in Tanzania.

The compound adjective usually appears before the noun it describes—but not always:

The city is smog-free most of the year.

One way to test for a compound adjective is to see whether either element may be eliminated without destroying the sense of the phrase. For example, in "6-foot challenger," both "6" and "foot" must be used as a single word to make sense. We can't say "the 6 challenger" or "the foot challenger"; we have to say "the 6-foot challenger."

A phrase which must be hyphenated when it precedes the noun often may be reworded slightly and placed after the noun without hyphenation:

A 16-year-old girl
A girl 16 years old

Newspaper usage has abandoned the hyphen in weekend, worldwide, nationwide, and statewide. Most compounds using the prefixes co, non, and re also are written as one word: coed, cooperative (but co-op), copilot, nonresident, and reinstate.

A common oversight is the occasional need for suspensive hyphenation:

The fifth- and sixth-grade classes

PRINCIPLES OF NEWSWIRE STYLE

"Style" has two meanings to newswriters. In the broader sense, style is the technique writers use to produce an effect on readers—the way they put words together. Because the desired effect usually is no more than the readers' understanding, the reporter's style is simple and unadorned but highly flexible.

In a narrower sense, style embraces the rules of capitalization, abbreviation, identification, and numerical expression. Style dictates whether you write "per cent" or "percent," whether you write "$4" or "four dollars," whether you identify a person as "Sen. Smith" or as "Senator Smith." In this sense, style freezes usage. The reason for uniform style is the same as the reason for uniform spelling: consistency leads to clarity.

Most daily newspapers follow approximately the same style, that agreed upon by the Associated Press and United Press International, with minor modifications to fit the whims of local editors. For that reason, an increasing number of schools of journalism require students to use the AP or UPI stylebook, which are identical except for the cover. Unfortunately for the student, the stylebook was written for professionals who already understand the general principles. Generalizations, therefore, were omitted. The result is a long list of specific rules with no visible pattern.

The pattern begins to emerge when you realize that the two major goals of style are clarity and brevity. And our goal here is to clarify briefly the newswire stylebook, not to replace it. Here are the basic principles and most important rules:

1. *Clarity comes first.*
   a. Capitalize proper nouns. The presidential mansion is the White House, not just another white house.
   b. Capitalize all parts of a proper noun. It's the Missouri River, not just a Missouri river. It's the First Methodist Church, the Senate Finance Committee, the Rocky Mountains.
   c. Spell out "alphabet" agencies on first mention, even if they are well known: the Central Intelligence Agency, the Volunteers in Service to America, the Rural Electrification Administration. (Exceptions are FBI and AFL-CIO.)
   d. Use adequate identification on first mention: Sen. Carl T. Curtis, R-Neb., . . . Ralph Jones, panel moderator.
2. *When there's a choice, say it briefly.*
   a. Omit the abbreviation of the state after a major city: New York, Chicago, Los Angeles, Miami, Boston, and many others.
   b. Omit "Mr." except in "Mr. and Mrs." or in subsequent reference to a clergyman.
   c. Omit titles after first mention. The second time you mention him, Sen. Rudyard T. Smith becomes merely Smith. This is true of military titles and most other titles. Exceptions: clergymen and the Pope.
   d. Omit the double zero in exact dollars and hours. You pay $3 at 4 p.m., not $3.00 at 4:00 p.m. When you get into higher finance, it's $3 million, $4.62 billion (two decimal places), which saves still more zeros. Exceptions to the rule of brevity: never use symbols for cents or percentages. It's five cents (spelled out), which is 5 per cent of a dollar (use numerals). Per cent is two words, percentage one.
   e. Omit the periods in abbreviating alphabet agencies: FBI, not F.B.I. Periods are used, however, in U.S., U.N., U.S.S.R., U.A.R., and academic degrees.

    f. Use the short form when there's a choice of abbreviations. He's Lt. John Johnson, not Lieut. Johnson. And he's from Minden, Neb., not Minden, Nebr.

       Approved short-form abbreviations for states include N.M., Pa., and S.D. Exceptions: Use Colo. and Calif., and avoid the two-letter abbreviations advocated by the U.S. Postal Service. Some states are always spelled out: Iowa, Ohio, Utah, Maine, Idaho, Alaska, and Hawaii.

    g. Omit the comma before "and" or "or" preceding the last element in a series: Churchill promised blood, toil, sweat and tears.

3. *Abbreviate in combination; spell out when alone.* This applies to titles and names, months and dates, streets and addresses, cities and states.

    a. A title is capitalized and usually abbreviated when it precedes the name; lower case and spelled out when it follows the name or stands alone: The candidate was Sen. Robert S. Kerr. Kerr was a senator from Oklahoma. Gov. Nelson Rockefeller was governor of New York.

    b. States are abbreviated only when the name of the state follows the name of a city: The tornado swirled into southern Kansas after smashing Blackwell, Okla.

    c. Months are spelled out when they stand alone, but those with more than five letters are abbreviated when followed by a date: He rested in September and went to work Oct. 1.

       Always spell out March, April, May, June, July.

    d. Street, avenue, or boulevard is abbreviated when a specific address is used, spelled out when you refer to the street generally: The car swerved off West Main Street and struck the corner of a building at 121 N. Oakland Ave.

4. *Always use numerals for exact time, temperature, measurement, ages of people, amounts of money above nine cents.* (The general rule for numbers is to spell out all below 10 and use figures for 10 and above—but so many exceptions exist that it's better to know the exceptions.)

    a. Use numerals for all human and animal ages: The 8-year-old boy had a 2-year-old pony. (But his mother was involved in a three-year-old lawsuit. And his father had been fighting a seven-year-old war.)

    b. Use numerals for votes, odds, and scores: Against 5-1 odds, the Yankees won 3-2. The Senate voted 90-7 to declare a holiday.

    c. Use numerals for dollars, but spell out cents up to 10: He broke a $5 bill to buy an eight-cent stamp.

    d. Use figures for precise measurements: The 6-foot-2 actor carried an 8 mm camera.

3. Use figures for exact time and dates: We'll have a test at 3 a.m. Jan. 1. But you'll have to work a nine-hour day and a seven-day week for two months to pass it.

BEYOND THE RULEBOOK

Winston Churchill, a master of the English language, said he followed a simple recipe. He limited each sentence to a single idea. Ernest Hemingway used a similar approach. He never forgot the advice he read in the stylebook of the *Kansas City Star:* "Use short words. Use short sentences. Keep everything short."

But there is more than simplicity and brevity in the works of Churchill and Hemingway. Like other great stylists, these men were in love with the language. They approached an oration or a narrative the way an ordinary person might approach a member of the opposite sex. Acutely aware of their love object's rhythmic movement, latent intensity, changing moods, and melodious voice, they transformed communication into art.

Neither love of language nor memorization of all the rules of grammar will make you a writer. But when both are coupled with reporting—when you have the necessary information and the ability to relate one fact logically and clearly to another—you have a good start. With this beginning you need only remember the prayer attributed to nuclear physicist Nils Bohr: "O Lord, never let me speak more clearly than I think."

SUGGESTED ASSIGNMENT

The instructor should ask an editor to save a week's accumulation of unused publicity releases. Depending on the length of the releases, each student should get at least three and perhaps five. Here is the student's task:

1. Using an AP or UPI stylebook and this chapter as a guide, edit each release for clarity, brevity, and style.
2. Rewrite each release, trying to improve the edited version. Submit both the edited releases and your rewrites.

CHAPTER NINE / HUMAN INTEREST AND THE DEPTH REPORT

In earlier days, in male-dominated city rooms, girl reporters and human interest copy had approximately the same status: that of stimulating but nonessential ornaments. At best, women and human interest were day-brighteners and occasionally circulation-builders. At worst, they distracted attention from the serious business of getting out the day's hard news. A man might secretly admire them, but many responsible journalists suspected that both belonged primarily to the scandal sheets.

The connection between women and human interest is more than a metaphor. For generations, editors tended to assign most of their light, bright stories to women. They did the same with stories calculated to cause the reader to shed a tear, and thereby created both the tearjerker and the sob sister. Human interest, like fetching coffee, was considered women's work; it was known to deal with the emotions, and everyone agreed that women were more emotional than men. In this view, writer and subject matter were properly matched. Besides, if the editor didn't get the story, nothing vital was lost—and he hadn't wasted a valuable male reporter in the effort.

The newsroom has changed, of course. The corner coffeepot has given way to coin machines, and the noise of yesteryear is muffled by carpeting and acoustic tile. The shirtsleeve deskman has shed his green eyeshade and traded his pencil for a video display terminal that enables him to edit with a keyboard. And the boss is not so much of a male chauvinist. Instead of automatically classifying every girl reporter as either a human interest writer or a candidate for the "women's department," he has assigned them to the police beat, the city hall run, foreign bureaus, and even the sports staff. Today women dominate many newsrooms numerically and are making inroads into the executive ranks. Women have improved their status considerably throughout journalism in the last generation.

The status of human interest copy, however, still varies greatly from one newsroom to another. "Hit the reader where he lives," some editors demand. "Forget the fluff," say others.

One reason for this wide range of attitudes is simply that any two editors may be talking about two entirely different things when they discuss human interest. No clear-cut definition exists. Perhaps all agree that human interest identifies copy that creates an emotional response of some sort, but just what sort are we talking about and how is it achieved? Is human interest intrinsic in certain classes of subject matter, or is it something a skilled writer can elicit from almost any story? If the answer is technique, does it require a certain psychological approach by the writer, or can it be achieved merely by following a few concrete guidelines? And, whatever it is, is it worth our time?

To many older reporters, human interest evokes memories of freckle contests, pancake races, eccentric recluses, trapped pets, and stray children—subjects that seemed more appropriate in an era when an editor still could argue that a dogfight on Main Street was bigger news than a revolution in Latin America. To others, whose thinking is related more to technique than to subject matter, human interest implies a hyped-up, huckstering style designed to lure the reader into a story which otherwise might be dry as dust. Many editors still equate human interest with trivia, bathos, and cutesy humor. And most use the label to describe all the "brites" or funnies, tearjerkers, thrillers, color stories, and outright fluff that rob space from more important news. Some tolerate these as salable commodities; others find them an embarrassment.

Unfortunately, the embarrassment is often deserved. Much of what passes for human interest is trivia. Further, it is often subjective and overwritten. In many newsrooms, the order to "featurize it" or "play up the human angle" is taken as a license to editorialize, sensationalize, indulge in purple prose, or make something out of nothing. It is as though the reporter suddenly were relieved of all responsibility to write with restraint—a depressing example of the way a label can shape behavior.

In defense of the label, however, we must admit that it also has inspired mountains of clear, lively copy from reporters who normally write wooden prose. Told to "featurize it," they magically discard their trite formulas and stilted phrasing and begin to write simply and vividly, the way they should have been writing all along. For every reporter who has lost his sense of balance at the mention of human interest, another seems to have gained it.

Call it a conditioned reflex or a semantic reaction, the fact is that the instant we suggest a story has human interest, reporters begin to view it differently from other writing. And here is where danger lies. Some portion of their output—either that which they call human interest or all the rest—is likely to suffer from this either-or classification.

TOWARD A DEFINITION

Let's try to put it back together. A story is a story, regardless of how it is labeled, and all that a journalist deals with must be factual, objective, and newsworthy. Moreover, in a general sense, every story worth publishing contains human interest. The concept of story itself—struggle—grows out of our interest in human problems and relationships.

In the technical sense, however, "human interest" refers to anything that appeals to virtually all readers, not necessarily because they are interested in the particular subject, but simply because they share the human experience. This can be any element with which the reader identifies, anything familiar that stirs his feelings or tickles his sense of humor. It may be embodied in a fragment—an anecdote, a pungent quotation, a vivid description, a folksy detail—or it may permeate the whole story. It may be culled from the circumstances of the story and cultivated, occasionally even capitalized upon; but you can't plant it unless the seeds are there. And whatever it is, its presence is no license to editorialize. Any increased freedom of expression must be subtle and restrained.

Perhaps the best way to determine the existence of human interest is to observe the readers' reaction. If they chuckle, swear, shudder, whistle, moan, or mumble "Ain't it the truth," you can at least suspect that the story has human interest. You are writing about something they understand, something that stirs them, and you are telling it in their language.

To achieve this level of reader involvement, writers must combine three things: a subject that is almost universally interesting, organization that "reads like a story," and words so concrete that the reader gets a vivid impression of the action. Ordinarily, no one of these elements is enough by itself.

The most interesting subjects are those that the reader can relate to his own life or those that he recognizes as universals of human experience, such as love, death, triumph, defeat, self-sacrifice, and hardship. Subjects high in human interest include crime, sex, violent action, and personal tragedy. Often the action has a touch of the commonplace—it describes something the reader has experienced or something that he could imagine happening to him. Almost as often, however, the human interest story focuses on the odd and unusual, what used to be called "gee whiz" news.

Some writers have tried to substitute the term "people stories" for human interest. And it is true that most human interest stories focus on the person as an individual rather than as a member of a group. The reason is that the readers can relate more easily to one person than to a multitude. (If you want to make them see a famine, first show them one starving child.) But it's wrong to think that all stories about individuals are automatically high in human interest. For example, routine weddings, obituaries, and police court news contain little interest for the reader who doesn't recognize the names. We can't measure the degree of human interest merely by counting the proper names and personal pronouns. If names were all that mattered, the Manhattan telephone directory would be one of the greatest stories of all.

One thing that has virtually universal appeal is a story that *looks* like a story. If it begins with an anecdote, an unexplained action or direct quotation, or the description of a scene, the readers know you are about to tell them something factual that resembles fiction, and they will stay with you at least long enough to find out what the something is. Human interest writers often use narration throughout, larding the body of the story with anecdotes and direct quotations, building up to a "snapper" ending. Occasionally, almost the entire story can be told in direct quotations, as if the witness or primary actor were speaking directly to the reader. This is a wordy technique, however, and few stories merit it. When the story is truly dramatic, it might be better to borrow the magazine writer's "as told to" form and give the source a by-line.

The third element of the successful human interest story, concrete diction, has universal appeal because it names and describes objects and actions with which readers are familiar. They therefore can imagine the people and scenes as if they were seeing them. The readers participate. Few writers master the language well enough to achieve this effect consistently without years of experience. It takes time to learn to change "tin cans" to "empty pork-and-beans cans" or "old furniture" to "tattered armchairs." It may take even longer to learn when to use "scurried," "scrambled," or "yelled," or when to plant a weather report into a story. But the effect you can achieve is worth the effort of learning.

STORY SENSE COMES FIRST

Almost any professional reporter may write a good human interest story occasionally, but only a few attain such recognition that they seldom are required to write anything *but* human interest. Writers of this caliber are constantly alert for significant "humanizing" detail: color, action, the characteristic gesture, a habit of speech, the telling remark. And they have a large vocabulary of sensory words and a store of effective techniques to convey what they see and hear. Most of all, however, they have a sense of story. They instinctively recognize adventure, tragedy, romance, and farce. They have a feel for the heroic, the ironic, the poignant, and the preposterous. This ability to smell the ingredients of a story is far more important than any conscious use of technique.

We have defined story as an account of a person or a group struggling against an opposing force—against each other, against their own impulses, against nature, against the conventions of society, or against fate. We can identify two contrasting varieties that are particularly high in human interest:

1. *Ordinary persons in extraordinary situations*—"people like us" involved in an adventure, a disaster, a tragedy, a triumph, or a farce.
2. *Extraordinary persons in ordinary situations*—"people we would like to be like" doing things that are familiar to all of us—for example, an ordinary day in the life of an astronaut or a Nobel prize-winning scientist.

A story also can be built around extraordinary persons in extraordinary situations, but the result may be low in human interest because it lacks anything readers can relate to their own experience. At least some element must be familiar to everyone.

Students sometimes ask whether a human interest story can be developed around ordinary persons acting in ordinary situations. This probably would be rejected as trivia. Still, the story is in the eye of the beholder; if a writer senses a story in something ordinary and if he has the skill to convey that same sense to the reader, then he *makes* it a story. Whether it is worth publishing, however, is a different matter. Few editors are interested in a story that is totally ordinary.

One way to measure the appeal of a story is to compare it with those that have become part of our cultural heritage: Greek myths, Aesop's fables, parables from the Bible, and the fairy stories of Grimm and Andersen. Do the action and its result parallel—or perhaps contradict—the story of Cinderella (the rags-to-riches theme)? Does the story remind you of the parable about the prodigal son? Does the outcome illustrate one of the Beatitudes (the meek shall inherit the earth, etc.)? Do the facts suggest that love conquers all, or that you never should put all your eggs in one basket, or that (as Prometheus discovered) you can't fight city hall? If your story exemplifies or contradicts such a proverb, you have a winner. But remember to limit your story to the facts; readers will participate more deeply if you allow them to discover the moral or mythic theme for themselves.

Some human interest stories are easy to recognize. A small boy, chasing his dog along the bank of an irrigation ditch, topples into the water and drowns. The readers realize that it could happen in any family, and they feel sympathetic. A chubby coed and middle-aged private pilot are marooned for weeks in the cold wilderness of northern British Columbia after their light plane crashes, and doctors credit their survival to the fact that both were overweight. The reader is both titillated and amused.

The appeal of some inconsequential stories, however, often surprises even the reporters who write them. For example, a widow decorates a leafless tree during the winter with milk cartons "because it looked so lonely." A story and a photograph of the woman and her tree get national circulation. Result: several proposals of marriage "because she must be a warm human being to be so concerned about a tree." And the proposals of marriage, of course, lead to a follow-up story.

Almost all people who have lived past adolescence may be good subjects for a human interest story if you dig deeply enough. Have they ever been robbed, shot at, decorated, wounded in combat? What strange things have they done to earn a living? What are their hobbies? Do they have an "impossible dream"? What is the greatest problem the subject ever faced, and how was it solved? The best subjects for such personality profiles, of course, are persons currently in the news or those closely associated with newsmakers. You can identify good subjects merely by following the news.

Any story can be humanized if you focus on the way a newsworthy event or situation affects an individual. The starting point may be anything: a serious social problem, a disaster, or a current fad. The inspiration may come from clinical statistics or from personal observation wherever you happen to be: on the street, at a theater or bar, or football game. Look for the stories that haven't been told—the small, individual stories within the bigger story.

On any university campus, the supply of potential human interest stories is virtually endless—professors engaged in odd and unusual research, students with odd and unusual causes, students past retirement age, foreign students, and pets that include alligators, boa constrictors, and declawed lions. Don't overlook the skydivers, rodeo clowns, puppeteers, or those who earn their tuition as professional boxers or human guinea pigs.

Ordinary Persons

An extraordinary person is rare. Most human interest stories, therefore, are about undistinguished people who somehow get involved in an extraordinary situation. And quite often this unusual situation is connected with something as common as love and marriage. Here is an example from the *Lincoln* (Neb.) *Journal:*

By DEAN TERRILL

DESHLER, Neb.—Sometimes, in this silver anniversary year, Gerd Kruse closes his eyes and sees the old barracks where he spent more than three years as a prisoner of war.

Not in Nazi Germany or on some Japanese-held island, but in Hebron. That's only eight miles across the furrows from his humming combine and comfortable brick farmhouse.

Gerd was a German sergeant fighting with Rommel when American troops overran his North African outfit in 1943. He didn't realize how the capture would change his entire life.

Today, 25 years after his discharge, he and his wife Ella own nearly a section of rich Thayer County farmland. Their wealth also includes two grown sons, countless friends and the treasured memories of a most unusual romance.

Gerd was one of 100 POWs farmed out to the small Hebron work camp from a much larger prison camp at Concordia, Kan. As far as he knows, he is the only one to return and locate here.

Although he had met Ella while assigned to some jobs for her father, the late Fred W. Kuhlmann of Byron, their acquaintance was casual. Not until the end of World War II and Gerd's return to Germany was there a hint of matrimony.

"I never gave her a second thought, even," he recalled in a crisp accent. "And it was not in my mind at all to return to America. But when my family began receiving packages from her, I sent letters of thanks, and soon we were writing back and forth. Now I think perhaps those packages were cheese to trap the mouse . . ."

By no means, insists Mrs. Kruse, though she does admit spending practically her entire paycheck as a grocery clerk to buy commodities for his family. Touched by the war-stricken people of her own German ancestry, she had chosen Gerd's name at random from among prisoners who had worked for her father.

Growing sweeter by the month, the couple's correspondence finally blossomed into love letters climaxed by a proposal. One catch was that the marriage had to take place in Germany before Gerd would be permitted to re-enter the United States.

The April, 1949, ceremony was performed in the 750-year-old church in which Gerd had been baptized and confirmed. Located in the village of Winkel bie Apen in northern Germany, it had survived the war's devastation.

"Although I had been sending home enough money to buy a nice house, it was by now worth next to nothing because of the devalued mark," Kruse said. "It took my entire account to buy a used bicycle. That's all I had to offer Ella, but she had 80 acres and a house in Byron for our start."

The couple soon moved to a farm east of Deshler which they bought from Mrs. Kruse's father. They gradually expanded their holdings. Sons George and Reinold, 21 and 19, are still home and involved in the family operation.

In 1953, only four years after his return to the United States, Gerd became a citizen. He has visited Germany twice in the last 15 years.

"Each time, after a couple of days I was ready to come back to America," he said. "Home is here now."

Extraordinary Persons

The less common variety of human interest stories—those about extraordinary persons involved in ordinary situations—are the stock in trade of certain popular magazines and newssheets. Catering to the adolescent yen (which many never outgrow) to identify with the rich, the famous, and the beautiful, such publishers operate on the principle that any bit of trivia their staff can dig up about Jacqueline Kennedy Onassis or Elizabeth Taylor is good for two picture-laden pages plus a screaming two-inch head. They try to convince us, of course, that the ordinary circumstances are in fact extraordinary—preferably scandalous.

In the more legitimate instances of this type of human interest, however, the stress usually is put on the ordinariness of the situation, the point being that the VIP puts on his pants one leg at a time just like everyone else. Humorous details about President Eisenhower's golf game, accounts of the Kennedy men and their children playing touch football on the White House lawn, and short bits about President Johnson's pulling his beagle's ears once gave many Americans a warm feeling about the basic humanity of their leaders, political differences notwithstanding.

Such stories tend to proliferate, generally as sidebars, when an extraordinary person dies. Here is a portion of a human interest story—one of many—published after the death of former President Truman in 1973.

> By MERRIMAN SMITH
> United Press International
> One afternoon during the late 1940s, President Truman was scheduled to leave for a month's stay at his favorite resort, Key West. Suddenly, the White House rescheduled his departure for the next morning. No explanation.
>
> We found out later what happened. Truman had learned that one news photographer's rotating tour of duty at the White House did not begin until midnight. Truman knew the fellow and knew how much he liked Key West. Had the president left on schedule, the man would have missed the trip.
>
> This was the Harry S Truman whom some of us assigned to the White House were fortunate enough to know. History will judge him as a president. But he had guts and compassion. Certainly, there has not been a man in the White House more considerate of the feelings and lives of others.
>
> Yet the real Truman frequently ran quite counter to his public image.
>
> For instance, he preferred scotch over bourbon.
>
> In public, however, he was expected to call for bourbon and he did, often going through an entire evening without so much as a sip of his drink. It was not that he disliked bourbon. Scotch was easier going.
>
> Not long after Truman was elevated to the presidency by the death of Franklin D. Roosevelt in 1945, it was

popular in some New Deal circles to de-
mean Truman because he lacked FDR's
regal air and class.

When he heard about old New Dealers
making fun of him, he sharply admon-
ished those around him not to overreact.

"Those fellows don't really mean it,"
he advised. "They're just heartbroken
and you would be too."

Because Truman identified so thoroughly with the little man, the little man
returned the favor and kept him abreast
of many matters which ordinarily escape
a president.

He knew when a stenographer's baby
caught a cold, when a White House servant lost a relative. He thought it was
hilarious when Leroy, the White House
leafraker for many years, fobbed himself
off as an important official and was shown
to a box at the Hialeah racetrack.

. . . .

For all his public image as a devotee
of poker and bourbon, Truman was a
square—even for his day. He was deeply
devout, women were to be held in rever-
ence, and I never heard him tell a dirty
joke.

A Cinderella Story

Good fortune is the subject of many stories. Sometimes these
parallel the Cinderella myth, in which virtue and hard work are
rewarded unexpectedly. The reader participates by wishing it might
happen to him. Here's an example:

MONROE, Mich. (AP)—Although Mrs.
Wesley Gray Jr. has become the bene-
ficiary of the multi-million dollar estate
of a brother she never saw, she has no
plans to retire from her job in the Monroe Evening News classified advertising
department.

"I hope I never forget the value of a
dollar," she says. But there will be at least
be some small changes right away.

"Now I realize I can have the carpet
I need for the living room as well as a
new refrigerator," Mrs. Gray said. "In

fact, if there is anything I want—just about anything—I can buy it."

Mike Padula, a saloonkeeper in the small northern California town of Castella, died Nov. 4, leaving $1.5 million in Lucky Stores supermarket stock and an estimated $1.5 million in property.

According to Atty. Howard Jones, the Lucky Stores stock will be divided equally between Mrs. Gray and her two daughters, Mrs. Michael Driessche of Monroe and Mrs. Harvey Miller of Sparks, Md. The disposition of the rest of the estate has not been determined.

Mrs. Gray, whose husband is a salesman, recalls that she never saw Mike, one of her nine brothers and three sisters. He left the family home in Marlboro, Mass., in 1918, a month before she was born.

Padula, who was 78 and a bachelor, had moved to Castella in 1919, and his first job was as a busboy. Nobody seems to know how he amassed his fortune.

In accordance with instructions he left behind, Padula's body was allowed to lie in state in his saloon for a wake. The long painting of scantily clad women behind the bar was draped in black while Padula's body was on view for an hour in a 500-pound copper casket.

James Padula, a brother, said at the funeral in California that Mike hadn't contacted or seen any of his 11 living brothers or sisters in 55 years.

He received a letter from Mrs. Gray in 1949, with pictures of her daughters, but never replied, James said. The will was dated 10 years later.

"All That Glitters . . ."

Some stories of good fortune take a different twist. Here is an example of a windfall with ironic results:

PERU, Ind. (AP)—Lowell Elliott was living the easy life of a retired farmer until he got curious about something that looked like a groundhog in his son-in-law's soybean field June 26.

What he found was a canvas mailbag containing $500,000 ransom money dropped by a skyjacker who had bailed out over north-central Indiana two days before. And that was the end of the easy life for Lowell Elliott.

Sunday the 64-year-old Elliott was in Wabash County Hospital, suffering from what was termed strain. He had been under a doctor's care following a heart attack when his discovery thrust him into the national limelight.

"I'm not supposed to talk about it," his wife Mildred insisted in a telephone interview. "If the newspapermen would just leave him alone, his life would be better. . . . If everybody would just leave him alone."

The Elliotts have evaded newsmen and have not answered their phone since harassing letters and telephone calls followed his refusal of a $10,000 "gift" from American Airlines.

He said he thought he should get 5 per cent, or $25,000. The original $10,000 offer still stands, but Elliott has said he doesn't know whether he will take it.

At first the national publicity seemed to appeal to Elliott, if not his wife.

"My picture's been all the way out in California," the farmer chuckled at the time.

Two weeks later his good nature seemed to wane. "We've got hundreds of letters," he said. "People are saying I'm a lousy person" for asking more than $10,000.

His wife added: "Life was so peaceful and nice before this happened. I just hope it can be that way again. I wish he had never found the money."

The Universal Experience

Birth and death are two subjects that never can be exhausted. They happen to everyone, and perhaps most are routine, yet they are never fully understood. And when the circumstances are in any way out of the ordinary, either birth or death is high in human interest. Note the restraint in this example:

SAN FRANCISCO (UPI)—Leonard Macchiarella, 16, died without ever knowing his last conscious wish was fulfilled—a visit with his convict father.

The end came last night at the University of California Medical Center, where doctors had kept Leonard alive by using an iron lung and a kidney machine. He had been stricken with a rare and mysterious kidney ailment.

Earlier in the day his father, Phillip Macchiarella, 35, an inmate in the California Training Facility at Soledad, was given a pass to travel to San Francisco to see his son.

Prison officials had decided to relax rules to grant the convict a leave because of public pressure.

Macchiarella stood by Leonard's bed for 45 minutes. Choked with emotion, he could not speak. He wept. His son didn't know it because he was in a coma.

Leonard was stricken with the disease last week. Before he lapsed into unconsciousness Saturday, he told nurses: "I want to see my dad."

Prison officials first rejected the plea. They said Macchiarella had served only two years of a five-year-to-life term for conspiracy to sell marijuana. They cited his "serious criminal record" and said he was a security risk.

PUTTING THE READER THERE

Reporters are only human. They see or hear something that stirs them, and they would like to convey this reaction to the reader. But the ethics of journalism bar writers from telling what they think or feel. They can present only the facts, with no inferences or judgments.

Beginners often chafe at this restriction. What they fail to realize is that facts are all a writer ever needs. They are far more persuasive than opinion and far more potent in creating the impression the writer wants. In the story about the convict's son, for example, the reporter might well have been tempted to add an editorializing word or two (such as "unfortunately" in the final paragraph). But the fact that he sticks to a bare narration of events is at least partly responsible for the story's emotional punch. Left to do their own editorializing, readers give their feelings fuller play.

Indeed, the only way to be reasonably sure that the reader will have the same reaction as the reporter is to give the reader the same information. The way the facts are presented, however, makes a difference. In human interest, as in fiction, skilled writers approach the emotions through the senses. Instead of telling, they show. They try to put the reader there, to make him see and hear the significant portions of what they saw and heard. They use number, color, movement, and everything else of consequence that can be seen, heard, felt, tasted, or sniffed.

Think of the high points of your story—the dramatic scenes—as a color motion picture with a sound track. As you try to function as a camera, remember that objects and motion are more important than color or sound. Not every story lends itself to this treatment, nor should it normally be used throughout any story. But it is one of the techniques that characterizes the effective writing of Truman Capote, Norman Mailer, Tom Wolfe, Gay Talese, Jimmy Breslin, Rex Reed, and other practitioners of the "New Journalism."

As a beginner, if you remember to avoid imitating their subjectivity, you can learn a lot from the "New Journalists." Breslin is particularly worth study because his technique is so easily analyzed. He gets his best effects with a mountain of detail, including many things that most reporters overlook. He seems to notice everything, to count everything, and to record its color. In "Alabama Schoolhouse" *(The World of Jimmy Breslin),* he observes that the building once was painted yellow, that its sits on small piles of loose red bricks, that it has 10 frame windows and five wooden steps leading up from the dirt. In "A Death in Emergency Room One," he describes the room where President Kennedy died—its gray tiled walls and cream-colored ceiling. He even observes how the surgeon was dressed and what he was eating in the cafeteria when his lunch was interrupted.

Skill at description doesn't develop overnight. And even with a lifetime of practice, you may never rival Capote's *In Cold Blood*. But you can make a start by learning to notice what your three primary senses tell you:

Sight	*Hearing*	*Touch*
units	units	units
movement	movement	movement
position	position	shape
shape	volume	size
size	pitch	weight
color	timbre	temperature
		texture

Notice how many of these qualities can be detected by more than one sense. Notice also how many can be measured and expressed in numbers.

Portraying People

It's natural for a writer to start looking for visual details when he wants to describe a person. But physical description in a news story must be more than a meaningless mass of sizes, shapes, and colors. It must make a central statement about a person—something that sets him apart from others—and it must somehow relate to the point of the story. Doing this economically, without interrupting the story's flow, isn't always easy. A student produced this terse example:

> Her blunt-cut, salt-and-pepper hair matched feminist Betty Friedan's words Thursday.

A common technique is to mix description with action. Sometimes an apparently trivial gesture makes a subtle point, as in the second paragraph of this student's story:

> "An ombudsman is functioning best when you hear the least about him," says James Suter.
> Propping a blue-jeaned leg on his desk, the 42-year-old Suter settled back Tuesday and explained his interpretation of his new job as university ombudsman.

A more complete—and traditional—form of description appears in this excerpt from a sketch of an English professor:

> Gaffney, white-haired and bearded, is overflowing with facts and dry humor. His glasses constantly slide down his nose —which seems too small for his broad face—and he peers over the rims.

However useful physical description may be, it is more dangerous than most beginners realize. Too often it results in adjectives that are highly subjective, perhaps even libelous. A beard that appears "unkempt" to one person, for example, might look "luxuriant" to another. And a voice and manner that strike one observer as "overbearing"—although no reporter would use the word—might be labeled "dramatic" or "forceful" by another.

Another pitfall of this technique is the temptation to use irrelevant details—description merely for the sake of description. When a student notes in a sketch of columnist Jack Anderson, for example, that "the color of his shirt and tie didn't match," the reader may well wonder "so what?"

Most human interest writers play it safe when portraying people. They use only neutral adjectives, if any at all, and they have learned to say a great deal about an individual without a single physical detail. They rely heavily on quotes—what a person says about himself and what others say about him—narration of specific actions related to the story's theme, and summaries of the major events in the person's life.

The following story illustrates these common techniques. Note, too, that it is about an ordinary person doing a more or less ordinary thing. Much of its human interest derives from the writer's translation of a simple action into rather startling statistics.

MIAMI (AP)—It's a good bet that Paul Morgan, 91, will be at the movies today. And tomorrow. And the next day.

With few exceptions, he has spent the last 9,125 days—25 years—at the movies.

"I get tired of sitting at home," explains Morgan, who has lived in a one-bedroom apartment for the last 36 years. "It gets so boring, I can't even stay home on Sundays."

So after his 9 a.m. breakfast of four dried prunes and two eggs, Morgan strolls to a nearby theater—the same theater every day, no matter what's playing there.

"He's always been the first in line every day since I came here nine years ago," says John McCormick. "He likes all the films. We've never been able to pin him down on a specific film or even a specific star he's enjoyed the most."

Morgan arrived in the United States from Yugoslavia in 1905 and worked in a Detroit auto factory painting Chalmers, an auto long faded from the scene.

A longtime widower, he figures he's spent 55,000 hours and at least $5,000 watching the silver screen over the last quarter of a century.

Morgan says that between Social Security and the money he earns cleaning rooms at his apartment house, he has no problem meeting the Rio's 75-cent matinee tab.

And he doesn't care if he sees the same movie four times in two days—the Rio changes the double-feature about twice a week.

Friday, for instance, he sat through two showings of "Nightmare in Wax" and one and a half unreelings of "The Wild Rebels."

"This is how I like to spend my time," he said while standing at the candy counter. "It's my life in there. Tomorrow, maybe I'm dead. I don't know what God is going to do."

Setting the Scene

Places, like people, are merely names in most news stories. The reader never really sees them. Yet the setting, often including the time of day and the weather report, can be as important as description of the actors in making a story come to life. Setting helps put the reader there, helps create a mood, and often constitutes an indispensable element of the story.

Some of the better examples of scene-setting can be found in United Press International's *Selections,* an annual paperback collection of the year's outstanding UPI stories. The *Selections* also are noteworthy for examples of narrative, first-person reporting, and a wide variety of other offbeat approaches.

An effective use of setting appears in this portion of a prize-winning story by a University of Nebraska student:

By JIM PRATT

HOLCOMB, Kan.—A harsh north wind whips dust through Holcomb, battering a few worndown stucco dwellings before losing itself in the western Kansas plains. Ponies tied to fence posts shake their manes in the wind and a dog lopes down a deserted dirt street.

Holcomb is a quiet town. Discounting the Mobil gas station (3.2 beer, soda pop, a few groceries), the only gathering place with refreshments is El Rancho Cafe, and in an adjacent room, a bar named Something Else.

Holcomb's few streets, mostly unpaved, often are empty.

Thirteen years ago today, however, the streets were jammed with cars belonging to law enforcement people, ambulance attendants and the curious. For Holcomb had just been stunned by four murders.

Subsequent reverberations would make the town known to millions.

It was early Sunday morning, Nov. 15, 1959, when Herb Clutter, 48, his wife, Bonnie, 45, and their two youngest children, Nancy, 16, and Kenyon, 15, were blasted point-blank with a shotgun by two ex-convicts with no previous records of violence. The motive was robbery.

The murders shocked the town. Herb Clutter was a prominent farmer, and he and his family were well liked. But the murders probably would have been forgotten had author Truman Capote not read a New York Times story about the killings and decided to use them as a vehicle for his book "In Cold Blood."

On a smaller scale, description of physical setting is used effectively to portray a person as well as a situation in this lead by another student:

By MARY VOBORIL

He'll be 93 May 12. His income includes $80 a month Social Security and $40 welfare. The black suit in which he will be buried hangs in his closet, a towel pinned around the shoulders to keep the dust off.

How does a 93-year-old man get along on an income of $120 a month? Apparently he gets along fairly well—if he lives in a one-room apartment, eats no meat, is in good health and has few desires.

Such is the case of Francis C., a widower who lives above a downtown health food store. For $45 a month he is master of a furnished, two-window room that includes a double bed, dresser, hot plate, sink, two chairs, a vintage refrigerator and not much of a choice of three bathrooms down a cavern-like hall.

The two windows, eight feet tall, are screenless and in need of winterizing. The paint is peeling. In July and August the heat becomes so intense that Mr. C can hardly stand it. He said the landlady provides him with a fan in the summer. His utilities are included in the rent.

He insists he is happy.

"We get so much here for our money," he said. "You'd have to look a long time to find a place like this for so little money."

Notice in both of these stories the number of concrete objects that the reader can visualize. Notice also that both mention the weather, one to create a mood and the other because it is an important fact about the austere existence the writer wants to make palpable for the reader.

Describing Action

Most news stories tell merely what happened with what effect; they seldom describe in detail *how* it happened. How, of course, is seldom as important as the outcome—why say *how* a person crossed the street when you can say simply that he crossed the street? In some stories, however, description of even minor actions makes the account far more vivid. Rarely are many extra words needed to achieve this effect; often, in fact, fewer words do the job best.

If you learned your sixth-grade grammar, you may recall that adverbs are words that tell "how." Forget all that. Occasionally, you may be forced to write "slowly," "hotly," or "deliberately." But the real secret to effective description of action lies in the choice of verbs. "Stalk," "creep," "prowl," "roam," "ramble," "meander," "poke," "dawdle," "dally," and "loiter," for example, all mean "to move slowly." Clearly, any one of them—whichever fits the context—is more expressive than the verb-adverb combination.

As a general rule, when tempted to tack on a descriptive adverb, look first for a better verb, one that includes the meaning of the adverb. Usually, your efforts will pay off in greater exactness, as well as vividness.

Here is an example from a student's account of an Indian invasion of a small western town. Key verbs are italicized.

By MARY HUFFMAN

GORDON, Neb.—Acting City Clerk Gerald Swick was on the phone to the county attorney Wednesday when he got the word: no statements to the press.

He *swung* in his chair and *reached* for a reporter's notebook.

"You can't have those!" he *shouted, ripping* a page from the notebook. He *crumpled* the page and *held* it away from the reporter.

"We're getting out of here," he said, and *burst* from the Gordon Community Center, the building taken over the night before by about 600 Indians angry over the death of Raymond Yellow Thunder, a Sioux.

A U.S. Justice Department official *tried to calm* Swick. Swick handed over the notes to the federal agent, who returned them—with apologies—to the reporter.

Like the town, Swick was *caught* in the middle of a swirling racial conflict, a confrontation between whites and Indians who seemed to hold each other in mutual fear.

"I don't want to become a statistic," Swick said, *reflecting* the fear and tension present here since the Indians *swooped* into town to *protest* the official handling of Yellow Thunder's death.

There were rumors. "The Indians are armed," said some whites. "The whites have guns," Indians claimed.

"It's just a mess," said Swick.

At the First National Bank, two blocks away, bank employes Keith Peterson and Gary Ruse discussed the conflict begun by the death of Yellow Thunder, 51, of Porcupine, S.D.

Yellow Thunder's body was found in a panel truck several days after he allegedly was *forced to strip and dance* at an American Legion club. Indians say he *was tortured and mutilated.*

Three white persons have been charged with manslaughter and two with false imprisonment.

The Case for Restraint

Description can be overdone, of course. It may require more words than the normal news presentation and may slow the story's progress unless it is woven piecemeal into the narration. And, as we stressed earlier, it can be misleading—even dangerous—when it is used for characterization. Ask yourself whether the image is the most important reality, whether the way a person looks and behaves at a given moment is as significant as his record of actions over a longer span of time. As a writer, are you only a camera? Only a tape recorder? Or are you something more?

In addition to the practical and ethical reasons for restraint, there is an artistic and psychological reason: the reader participates more deeply if you leave something to his imagination. Producers of radio dramas were reminded of this, sometimes joltingly, when they made the transition to television; the creaking door of "Inner Sanctum" was far more effective when it was left unseen. And fiction writers have known for ages that the reader will not identify with a character who is described too clearly.

Many newswriters have found what they consider the ideal amount of description in the works of Ernest Hemingway. Read especially *Byline Ernest Hemingway,* the beginnings of his short stories, and the first and final pages of *A Farewell to Arms* to see how much can be accomplished with only a few words. Hemingway is almost the opposite of Breslin in his approach to detail; where Breslin uses a mountain, Hemingway uses the bare minimum. His secrets are superb selection and painstaking arrangement.

Perhaps the best approach to description—and indeed to each individual detail—is to evaluate it much as you would a direct quotation: it should say something essential to the story, it should not be taken out of context, and it should not be prejudicial. Above all, it should not be meaningless clutter. If you can get the reader involved without it, don't use it.

THE FEATURE: DEPTH PLUS HUMAN INTEREST

A feature is any story that doesn't depend on immediacy for its appeal. It may be a historical article with an anniversary as its news peg, such as Jim Pratt's story about Holcomb, Kansas, 13 years after the Clutter murders, or it may be a how-to-do-it piece that tells you how to prepare your income tax return or winterize your car. It may provide background about some situation currently in the news, or it may be the report of a month-long investigation. The only characteristics common to all features are an intrinsically interesting subject and thorough treatment.

Many features, such as the personality sketch, are automatically human interest stories because of their subject. Others, however, are not; their subjects may interest only a small portion of the total audience. Whatever human interest the latter contain often is heightened by the reporter to (1) hook readers at the beginning, and (2) keep them reading to the end. In such stories, human interest is a strategic tool rather than an essential element. It results more from the reporter's approach to the story and the technical treatment of details than from the raw material itself.

Depth as the Foundation

The best read newspaper feature stories today are commonly described as depth reports, a term that gained general acceptance after Neale Copple of the University of Nebraska published a book called *Depth Reporting* in 1964. Copple defined depth as the opposite of deadline dictated superficiality. He showed how it could be achieved by any reporter with the will to work hard and the time to do it. Best of all, perhaps, he swept aside a lot of semantic quibbling over interpretation, feature writing, backgrounding, and investigative reporting. We can almost forget these categories; depth reporting includes them all.

Depth means thorough, explanatory reporting. It requires an investigative attitude, a lot of hard work, and the ability to tell a story in terms of what it means to the reader. The depth report may be as long as a magazine article, or even longer, but it lacks the subjectivity so often found in magazines. It may be presented in one piece, or it may require a series. But it is not just another long story or another series; length alone doesn't spell depth.

Research and legwork for the typical depth report are both expensive and time-consuming. At least a few days and often several weeks may be required to gather documents, conduct interviews, and digest previously published material. Depth treatment, therefore, must be limited to a subject worth the price. And it usually must be applied to a continuing situation, rather than an immediate event. Unless an editor uses a large, well-organized team, he can seldom produce a spot news story of any depth. Rather than something that occurs unexpectedly, the typical depth story is *developed* news—what editors once called enterprise copy.

THE INVESTIGATIVE APPROACH

The depth report begins in the mind of the reporter. It often starts with nothing more than a cloudy knowledge of a situation and a vague feeling that there is more to be told than anyone has yet published. You begin to form questions and to study the situation at a distance, searching for the one key question that will interest the reader most.

At some point early in the investigation, you get a glimmer of an idea, an "angle" or a working hypothesis. You think you know what the situation is. And this is the most dangerous stage. As you move into more detailed investigation, you must remember that all you have thus far is a *working* hypothesis; you don't yet have all the answers. Until you have, you must keep an open mind. You must avoid searching only for information that fits your hypothesis.

The wrong approach is illustrated by a message that a national news magazine sent its Oklahoma City correspondent in the mid-1950s. The correspondent was asked to supply a story and photographs of a large farm family forced off the land by dust storms. The New York editors further stipulated that the family should include at least 12 children. The correspondent had a difficult time convincing the editors that (1) the dust storms of that era were relatively mild and nobody was being forced off the land, and (2) that Oklahoma farmers no longer specialized in producing large families.

A similar error was committed by a reporter who once proposed a series on "discrimination against Indians in South Dakota." Without investigation, the reporter already had jumped to the conclusion that discrimination was practiced to a newsworthy degree. Perhaps it was—certainly it was often charged—but the reporter erred in assuming that the charges were true before checking into them. The reporter should assume as little as possible. The investigation must take the form of a question, and any suspicion of an answer must remain tentative until all the evidence is assembled.

The proper approach can be illustrated by two student stories written for a depth reporting class. Each story studied an entire community.

One student set out to determine how national attention had affected a small town in western Kansas. (A portion of his story appears earlier in this chapter.) The town was Holcomb, where four members of the Herb Clutter family had been murdered 13 years earlier. The crime was the subject of Truman Capote's factual novel, *In Cold Blood,* and a motion picture by the same name. The student's question: Had notoriety and the association with New York and Hollywood deeply affected the lives of the townspeople? His working hypothesis was that it had. He visited Holcomb and conducted interviews for several days to test his hypothesis. It didn't hold up. Actors, jet-setters, and tourists had left Holcomb residents and their prevailing lifestyle relatively unchanged. So the young reporter developed his story around that point instead of his original idea, and it won him a $900 scholarship.

Another student was curious about the psychological aftermath of a major disaster. Her hypothesis was that Rapid City, South Dakota, would have a serious mental health problem as a result of the 1972 flood that killed more than 230 persons. She spent several days in Rapid City interviewing public officials, therapists, social workers, survivors, and ordinary townspeople. Her findings supported the hypothesis.

As thorough as these student-produced stories may seem, they are overshadowed regularly by the work of professionals. Just before New York's liberalized abortion law took effect in 1970, Kathy O'Toole of the Gannett newspapers in Rochester spent six weeks developing a series of articles assessing its probable impact. She covered several counties in upstate New York, interviewing hospital officials, doctors, clergymen, social workers, and women who had had abortions, both legal and illegal. She also investigated the outlook for neighboring counties in Pennsylvania.

Another noteworthy series was produced in the 1950s by a reporter for the *Norman* (Okla.) *Transcript*. It was the era immediately after Sputnik, the Soviet Union's first space vehicle, and many Americans were seriously worried about the relative quality of education in the United States and the Soviet Union. Three University of Oklahoma professors had just returned from the Soviet Union, where they had studied the entire school system. Armed with notes and photographs, they agreed to make their findings available to the *Transcript*. The three professors were interviewed together, then each was interviewed separately. Then the writing began. As the first draft of each installment was completed, it was submitted to the appropriate professor for corrections and suggestions—something that newsmen rarely do. Each first draft led to another interview. The typical installment—there were more than a dozen—went through three drafts before it was finally approved, and the entire project took more than a month. But the result was both authoritative and exclusive.

The goal of such reporting is to present things as they are, which is not necessarily as people *say* they are. We set out to find a deeper reality, to answer a question that may never have been raised before, or at least has never been answered satisfactorily. Reporting of such depth requires that writers look at situations from every possible angle, through their own eyes as well as those of others. It requires walking all around the subject, both literally and figuratively, searching for the one perspective that shows it best. And sometimes it means getting inside. This occasionally happens with no effort on the reporter's part, as it did to Jim Buchanan of the *Miami Herald* when he landed in a Cuban jail during the early days of the Castro regime.

Ideally, the reporter begins with an intrinsically interesting subject and develops it as fully as possible. But any reasonably newsworthy subject will suffice if the writer can find a provocative angle. All a reporter needs is an approach that offers the reader something new, plus a small mountain of supporting information and the skill to hold the reader's interest until the end.

Human Interest as Bait

A few depth reports, because of the sensational nature of their disclosures, can grab readers and hold them with little more than cold statistics. But these are rare. More often the subject is one that has been hashed over frequently, and a straightforward approach would interest nobody. The best way to hook readers and keep them nibbling is to use human interest as bait.

The longer the story is, the more important it is to salt it throughout with anecdotes, description, and direct quotations. Particular attention, however, must be paid to the lead; you can't hold readers unless you hook them in the first place.

The common devices already have been described: the anecdote lead, description of a scene, the narrative introduction. Here are some additional examples:

> The people sat in groups on the thick, orange-and-yellow shag carpet. In the middle of the room, four people sat around a low orange table and talked. From time to time their laughter drifted over to the other group playing cards in the corner.
>
> Someone read from the *National Lampoon,* accompanied by alternating moans and choruses of laughter. Another person walked to a table in the back of the room to get coffee and cookies for a friend.
>
> The occasion was the third meeting of the Gay Action Group's new open house program.

This narrative-descriptive lead accomplishes several things: by withholding the subject of the story for the first two paragraphs, it arouses curiosity; through the concrete imagery it "puts the reader there," thus getting him involved; and with impressive subtlety, it conveys an unstated message that both prepares the reader for and reinforces the writer's approach in the report on homosexuality that follows.

Illustrating a general situation with a single case history often leads nicely into a story about a social problem or institution. By suggesting universal experiences—waiting, lonliness—and eliciting identification with one individual's plight, the writer of the following lead tries to arouse enough human interest to carry the reader through a documented discussion of the aged in America.

> There is nothing to do but wait. His children come dutifully to take him home for the holidays. But they have their own families now and somehow he doesn't fit.
>
> Ernest Sampson is 78 years old. He waits with the others in the Valley View Nursing Home. Although he is still good with his hands and spry on his feet, he is a burden to his relatives. So he has been put aside.

Had the story begun with the statistics on senior citizens, however startling they might be, chances are it would have attracted fewer readers. Similarly, a story about a federal program called "Title I" would fall flat in a hurry if the bureaucratic terminology were the first thing readers faced. Again, in this example, the writer boils it all down to an individual for the lead, combining this approach with direct address.

> You've seen this child in school. He's either so active—perhaps ornery—that he demands all the teacher's attention, or he is uncooperative and refuses to do anything.
> Years ago the classroom teacher would have thrown up her hands in despair and said there was no hope. He was simply a problem child.
> Today she has outside help from teachers who understand. These teachers are part of the Title I program, a federally supported effort to help educationally deprived children.

Posing a puzzle, tossing out only clues to your subject, is a device easily overdone. Before long, readers decide that if you're not going to tell them what you're talking about, they're not going to fool around trying to find out. But used discreetly with a couple of intriguing images as part of the bait, this approach can produce effective leads, as in the following example:

> The glare from its spotlight can interrupt a romantic moonlight walk and its noise can disturb a good night's sleep. But the city has appropriated $26,220 this year to finish paying for that glare and noise because they help fight crime.
> Last summer the light and sound of the police helicopter routed a man who was assaulting a woman. He was captured by ground units summoned by radio from the chopper.
> The helicopter has made skylight burglary obsolete, according to Curtz Snoberger, assistant coordinator of police-community relations. Rooftops are no longer a place to hide.
> As a result, more cities are using helicopters to fight crime. Kansas City has

> 12, Snoberger said. And Tucson police estimate that one helicopter does the job of nine patrol cars.

Are romantic moonlight walks and a good night's sleep more widely appreciated than helicopters? Are you more interested in one attempted rape than a mass of statistics? If so, the writer is on solid ground with this approach to a report on the growing use of police helicopters.

TYPOGRAPHICAL INTEREST AND THE SERIES

Regardless of the content, a story can be made to *appear* interesting by using several typographical devices. Most of these—subheads, indented or odd-measure body type, boldface read-ins, and italicized paragraphs—are tools that are reserved only for editors. A few, however, are in the reporter's province. These include quotation marks, dashes, ellipses, the ultra-short sentence, and the one sentence paragraph. Any of these, used judiciously and spaced out in a long story, has a tendency to shake readers gently and keep them from going to sleep.

One of the most common devices used to sustain interest is simply breaking a story into several parts and publishing it in installments. This calls for a joint agreement between editor and reporter—and a decision that usually both would prefer to avoid. Many editors dislike the series because they must reserve space for it before they know what spot news may be competing for that space. Ordinarily they will approve a series only when the story is such a blockbuster that there is no hope of getting it into a single edition. And some reporters dislike the series because it means extra effort in organization. Each installment must make sense by itself, yet fit logically into the overall plan. Each must have a separate lead, an editor's note preceding it, and (except for the final installment) a note at the end telling what's coming next.

A simple three-part series typically is written first as a single story. Then the reporter hunts for logical places to divide it into three approximately equal parts. Once the story is split, a certain amount of rewriting is necessary, along with additions, to make it work as a series.

When reporters are told in advance that the story will be treated as a series, they may write each installment separately. Typically the first and last installments will be summaries, and each of the other installments will treat a different aspect of the story.

HAZARDS OF HUMAN INTEREST

Human interest stories require special warnings because of problems that seldom occur in straight news reporting—problems that are certain to test the reporter's devotion to accuracy, neutrality, and sense of fair play.

First is the problem of hoaxes. Thousands of journalists have been taken in by "cute stories" that never happened. One tells about the clergyman who lacks a coin for the parking meter, so he leaves a note on the windshield, explaining the situation and ending with "Forgive us our trespasses." When he returns, he finds a parking ticket and a note that says "Render unto Caesar what is Caesar's." Another classic tells about the stalled motorist who explains to a helpful neighbor that his car needs only a push, but that it has an automatic transmission and won't start until it gets up to 35 miles an hour. The good Samaritan gets into his car and backs away. The stalled driver settles down behind the steering wheel and waits. Nothing happens. Then he looks back and sees his benefactor's car coming toward him—at 35 miles an hour. Each of these stories has been published several times as legitimate news, yet it is doubtful whether either ever happened. So many similar stories have been passed on to newsmen that professionals have learned never to accept a story that doesn't contain names they can check.

Another danger related to humor is the possibility of libel. Anything that holds a person up to public ridicule or contempt is libelous, and the dividing line between innocent humor and public ridicule is often hard to determine. If a funny story tends to make a person look stupid, naive, or otherwise ridiculous, the best advice is to leave it out.

The third pitfall is more subtle. Reporters with a well-developed story sense often have a tendency to sympathize with the people they are writing about. They may create heroes or villains, allow themselves to become advocates, or otherwise let bias color their stories. Perhaps there is no way to prevent this entirely; writers can only subject themselves to a continuing self-examination. Are they seeing things as they are? Or are they allowing their emotions to influence their perception? The better the story sounds, the more the writer should suspect himself. Sensitivity to other people certainly characterizes the best reporters—as well as the best human beings—but in both cases, self-discipline is also a vital quality.

SUGGESTED ASSIGNMENTS

1. Select a published story about a natural disaster, such as a tornado, a hurricane, a flood, an earthquake, or a major blizzard. Interview two persons who were injured or suffered newsworthy hardship and try to recreate the disaster so that the reader can see it.

2. Select a published story about a common social problem, such as poverty, alcoholism, or drug abuse. Interview a case worker, then a person who has the problem. Fictionalize the person's name and focus on the individual to illustrate the more general problem.

3. Make appointments with a public figure to interview him or her both at home and at work. If possible, follow your subject throughout the day. Write a personality profile that includes the person's private way of life as well as the face he or she shows to the public.

4. Collect fragments of conversations that you overhear in public places, such as elevators and restaurants. Select the most amusing or mystifying and weave them into a story without identifying the speakers.

5. Attend a sports event. Pay relatively little attention to the contest and concentrate on the spectators, the officials, and any incidental ceremonies. If it is a football game, watch the band, the cheerleaders, the characters on the sidelines, and any halftime activities. Write a color story that puts the reader there.

6. Think of something that almost everyone looks forward to, such as vacation or an income tax refund. Then telephone a dozen or more people whose names are often in the news and ask them how they plan to spend theirs. When you write the story, concentrate on the odd and unusual.

CHAPTER TEN / FINDING AND USING NEWS SOURCES

More than a century ago, Henry M. Stanley of the *New York Herald* searched Africa for two years until he found a missing missionary, Dr. David Livingstone. Stanley's expedition, along with the 72-day round-the-world trip of Hearst's Nellie Bly in 1889, helped create the popular belief that a reporter will do anything to get a story.

Although some journalists are reluctant to admit it, the myth has considerable foundation. Reporters have crashed parties and spied on closed meetings by crouching on window ledges. They have evaded police lines, smuggled film past federal officers, and commandeered or chartered vehicles without money or authorization. A few have joined volunteer fire departments or got themselves elected constable in order to drive cars with sirens and flashing red lights. They have used deception, impersonation, pursuit, and outright invasion—every tactic that was legal and a few that weren't. They have risked—and often lost—their lives in combat, criminal investigations, exploration, and daredevil adventures. Like Ernest Hemingway, they have captured cities—or at least saloons—in advance of approaching armies. Like George Plimpton, they have taken physical punishment merely to write about it.

But, however frequent, such dramatic reporting stunts remain the exception rather than the rule. Few reporters find it necessary to comb Africa, travel around the world, or venture into outer space to get a story. Indeed, the successful reporter often does nothing more exciting than pick up a telephone and make a half dozen calls. Reporters can do this, however, only if they have sources.

Perhaps unconsciously, reporters usually define "source" as a human being, an acquaintance in a key position who can be trusted to supply straight information. Many editors quarrel with this limited definition, criticizing what they consider a tendency to rely too much on word-of-mouth information. They argue with considerable justification that the best source is a written report or document because of its legal status and the care that has been taken in preparing it. Unfortunately, documents aren't always available, especially when you are dealing with fast-breaking news. Reporters still must rely heavily on word-of-mouth information from newsmakers, their clerks and go-betweens, and tipsters. More often than not, you must rely on such sources in order to obtain documents as well.

To make certain they have plenty of sources, professional reporters are constantly compiling and revising lists. Some of the names on the list probably were supplied by the city editor, others inherited from other reporters, and still others culled from directories. Regardless of how they were acquired, the lists are constantly changing. Each election—general, municipal, or school district—calls for an update. So do the private elections of lodges, professional societies, chambers of commerce, corporations, and trade associations.

Reporters fill address books and file folders with names, telephone numbers, standard biographical information, and other pertinent facts about their sources. Some of the personal information, however, may be kept only in their heads. They learn where their sources eat, drink, and play, as well as where they normally work, so that they can be reached at any hour. Reporters learn which documents their sources handle routinely, which subjects they will talk about and which they won't, and how they can be coaxed or pressured. Reporters trade some of this information with fellow reporters and keep some to themselves. After all, some of the information is confidential, and a reporter's success often depends on his ability to respect a confidence.

Good news sources first must have access to special information. Second, they must be much like reporters, in that they recognize the makings of a news story and act immediately. Instead of waiting to be called, good sources telephone the reporter day or night with any scrap of information that might be important. Such sources seldom spring up overnight. A few—for example, public relations practitioners—may have journalism training, but most are the product of long and careful cultivation by a journalist who has earned their trust.

Cultivation of the source is a form of low-key salesmanship. It may amount to nothing more than a few minutes of conversation each week on the street, in the coffee shop, or at social events. The goal is merely to keep the source aware of your interest and expectations. A beat reporter may achieve this automatically during normal rounds. But reporters with no clearly defined beat may find it necessary to go through their address books occasionally and telephone those sources whom they haven't seen recently "just to visit."

No amount of cultivation, of course, will make some potential informants cooperate regularly. These are sources who have information but are chronically reluctant to talk because some degree of secrecy is essential to their activities. They may be FBI agents, diplomats, bank examiners, or persons on the fringes of the underworld. News reporters often must take unusual steps merely to keep track of their source's movements. For example, during the last years of prohibition in Oklahoma, the police reporter of the *Daily Oklahoman* found it helpful to memorize the auto license numbers of all the known bootleggers and gamblers in two counties. Some of his sources rewarded this effort by running his car off the road and shooting at him. Others, however, reluctantly cooperated after he pursued them.

RECOGNIZING THE SOURCES
Anyone may on occasion become a news source. He or she need only (1) participate in a newsworthy action, (2) observe it, (3) know some person who did, or (4) have access to special information. To borrow an example from sports, a news source may be a player, a spectator, a confidant of one of these, or a statistician. He may also be a club owner, a coach, or the fellow who tried to fix the game—anyone who knows something about the subject.

Some sources are acquired literally by accident. Examples would be survivors and witnesses at a disaster scene. Unless you learn otherwise, you must assume that these are "untrained" sources, unaccustomed to speaking for publication. Such sources must be treated, although diplomatically, much the way witnesses would be treated in court: Are they mentally competent? Were they actually at the scene? Were they in a position to see and hear what happened? Was the light adequate? Are they impartial? And how much of what they are telling is merely hearsay?

Accidental sources may never be useful again. This may be the only time they will ever experience or witness anything worth putting into print. But you can't be sure. It's best to spend a few seconds getting acquainted, learning about an informant's occupation, and taking his or her telephone number and address. Tell the source that you may want to phone later; never close the door to possible future use.

Everyday Informants
The sources you want most are those you can use day after day.

They can be divided roughly into two groups: (1) the highly visible sources, newsmakers and lesser public officials, whom the reporter must share regularly with competitors and fellow workers, and (2) those who are virtually the reporter's private property by right of discovery or special attention. Each reporter tries to increase the membership of the second group without overlooking or failing to cultivate members of the first.

Shared or private, most sources are in some sense members of the community power structure. They can be found in government, business, the school system, charitable agencies—even in the organized antiestablishment forces. Many are the "doers" of the community. Some hold offices of statutory power; others merely aspire to such positions. As a reporter, you must know both the person in charge and the person who would like to be. You also must know those on the fringes of power—the clerks, records-keepers, and political errand boys who make few decisions but are in positions to know what is happening.

Names of high-visibility sources can be found in directories of public officials or lists of corporation officers, labor union executives, and service organization directors. Here is where you find the newsmakers—the legislators, judges, executives, and others who routinely and publicly make decisions that affect your public—and often those who keep the records of newsmakers' decisions. In any community, you can easily identify most of these sources by studying the newspaper for a week or two. But when you have done this, you know little more than average readers do, and you are in no position to give them any more news than they already have been getting.

Less Visible Sources

Digging beneath the surface, you will find that some of the best informed and most powerful members of the community hold no major public office and therefore appear in no official directories. Even their names may seldom appear in the news. Some of these are specialists: medical scientists, architects and engineers, law professors, or scholars in little-publicized fields. Others are persuaders: teachers, salespeople, clergy, and opinion leaders in various social and professional organizations. Still others are the true kingmakers of the community: bankers, major property owners, political bosses, and crime syndicate leaders. All are persons of influence, whether it is exercised by words, money, patronage, or the threat of violence.

Some persons loudly proclaim themselves as "influentials" by habitually writing letters to the editor, voicing their opinions at public meetings, and regularly running for office. And they may indeed gain influential status if their names appear often enough in print. Normally, however, such self-advertising must be viewed with skepticism. The truly powerful (for example, slumlords and racketeers) tend to shun publicity. They can be identified, however, if you listen carefully, ask questions, and dig through enough public records. You need only observe the frequency with which certain names are mentioned in certain contexts. Not all of these backroom powers can be converted into news sources, but occasionally you may score an unexpected success. Mafia families once were considered virtually inaccessible; all that ended with Gay Talese's *Honor Thy Father.*

The Go-Betweens

Many reporters view public relations practitioners as nuisances bent on grabbing space for trivia or keeping embarrassing stories out of print. Most PR practitioners, however, know their business too well to stoop to such practices. They offer only what they believe to be news, and they never try to kill a story. The most they ask when their client or employer is in trouble is time enough to prepare a defense. Nor will ethical PR practitioners lie to you or mislead you. Without credibility, they are out of business. They are therefore some of your best sources—as long as you recognize their bias and the danger of coming to depend upon them.

Remember that PR practitioners are working for their employers, not the general public. They will be on your side when the employer's interests coincide with the public's, but they will be of no help when the boss's best strategy is silence. If PR people are wise, they will avoid the politician's "no comment"; they will say only that they can't talk about the subject at the moment.

One of the commoner public relations ploys is the staged event: the anniversary celebration, groundbreaking ceremony, check presentation, open house, president's speech, or press conference. All of these are what historian Daniel Boorstin *(The Image)* calls pseudoevents; they are planned primarily to gain favorable publicity. Your approach to these events will be dictated by your organization's policy and your boss's instructions. Usually you will give them no more space than they merit as legitimate news.

The biggest danger in dealing with PR practitioners is the subtle matter of seduction. Most PR people probably were once reporters themselves. They know what you want, and they give it to you. And you are tempted to do favors for them in return. Up to a point, reciprocation may be justified. You have crossed the line, however, when you begin to serve the PR person's interests instead of the public's.

Perhaps the most frustrating go-betweens are those who serve government agencies, especially the armed forces. They often conceal information or supply misleading "leaks"—practices considered both unethical and self-defeating in corporate or institutional public relations. Government information officers have gone so far as to justify outright lies in the name of national security. In one respect, however, government go-betweens are less dangerous than more subtle practitioners; their misbehaviors have been so widely publicized that even the beginner seldom is seduced. An interesting book in this area is

All the President's Men by the two reporters on the *Washington Post* who helped expose the Watergate scandal.

Sources Closer to Home

As a beginning professional, you may easily overlook potentially productive sources simply because they are not "official." These include the people closest to you—relatives, friends, people you have known for years, and people you meet every day. Here are a few potential sources for offbeat stories:

Your own experience and acquaintances—are you a Sunday painter, an amateur musician, a radio ham, a gun collector, or a bird watcher? If so, you probably come into contact with a hobby group that is doing something newsworthy. Or perhaps you had some unusual job experience before you entered journalism. One reporter, a gold miner until he was 30, regularly uncovered stories among the miners with whom he once worked. Another, who grew up in a small-town telephone exchange, frequently used his knowledge of electronics and the telephone industry. Many more have put their military experience and acquaintances to good use years later.

People you work with—printers, advertising salesmen, circulation workers, and other newsmen. Circulation people regularly hear stories that seldom reach a reporter, and advertising salesmen often know more about business activities than the editor who is supposed to be covering them. Printers, who deal with circulation and advertising as well as news-editorial staffers, provide an additional listening post. In the newsroom itself, a casual chat with a fellow reporter may yield a scrap of information that completes a puzzle that has baffled you for weeks. Even a competitor may give you a clue to a story—sometimes inadvertently, sometimes because his employer's policy prevents the reporter from using information which he thinks should be published.

People who regularly hear a lot—salespeople, barbers, waitresses, hotel porters, receptionists, taxi drivers, and beauty operators. Much of what they hear is fragmented or distorted, and a lot is unusable personal gossip. But some of it may lead to legitimate news stories. The first inkling of a price increase, an impending strike, a major business deal, a transportation delay, a vice operation, or mass food poisoning may come from sources who sometimes are referred to patronizingly as "the little people." Their rumors must be checked carefully, but you can't afford not to listen.

Routine Written Sources

Many standard fixtures that appear on the inside pages of newspapers are culled from reports and documents kept at the police station and the county courthouse. These include traffic accidents, complaints, arrests, fines, the filing of civil suits, and the daily lists of marriage licenses and divorces. The custodians of these records are the police dispatcher or booking sergeant, the sheriff or his chief deputy, highway patrol headquarters, the county clerk, and various court clerks.

Each day police reporters must read stacks of complaints and reports of investigations, only a few of which ever result in stories. Many are so similar that reporters can easily lose their place and discover later that they have been wasting time by reading something that was read and rejected the day before. One way to avoid this is to pay close attention to the date and hour of the report. If the complaints are numbered, reporters can keep their place by jotting down the number of the last one examined, then starting with the next number the next day. In small-town police departments where the complaints may not be numbered, reporters often leave their initials or some small identifying mark on each report read. Some such system is necessary, particularly when a substitute reporter must cover the beat.

Dates should be observed carefully when you are examining court records. Occasionally a lawyer checks out a file and keeps it for months. When it reappears, a clerk may place it among the recent dispositions. And if you aren't alert, you may find that you have written a "news" story about a case that was disposed of two years ago. This can be embarrassing if you have reported the divorce of a couple long since remarried.

Both police and court records are notoriously inadequate in some respects. Ages and street addresses seldom appear in court records. Police reports may include these details, but they may omit marital status—and misspell all the names. Much of what you get from official documents must be verified by asking questions and consulting the city directory.

GETTING ACQUAINTED

One of a reporter's more important assets is the ability to "talk shop" with almost anyone. This is because it offers a means of establishing rapport, a way of getting the source to talk. And it usually leads quickly to a newsworthy subject.

Because so many sources are part of the community power structure, the first step in learning to talk shop is to study government, economics, institutions, and procedural law. Learn all you can about each newsmaking agency or information collection center: its budget, the scope of its powers, and to whom it is responsible. Determine where it fits into the overall community structure, then get acquainted with its internal operations. Mere textbook information isn't enough.

You must understand the daily routine of each office, the documents that it collects and issues, and the enthusiasms and frustrations of the people who work there. You must learn how your sources think and feel, as well as what they do.

People and Power in Government

No matter what your beat or assignment, you will come into contact with government agencies at some point. If you are a sports writer, you may find the federal courts settling a dispute between professional athletes and their employers, or the attorney general's office investigating a fixed race. If you work for the home and family or "women's" department, you may keep watch on the activities of the Consumer Protection Bureau, the Food and Drug Administration, and the Equal Opportunity Commission. As an education writer or police reporter, you will encounter government at every level—local, state, and national.

No one textbook can describe all you need to know about political structures, the court system, or principles of law. This can come only from detailed study and experience. You may speed up the learning process, however, if you approach each government source with the goal of analyzing his power—the nature of that power, its scope, and its source.

The first consideration is whether an official makes law, interprets it, or enforces it—whether he or she belongs to the legislative, judiciary, or executive branch. But this is only the starting point. It is equally important to determine the control this person's office exercises over money, jobs, information, and other branches of government. Can it levy taxes and appropriate funds? If so, is there a statutory limit on how much it can tax? If it has no taxing power, how large is its budget? What kinds of contracts may the head of the office negotiate? Does the official have full authority to determine who gets these contracts, or does law require acceptance of the lowest bid? How many people are employed in the office or department? Is the person in charge empowered to choose these people freely, or are there some restrictions? Can the official remove employees at will, or must a hearing be conducted in order to discharge tenured personnel? What special information does the person collect or have access to? What other branches of government can be overruled by the office?

The scope of an official's power may be limited in many ways. It may be a personal power, as is the case with executives and many judges, who are answerable only to the law. Or it may be a power shared with others, as in legislative bodies, regulatory commissions, and the Supreme Court. It may be a national, state, or merely local power. It lasts only as long as the term of office, which may be a

specified number of years, a lifetime, or only as long as the person
pleases some higher official.

The reporter must know who put the source in office, to whom he
or she must answer, and how the official can be removed. Is it a constitutional office, one established by statute, or one created only by
executive order? Is the source answerable directly to the voters, or
only to the leaders of a political party? Who can fire this official—
when, and by what method?

Except for the few who are wealthy, the average person in government is in one respect like almost everyone else. The public official—
male or female—is concerned about his job: how much it pays, how
long it will last, how he can gain recognition for good efforts and
make them more effective, how he can use this current job as a spring-
board to something better. If you recognize these interests, you have
a good start toward learning what makes the source tick. But to deal
with this person effectively, you need to know still more. To what
individual or pressure group does the official owe his present position?
If he is an elected official, who supplied the money for the last campaign? And how are political debts being repaid? What are his ambitions, political philosophy, personal loyalties, and occupational prejudices?

If you can answer all these questions about the government source,
you can explain many of his actions and evaluate the extent to which
this person is influenced by public opinion. And you can get a fair
idea of how well he will cooperate as a news source. To illustrate,
let's examine some of the people you will meet.

LEGISLATORS

Money is power, and legislative bodies are the source of all money
in the American political system. They alone have the authority
to levy taxes and appropriate funds. They determine their own
salaries, those of judges and executives, and the amount of money that
shall be spent for specific programs. They may either build or destroy
through the power to tax and appropriate. This is, of course, a shared
power; it is invested in the body as a whole, rather than in any one
legislator. Indeed, a freshman legislator may feel that he has no
power at all.

Members of Congress and most state legislatures are elected on a
partisan ticket. They are first responsible to the laws of the state and
nation, to the public as a whole, and to the specific constituency that
elected them. But they also owe political debts to their parties, its
titular leaders, and individual campaign contributors. And, because
legislation is accomplished by compromise, they owe many debts to
their fellow legislators. They vote for the other fellow's bill in order
to get him to vote for theirs. If they are adept at compromise, they are
in a strong position to pay political debts to campaign contributors
through special-interest legislation. The major brakes on their activi-

ties are public opinion, the court system, and the opposing party. Another brake on the individual legislator may be personal ambition for a higher office.

Elected officials operate on the principle that a politician's first duty is to get into office. Otherwise, he or she can accomplish nothing. And the person who gets elected usually wants to be reelected. Elected officials are therefore sensitive to public opinion; they read published polls and often conduct polls of their own. The extent of this sensitivity depends largely on how often an official must run for reelection. Members of the U.S. House of Representatives and others who serve two-year terms never stop campaigning. They are readily accessible to reporters, but they may provide more opinion than hard fact, in some cases flooding the press with self-serving publicity. U.S. senators, on the other hand, campaign only once every six years, and are therefore under less pressure to court the press and public regularly.

An individual lawmaker's power derives from committee assignments, seniority, and political affiliation. Bills are drafted or amended in committee, and the chairmanships of these committees go to senior members of the party in power (although recent reform legislation has been making some dents in the traditional seniority system on Capitol Hill). If the legislator also is a member of the chief executive's party, he or she has the opportunity to fill many patronage jobs back home.

PRESIDENT AND GOVERNOR

Elected chief executives are automatically the leaders of their parties. They have the power to appoint many officeholders and even to create new jobs, which gives them a lever to use against legislators who would like to repay faithful supporters in patronage. The power to award large contracts gives the chief executive another important lever.

Presidents historically have tried to limit the flow of news from the executive branch, usually in the name of national security. As a result, both legislators and the general public often are in the dark about where certain tax money goes. Much of the excitement of Washington reporting comes from trying to knock holes in this wall of secrecy. It is easiest, of course, during a president's first term when he must listen to public opinion in order to be reelected. In a second and final term, the president may be virtually inaccessible.

Unlike the president, who has no higher office to seek, many governors may be strongly motivated by a more attractive future. Perhaps they serve their parties faithfully in the hope of getting lifetime appointments to the federal bench. More likely, however, many of their actions are designed to make them attractive candidates for the U.S. Senate, or even the presidency. A governor is therefore far more cooperative with the press than is a president.

One way to understand governors is to compare their salaries with

those of other state officials. In many lightly populated states, the
governor's pay is exceeded by that of serveral other officials—perhaps
the state engineer, the director of a mental hospital, and several college
presidents. Much of what a governor does may be explained by a
desire for money.

ELECTED STATE OFFICIALS

Unlike national government, executive power at the state level
isn't all centralized in one office. Whereas each president picks
the members of his cabinet, a governor must get along with several independently elected constitutional officers, some of whom may not be
of the same political party.

Few elected state officers bear names that are household words.
Indeed, citizens may recognize none of the candidates on election day,
so they usually vote for their party's choice. Such officers seldom
campaign vigorously for reelection. They need only serve the dominant
party faithfully, get the nomination, and return to office term after
term.

These often faceless state officials, together with the county courthouse crowd, are the backbone of party politics. United, they can
make or break a candidate for governor or senator. It would be a
gross misconception, however, to regard them all as party hacks. Some,
such as the attorney general, may be highly trained professionals.
Others often achieve expertise from years of experience.

Within limits, state officers can reward their friends and punish
their enemies by approving or refusing contracts, issuing or canceling
licenses, and releasing or withholding information. Their routine
activities and periodic reports can be a gold mine for the alert reporter.
Here are three of the most important news sources in this category:

Attorney General—The state's chief prosecutor also is the legal
adviser to all state agencies. He or she usually is assisted by a staff of
junior prosecutors and a criminal investigation division. The attorney
general's name gets into the news frequently when legal opinions are
issued at the request of other officials, making this official second only
to the governor in visibility. Unlike most other state elective offices,
the attorney general's office is an excellent stepping stone to either a
higher political office or a court appointment.

Secretary of State—Don't confuse the state officer with the presidential cabinet member who has the same title. At the state level, the
secretary of state is concerned with internal affairs, not diplomacy.
Duties of the office usually include regulation of corporate charters
and supervision of elections. Here is where you can find out who has
incorporated a firm, for what purpose, and with how much capital.
Here also is where you can check the official election returns or the

number of signatures on an initiative petition. By the way he or she interprets the law, the secretary of state may at times have the power to decide whether a candidate or an issue gets on the ballot. This obviously can be a political power.

Controller or Auditor—This person, whose title varies from state to state, is the state's financial watchdog. The job is to keep fellow officials honest by auditing their accounts. This office could be described as the state equivalent of the U.S. General Accounting Office, charged with the duty of making certain that all expenditures are legal.

The auditor normally has no power to punish wrongdoers. If, for example, there is an irregularity in a sheriff's claim for travel costs, the auditor's only weapon is to publicize what has been found. Some auditors release their findings directly to the press; others merely send their reports to the appropriate supervisors and let reporters uncover them at that level.

Because the auditor's work is vital to honest government, some states have removed the office from the list of elective positions and placed it under the merit system. Law usually requires also that the auditor's office be subjected to private audit.

POLITICAL APPOINTEES

Presidents and governors traditionally reward major campaign contributors and loyal party workers with a host of jobs that vary dramatically in pay, prestige, and actual power. At the top are federal court appointments (a special class to be examined later), cabinet posts, and ambassadorships. At the bottom are assignments to commissions that seldom meet, pay nothing but expenses, and perhaps accomplish only lip service toward studying some problem that the executive never intends to act upon.

Some of the most powerful positions also are the least secure. These are spoils-system offices which appointees hold only at the pleasure of the person who appointed them. The most prominent are members of the president's cabinet. Their jobs end when the president leaves office—and may end much sooner if the chief executive chooses. They tend to share the president's political philosophy, support him firmly on specific issues, and deal with the press much as he does. Their comments usually are predictable. If, however, a cabinet member differs with the president, you have a story. And you soon may have a follow-up—a resignation story.

At the state level, the most powerful post that traditionally goes to a political appointee is that of highway director. The person who holds this office very likely was the governor's campaign manager in the last election. Without breaking the law, highway or transportation heads often have the opportunity to route highways to benefit themselves or their friends, write contracts that favor the "right" people, and fill many small positions with members of their party. They may also control promotions and geographical assignments for highway engineers, and they usually spend more money than any other department heads. Despite these powers, however such officials are far from being free. They are still part of the governor's "team," and they also must comply with federal regulations that govern roads built with federal aid.

A few positions, often on regulatory commissions, are filled by political appointment for specified terms. These may exceed the term of the person who made the appointment, which gives the appointee a large measure of freedom. Members of these commissions often are experts who return to office term after term under different chief executives. They may be virtually independent of political influence.

THE "UNTOUCHABLES"

Headlines sometimes give the impression that government in the United States is in constant upheaval: frequent turnovers of executive control, sudden policy reversals, cabinet shakeups, corruption, and various forms of wheeling and dealing. It also seems that we are eternally throwing the rascals out and installing new rascals in their places. An outsider might wonder how anything ever gets done.

One answer, of course, is that the system makes it impossible to throw out all the rascals at the same time. Varying terms of office and staggered election dates are designed to make certain there are always at least a few old hands around at the policymaking level. Further, the voters tend to fill major offices with candidates who already have government experience, then reelect them. This is particularly true of the U.S. Senate.

But the real reason the system works is that a few people near the top—and a vast number farther down—are never thrown out at all. Some serve for life, some for 20 or 30 years, and some to the age of 65. They keep on minding the store as administrators come and go; they are interested spectators to the political turmoil around them, but generally insulated from it. These are the judiciary, the military, and the civil servants whose jobs are protected by the merit system. State or federal, they conduct most of the routine business of government, and they are largely untouchable by public opinion or political influence. They can be removed only by due process of law or abolition of their office. Their long tenure constitutes an effective brake on sudden change, giving some branches of the government a stability that borders on inertia. Here are some of the "untouchables" you will meet:

Federal Judges—A federal judge is perhaps the most powerful person in American government, answerable only to the law and restricted only by the constitutional division of powers. Federal judges are appointed by the president, subject to Senate approval, and serve for life. Politics plays an important role in their selection, but need not influence their behavior in any way thereafter. They usually reflect the political philosophy of the president who appoints them and are members of the president's party, but they tend to rise above partisanship on the bench. They can be as independent as they like, as long as they adhere to the law.

Federal judges are important newsmakers, but they seldom grant interviews or hold press conferences. Reporters usually must cover their actions in court or read the record of their decisions available from clerks.

State Judges—Some states elect district or circuit judges, but many have tried to take the office out of politics. Under one system of selection, the judge is appointed by a commission that works from a list supplied by the state bar association. After the judge has been in office for a term of four years, his name is submitted to the voters without opposition for approval or disapproval. The result almost is equivalent to the federal judge's lifetime appointment.

State judges, like their federal counterparts, seldom seek publicity. They tend to be aloof to public opinion and as politically independent as they care to be.

Career Military Personnel—The Defense Department spends more money than any other federal agency. This alone would make its activities of major interest to every reader—even if personal security were not involved—yet the coverage of military spending seldom is adequate. The public hears mostly about the construction of bases and spending for military hardware—big-ticket items subject to congressional approval. Far less is heard about the cost of operations; the civilian payroll; or the outlay for food, clothing, and supplies.

Although civilians ostensibly are in charge, major spending decisions may be made by—or influenced by—career military personnel ranging from generals and admirals down into the enlisted ranks. And those decisions sometimes are influenced by personal considerations. A general might favor a firm that has offered him a job after retirement. Mess sergeants, supply sergeants, and post exchange officers have been known to get rich by manipulating contracts and taking kickbacks.

In dealing with the military, you will often be at the mercy of security-conscious officers who may be mildly paranoid about civilians in general and the press in particular. On the one hand, they are secretive; on the other, image-conscious. Often they have been made to feel like outsiders among the civilians they protect. As a result, they have developed the habit of talking mostly to each other; you may get little more news than the public information officer wants you to have.

A helpful approach is to remember that military sources are human beings, not computers in uniform. They were born somewhere, went to school somewhere, and presumably still have family and regional ties. If you investigate their personal histories, you will have a better idea how to communicate with them. Is the source a reservist, or an academy man? A combat veteran, or a desk pilot? Is he committed to his career, or is he only putting in his time?

Civil Servants—Few generalizations can be made about the vast numbers of federal, state, and municipal workers whose jobs are protected by some form of merit system. Most are barred from active participation in politics, and most must retire at 65. Perhaps all resent being called bureaucrats. Otherwise, it is an extremely varied group: clerks, stenographers, shop workers, scientists, engineers, diplomats, educators, and investigators and law enforcement officers of many kinds. It covers most of the people in such diverse agencies as the U.S. Department of Agriculture, the General Accounting Office, the Public Health Service, the Internal Revenue Service, the Central Intelligence Agency, and perhaps your local fire department. It may also cover state health and welfare specialists.

One oddity that characterizes the federal civil service and many municipal police departments is the employment preference given to veterans of the armed forces. As a result, many government jobs are filled with older persons already drawing military retirement pay and working toward a second pension. This is particularly true of the Veterans Administration. This means that the reporter can expect many civil servants to take a dim view of the public's right to know; they have been conditioned too long to the military view of security.

In such a large and varied class, however, you will find all ranges of attitudes toward the press and public opinion. Some agencies—like the U.S. Department of Agriculture—employ a corps of writers and editors to make certain the public is informed. Others operate as if the government were their private business. And workers in more than a few agencies are disappointed that "nobody seems to care what we do."

LAW ENFORCEMENT OFFICERS

As a group, peace officers share many of the attitudes of military personnel. They are sensitive to criticism, conscious of their public image, conditioned to secrecy, and somewhat suspicious of "civilians." Most consider themselves underpaid and overworked, and they usually are. They are convinced of the guilt of every person they bring to trial and often complain that courts are "too permissive." They doubt that outsiders ever understand their work, and they usually are glad to talk with reporters about procedures, systems, and equipment. About pending investigations, however, they may be silent.

Law enforcement involves much more than investigating crime. Policemen regulate traffic, investigate accidents, search for missing persons, and conduct rescue operations. They often must open cars or homes for people who have locked themselves out. And at some levels —notably the sheriff and the U.S. marshal—they are responsible for serving civil legal papers. In some communities they spend a considerable amount of time making sure that business doors are locked at night; in other places this chore is left to private security agencies. Many policemen moonlight as company guards or nightclub bouncers. The result of all this activity is that the police station and the sheriff's office yield much more information than merely the overnight list of investigations and arrests.

The amount of information you get from any law enforcement agency, however, depends largely on your personal powers of persuasion. You can't force an officer to tell you more than who was arrested, on what charge, when, where, and under what circumstances—and some will try to conceal even this minimum. In some small communities, the police department may be so secretive that your only source is the chief. In most, however, the custom is to allow reporters full access to the arrest book, the complaint file, and all accident investigations. Getting access to an individual officer's report of a continuing investigation usually is more difficult.

In a medium-sized city, the usual sources at the police station are the chief himself, the dispatcher or desk sergeant; the duty officer in overall charge of the shift; the heads of various divisions, such as the detective bureau, vice squad, traffic division, and juvenile branch. At the sheriff's office, they may be only the sheriff and the chief deputy. A large sheriff's department, however, may comprise many of the same departments you find at police headquarters. None of these "usual" sources, however, is as good as the officer who actually conducted the investigation or made the arrest.

Personal ambitions and interdepartmental rivalries often help a reporter. Among law enforcement people, these rivalries may be focused on the sheriff's office, because it is elective. Perhaps the sheriff has an ambitious deputy, or some police captain is interested in running for sheriff because the office pays more. People with political ambitions like to see their names in print and are quick to cooperate.

Another pressure point in crime coverage is the district or county attorney's office, which usually is elective. Is the district attorney seeking a court appointment? Would he or she like to run for governor? Is there an assistant prosecutor who wants the district attorney's job?

Police reporters often are asked to withhold information while an investigation is in progress. The usual reason given for this request is that you may alert a suspect and give him a chance to get away before an arrest can be made. Sometimes this is a legitimate request; sometimes not. A police reporter must "play ball" occasionally, but each case must be decided on its merits.

SOURCES AT CITY HALL

City government is organized much like national government, except that the judicial branch is much weaker and the legislative body seldom consists of more than one house. The city normally has a single strong chief executive (an elected mayor or council-appointed city manager), a one-house city council, and a municipal court limited to small civil claims and the prosecution of misdemeanors or infractions of city ordinances. City government also may include several independent or semiindependent agencies, such as a housing authority, a zoning board, and an airport authority.

Covering city hall can be a day-and-night job. Like Congress, the city council does much of its preliminary work in committees that meet at odd hours throughout the week. Most of these sessions, as well as the regular meetings of the complete council, must be staffed, and usually by the same person. Except in the largest cities, one reporter covers it all.

The executive branch is somewhat easier to cover because all, or nearly all, authority is centralized in the office of the mayor or city manager. If you can't reach the top officer, the next best source is the city clerk or city finance director. Other helpful officials are the city attorney, whose most important role is that of legal adviser to the council, and the city engineer.

The primary function of municipal government is to provide basic services: water and sewer systems, streets, public safety and fire protection, parks and recreation programs, garbage collection, and animal control. The appointed heads of these departments, all answerable to the chief executive, can be useful sources.

The branch of city government that gets the briefest coverage is municipal court. Small claims usually are ignored and fines for misdemeanors may be carried only in list form, if at all. Still, the court can't be overlooked entirely, because it has the power to conduct arraignments and preliminary hearings in felony cases. But municipal court usually is only a small part of the police reporter's job and no concern of the person who covers city government.

THE COUNTY COURTHOUSE CROWD

Covering county government is one of the toughest jobs in journalism. The reason is that, unlike the city, the county has no single chief executive. It is a branch of the state and is governed by several relatively independent elected executives and a board of commissioners that exercises budgetary control over each office. The commissioners have the power to levy taxes and in some states to pass ordinances.

The principal functions of county government are to build rural roads, provide welfare assistance and health service, collect taxes, zone rural property, keep the peace and investigate crime in rural areas, and keep a wide variety of public records. The county also may have some control over school systems.

In heavily populated counties, the board of commissioners may function much like a city council, with regular meetings well attended by the public. But in predominantly rural states, commissioners' meetings often are long, informal, and unattended by either the press or the public. Debate may be nonexistent. The commissioners sit at a table, pass papers around, and conduct the county's routine business with a minimum of conversation. At some meetings they may do little more than approve payments and ratify decisions made by the independent elected executives. Occasionally, however, they make news. They can withhold welfare payments, refuse the sheriff's claim for travel expense, or fire an appointed health officer. And if they are dishonest, they also can make money in kickbacks from contractors and suppliers, because they are seldom watched closely.

One reason that county commissioners' meetings are poorly covered is that most of the time they do nothing out of the ordinary. The biggest reason, however, is that meetings are seldom finished in the two to four hours customary for city councils. A short commissioners' meeting may be an entire day; in at least one state, they are required to meet for four consecutive days once a month. Few newspapers can spare a reporter this long for a single assignment. So instead of staffing the meetings, reporters are forced to cover them as best they can by checking with the clerk or auditor who acts as secretary.

Most of the news that comes out of the county building comes from the courts and the elected officers: the sheriff, county attorney, county clerk or auditor, assessor, treasurer, superintendent of schools (an office rapidly being abolished), and the recorder or register of deeds. These are only a few of the more common offices. Some states also have elected coroners and surveyors.

The exact title and duties of each office vary from state to state. But each is a collection point for records that are open to the press and public. Here are a few examples of how the major work may be distributed:

County Clerk or Auditor—This officer usually is the most important source of county news that doesn't deal with criminal investigation or court action. The clerk or auditor serves as secretary and purchasing agent for the board of commissioners and to some extent oversees the financial operations of other county officers. He or she also may supervise elections and compile the returns. In some states this person functions as recorder and clerk of the county court.

Sheriff—The sheriff is the county's chief law enforcement officer. In criminal investigations, the sheriff's office usually works under the direction of the district or county attorney's office. He cooperates closely with the state police or highway patrol in maintaining order in rural areas. His office serves many civil papers for the court system, conducts sales of property for delinquent taxes, and operates the jail. In addition to the salary, the sheriff often receives fees for legal service, a liberal travel allowance, and payment for feeding prisoners. A sheriff may become prosperous after a few terms in office and in some sections of the nation can become a major political power.

Treasurer—The treasurer collects property taxes for the county and all the towns and school districts within it, then distributes the money to the appropriate branch of government. The treasurer also may collect taxes on motor vehicles and sell license plates and hunting and fishing licenses. In some states, the treasurer's office has been combined with that of assessor, who determines the value of property for tax purposes.

Court Clerk—A single clerk may serve district and county courts, or each may have a separate clerk. The most important information found at the clerk's office is the complete record of each criminal or civil case the court handles, from arrest warrants, subpoenas, and the original filing to the final disposition. All this is open for your inspection, unless the record has been sealed by court order. In addition to major litigation and criminal prosecutions, the clerk's office is the source of information about divorces or marriage dissolutions and the distribution of estates.

In many states, the court clerk issues marriage licenses and records birth and death certificates. In others, these functions are performed by the county clerk. In any state, both offices must be covered daily.

Recorder or Register of Deeds—The chief function of this office, which goes by many names, is to keep records of ownership. Land titles, mortgages, subdivision plats, and the complete history of each piece of real estate in the county are available here. So are the records of liens on such personal property as automobiles, boats, and trailers. And in some states, this is the office where military veterans are required to record their discharge papers. The only news that comes from this office regularly may be the routine list of real estate transfers, but it is an important source of information for abstractors, attorneys, credit investigators—and investigative reporters.

Researching the Source

Before you approach a recognized news source for the first time, take a few minutes to find out who he or she is. Use *Who's Who in America,* the state directory of public officials, or some other standard biographical reference. If the person isn't listed there, try your newspaper's clipping files. Find out where the person was born and reared, what kind of education the person has, what previous positions he or she has held. Find out everything that will help you communicate with the source. Then ask the city editor what kind of person this is. Does he or she have any known eccentricities? Any outspoken opinions? Any blatant vices? Has the individual cooperated with your newspaper in the past? Above all, can this source be trusted?

Many reporters make it a practice to write a feature story about a newly acquired source as soon as they can find a legitimate reason. This is designed to (1) make the source friendlier, and (2) collect additional biographical information for the office files. It must not, however, be merely an attempt to butter up the source; it must serve the reader's interests as well as the reporter's.

The Testing Period

One encounter, even if it results in a favorable personality profile, is seldom enough to cement a lasting relationship. More often, reporter and source go through weeks of mutual testing, until each is assured that the other knows his or her business and can be trusted. During this getting-acquainted period, a source may either conceal information or deliberately mislead you to see how much you will swallow. Similarly, you as the reporter may check everything important that the newfound source tells you with some other person known to be trustworthy. If you discover that you have been misinformed, you must let the source know of your discovery. The source must know that he is dealing with a person who can't be deceived, or he will never respect you. And without respect, the relationship may be permanently blighted.

You also must make it clear that you can play no favorites. Your job is to write the news, no matter who gets hurt, and this includes the source. A reporter is neither the partner of the source nor his antagonist. Unless this is established immediately, the source may tend to discount the journalist as just another one of the gang. The source must understand that he speaks at his own risk, that everything he says is presumed fair game for publication unless there is a prior agreement that comments on a specific subject will be "off the record."

THE TRANSACTION

Newspapers and news agencies seldom buy information directly from the source. It may happen occasionally, when a publisher wants exclusive rights to a first-person account, but this is rare. Usually the publisher expects reporters to operate with no more cash outlay than that required for telephone calls and transportation. In layman's language, this means that most newsworthy information is provided free.

Behavioral scientists, however, see it differently. They describe the news interview as a *transaction* in which both persons expect to gain something, regardless of the fact that no money changes hands. What the reporter expects, of course, is usable information. But what the source wants from the transaction may differ from person to person—and from encounter to encounter with the same person.

Sources often can't tell you what they expect. Indeed, they may not be aware that they expect anything at all. But they do, and reporters should discover what it is if they are going to use sources effectively and avoid being used in return.

Many sources have strong personal motives for talking for publication. They want to smear a rival, promote a cause, defend themselves in a controversy—or merely get their names into print to achieve a status they hope to use later. They have a message, often biased, which they would like to tell the world—or, in the case of public relations practitioners, a particular audience. Such obvious self-interest is easily turned to your advantage. You have no trouble getting information from this source, only difficulty checking it out, balancing it with opposing viewpoints, and determining how much to use.

But what of the source who has nothing tangible to gain? What do you have to offer the secure public servant protected by the merit system, who isn't subject to the influence of public opinion or the whim of a higher executive? What benefits are expected by the person who is angry at nobody and promoting nothing?

One benefit may be simply the pleasure of your company. Don't underrate this possibility. To many sources, you represent a break in the day's routine, a welcome excuse to quit work for a while. And you bring with you information about the outside world, tidbits about what is happening in all the other offices around your beat. The source may well consider you an engaging conversationalist, even something of a glamorous figure. And the fact that you are spending a few minutes with him or her may produce a feeling of importance rarely experienced.

But perhaps the most important thing you have to offer is the opportunity to be of public service. You are not, after all, the only person who believes that the free flow of information is the cornerstone of democracy. Many sources cooperate for nothing more than the feeling that they are contributing to the general welfare of the community. You still must convince them, however, that you personally are the means to that end. Sources must know that you share their ideals; they must perceive you as a dedicated, honest, disinterested professional.

The foundation of any lasting relationship is ethical performance. Sources expect you to tell them the truth, to keep any promises you make, to give them recognition for their cooperation, and to protect them from those who could harm them. There are a few specific guidelines you must follow.

Identify Yourself

You owe it to your sources to let them know who you are. At the minimum, this means telling them your name, position, and employer. Don't try to conceal the fact that you are a reporter; sources who discover that they have been deceived are unlikely to help you a second time.

Identifying your employer may be either an asset or a minor handicap. If you work for *The New York Times* or the Associated Press, the prestige of your organization may be a big help. If you work for a newspaper or broadcasting station with a low prestige in its community, you may have to work a little harder. Regardless, it is usually better to leave your organization in the background. Instead of saying "My newspaper would like to know," tell the source "I would like to know." It's better to be personal than pompous.

Promise Nothing You Can't Deliver

The source must understand that your only job is to collect and write the news. What happens to it afterward is beyond your control. You can't always promise that a story will appear today or tomorrow—or even that it will be used at all. You especially can't promise that it will be used on the front page. Such decisions are made by editors, not reporters.

Conversely, you can't promise either that certain information won't be used, unless you first consult your editor. You may agree to a delay only to discover that another reporter has picked up the same information from another source. All you can ever promise is what *you* control.

When sources use the phrase "off the record," interrupt quickly and make them explain what they mean. Does the source mean that you can't use what he or she is about to tell you under any circumstance? Or does the person mean that it's all right to use as long as you don't attribute it. Is the source trying to tell you something for

publication, or only for background information? You may want to
go along, or you may want to tell your informer you're not interested
in anything that's off the record. The latter course often is best. This
way, if you get the same information from another source, you can
use it without violating any promise made to the person who wanted
it off the record.

In Washington and in many state capitals, the off-the-record briefing for reporters has become an institution. The official who stages
such a briefing establishes the rules, and reporters who attend must
agree to follow them. A common rule at such background sessions is
that nothing the reporter uses shall be attributed to the official who
said it. This allows the politician to "leak" information about actions
under consideration without taking public responsibility for them.
The official thereby uses the press to determine public reaction before
making a final decision. In another variation, the background briefing
is solely for the reporters' information, and it is open only to those
who agree to use nothing they hear. Many newspapers boycott such
sessions. Editors have found that they usually can get the same information on the record from another source.

Show Courtesy in Attribution

It is common courtesy to attribute a story to its source, even when
attribution isn't essential to the reader. After all, the source
helped you get the story, and most will be disappointed if their
names aren't mentioned. This is particularly true of arresting officers,
records keepers, and other government underlings who seldom fall
into the category of newsmaker.

Attribution, however, can be overdone to the point where it becomes an embarrassment to the source, especially if he or she is someone who supplies you with information daily. Further, readers may
begin to wonder whether you ever talk with anyone else. Therefore,
when you know all the facts to be true, don't make the source obvious
unless he or she is a legitimate part of the action. One mention of the
person's name may be enough.

Consider Quotes Carefully

Although sources must understand that everything they say normally is "on the record," they have a right to expect you to exercise
restraint when you quote them directly. Normally you won't quote
profanity or grammatical errors. If, however, a source makes a sensational charge or says something which you think might be com-
promising, courtesy requires that you ask permission to quote directly.
This can be a delicate problem; you owe the reader the information,
but you also must avoid alienating the source entirely and thereby

undermining future cooperation. The difficulty lies in drawing a line between treating the source fairly and becoming a public relations adviser.

Provide Protection

Sometimes the only way to get a story is to agree first that the source will remain anonymous. Perhaps every reporter has made such agreements to protect a source from losing life or livelihood, yet it is a risky business that often has put newsmen in jail.

The problem is that present law in many states fails to recognize any confidential relationship between reporter and source, such as the relationship between lawyer and client, physician and patient, or husband and wife. You may be subpoenaed, therefore, and ordered to testify against your source. Sometimes a court or grand jury will demand information you received but didn't print; more often it merely wants you to identify the source of something you did use. But if you have agreed to conceal your source's identity, you are bound to keep your word—even if it means going to jail for contempt.

The Telephone Transaction

The best way of dealing with a source normally is face to face.

By reading a person's smiles, gestures, and blank expressions, you can tell whether he understands the questions, how he feels about the subject, and perhaps whether he knows much more than he is telling. This visual feedback enables you to judge the information much better than mere words would.

But at times the face-to-face interview is impossible or too time-consuming to be practical. On a heavy day, you may have to write as many as 30 routine stories in an eight-hour shift. Or perhaps you will have a single assignment that requires more than 20 brief interviews. At times like these, the telephone is indispensable. You also will have to use the telephone when (1) a source is in a distant city or away from his usual haunts, (2) you have so few questions that a trip away from the office would be wasted, or (3) you must check a few facts just before deadline.

The telephone also may help you reach a source who refuses to see visitors; a call often gets through while reporters on the spot are kept waiting.

A few simple rules will improve your telephone technique:

1. *Identify yourself fully.* The person at the other end can't see your face, and even a close acquaintance may not recognize your voice. Remember, too, to name your newspaper.
2. *Keep it brief.* Know what you are going to ask, and get to the heart

of it immediately. Try to avoid using the phone for any conversation that will require more than five minutes.

3. *Use more verifying techniques than usual.* Repeat words and phrases frequently for confirmation. Paraphrase what the person has told you, and use short summaries.

4. *Be especially careful about spelling.* Did he say "s" as in "Sam," or "f" as in "Frank"? Many letters sound alike over the telephone, so it pays to adopt something like the military system for verifying spelling.

SPECIAL PROBLEMS

Reporting is seldom as simple as staffing a speech or roving around a beat and picking up lists of names and numbers. You deal constantly with gossip and rumor, with people who try to use you, and with sources who disappear when you need them most. An investigating officer cleans up an accident, then goes to a movie without filing a report. Days pass when every regular source either is missing from his office or has no time to talk. Then there are other days when you have no time to talk with them.

Similar frustrations are found in other occupations. But in journalism they create more difficulty because of the pressure of deadlines and the necessity of being thorough and accurate. In another occupation, you might write off a series of such problems as just a bad day; in journalism, you must find quick solutions. Perhaps it will help to review a few typical problems and the professional's way of handling them.

The Missing Source

Each term, beginning newswriting students return from their campus beats the first day without stories. The reason, they explain, is that the source wasn't in his office. Where is he? They don't know. So the instructor sends them back to find out where the source went, when he left, what he is doing there, and when he is expected to return. This information alone may be enough to make a brief story, and occasionally it turns out to be much more important than the student expected.

Remember that most newsmakers are on the public payroll. If sources aren't in their offices, they may be (1) on official business elsewhere, (2) coping with a personal emergency, or (3) taking an unannounced vacation. Whatever they are doing—unless it is merely taking a coffee break—is the public's business. As a representative of the public, you have a duty to find out what that business is. It may not amount to a story, but don't stop asking questions until you are certain.

If you need a specific item of information and a source can't be reached, the logical course is to ask who else might know. Usually this is the next highest person in the chain of command. If you don't know who that person is, ask a secretary or receptionist for the name.

The Overtalkative Source

Occasionally you will have less trouble getting people to talk than getting them to stop. As a beginner, you may botch this problem either by allowing the source to detain you far too long or by insulting him in your haste to escape. The professional usually solves it by rising, smiling, thanking the source, and explaining that he has a deadline to meet. Sources may be disappointed, but they probably understand about deadlines, and they hardly will be offended.

Sources who visit the newsroom present a different problem. If they trap you at your desk, you can't very well ignore them and start writing again. But sometimes you can signal your plight to a fellow newsman, who then can use an extension phone to call you. This interruption usually provides an excuse to smile and wave good-by to the person who is wasting your time. If neither this nor anything else works, you may have to walk the offender to the nearest coffee shop, have a quick cup, then make your exit.

The Sophisticated Source

At some point, most reporters encounter a source who makes them feel slightly foolish. This person may be the head of a foreign state, an astronaut, a sharp-tongued senator, or author, a super-spy, a prominent feminist, or a show business celebrity. Such a source's reputation may be so awesome that beginning reporters feel intimidated. Here is somebody they never expected to meet and probably will never meet again, and they don't want to muff their only chance.

An editor may try to reduce the reporter's nervousness with the homely observation that the Great Man puts on his trousers like anyone else, one leg at a time. This may seem largely immaterial, but it isn't. Unless reporters overcome their awe and recognize that the source is only a human being, the interview is doomed from the start. Reporters must show neither fear nor fawning admiration. To establish and maintain control, they must be relaxed and mildly friendly, yet businesslike. They must approach the person of reputation much as they would approach any other, with the goal of getting a news story—hard news, not just a fan story.

Yet this is no ordinary source. This is a person who has survived hundreds of interviews and dealt with reporters for years. He or she knows all the stock questions, has all the stock answers, and may be slightly bored by it all. If you ask the obvious questions, you will get nothing the reader hasn't seen a dozen times before.

What to do? You can't very well ask him how he likes Durango or Dubuque or what he thinks of the potholes in Main Street. Nor, as Rex Reed has observed, should you ask whether he sleeps in the nude; it's doubtful whether anyone cares. You will have to prepare questions that deal with more important matters, yet in a way they never have been investigated before.

Both before and during the interview, you should keep in mind a few characteristics of the sophisticated source—male or female—that set him apart from those you deal with regularly:

1. His activities, past and present, are of national or international consequence. Library research will tell you what he has done; the question now is to find out what he plans to do next.
2. His opinions about current events in his field will carry weight. And because of his position or background, his attitudes toward the universal experiences of life are likely to be unique.
3. Like a veteran fighter, he knows how to protect himself in the clinches. He recognizes and accepts the risks involved in talking with a reporter and would rather be challenged by a tough question than bored by one that is inconsequential.
4. Unlike your everyday sources, he is not someone with whom you must build a lasting relationship. You do not have to "play ball" with him. You needn't hesitate to ask a question that may anger him—as long as it is a *fair* question and is timed late enough to avoid ending the interview prematurely.

Perhaps the best preparation for interviewing the elite source is to study the techniques of a master reporter. One of the most successful has been Oriana Fallaci, who started her career as a police reporter in Florence, Italy, when she was 17. Her interviews with heads of states are particularly instructive because they are published verbatim in question-and-answer form. In December of 1972, she directed a series of what she called "rather brutal" questions to President Nguyen Van Thieu of South Vietnam. These asked him to react to charges that he was an American puppet, that he was corrupt, and that he had bank accounts and property in several foreign nations. She also asked whether he had considered going into exile and whether he was afraid of being assassinated. In an interview with Israel's Prime Minister Golda Meir in 1973, Miss Fallaci asked the subject whether she was puritanical and inflexible and whether she liked herself. She also asked whether Mrs. Meir had ever killed anyone.

Another interviewer who takes the tough approach is Mike Wallace of CBS. Wallace is quick to call attention to contradictions and discrepancies and has been known to tell a source, "But that's not true." His penetrating technique has been criticized, however, by many who consider it abrasive. An equally incisive television interviewer worthy of study is William Buckley.

Gossip and Rumor

When you encounter a rumor of a newsworthy action or situation, the first step is to ask your sources how they know. Who told them? What evidence do they have to believe that this is true? Who else has heard about it? Who, supposedly, is behind this action? Trace the rumor backward until you find a person who actually has the information. Often you will find that your original information was badly distorted—sometimes twisted as much as 180 degrees.

Personal gossip—the eyebrow-raising whispers about the escapades of certain newsmakers—is a somewhat different matter. Normally it doesn't concern anything you could print, so you have no public justification for inquiring into its truth or falsity. Still, you may need to know so that you aren't caught unaware if the subject suddenly loses his or her job or spouse. Perhaps you can approach the matter indirectly by hinting about it to a trusted source; more often the better course is to say nothing and continue to listen. Remember that the person who passes along gossip may be guilty of slander. Remember also that gossip, even if true, is never more than *part* of the truth about the person or situation.

SAFETY IN NUMBERS

A newsroom proverb holds that a reporter is only as good as his or her sources. By "good," editors mean sources in the best position to know. In government, these usually are the people in charge or their clerks.

Quantity, however, often makes up for a deficiency in quality. If you have enough sources, somebody always will have the information—and somebody always will talk. Not only can few people keep a secret; few even want to do so. Often after a closed meeting of only three persons, at least two beat a path to the reporter to tell their differing versions of what happened. The reason may be political rivalry, personal or professional jealousy, or an idealistic urge to tell the truth. In any case, it is a phenomenon that the reporter can use. If the sheriff won't talk, somebody in his office or the district attorney's office probably will. If the FBI isn't telling, try the U.S. marshal's office. Always ask yourself who else might know. Ask also whether anything exists in writing.

Having a large number of sources also may help you pry information out of one key person who has been balking. All you may need to persuade a source is the mere mention of other persons with whom you have talked or intend to talk. Once the source realizes that you already have one version of the story or that you are likely to get information from any number of other people, he or she may be more willing to talk.

SUGGESTED ASSIGNMENTS

1. Imagine that you are the city editor of your local newspaper. The managing editor has allowed you five reporters to cover all the news in town, exclusive of sports and home and family or "women's" news. Organize your operation into a rewrite desk and four beats. List the rewrite duties and the major offices that each beat must cover.

2. Select two of the beats you have organized and list all the sources for each. Name the source, give his or her position and place of work, and list the person's office telephone number.

3. Clip a major local story from your newspaper and underline all the sources who are identified. For each source who is named, list one other person not named in the story who should be able to provide the same information.

4. Interview a newsmaker with a national or international reputation. This may be either a visitor or someone who lives in your city. Prepare for the interview by writing a three-paragraph biography of the subject and making a list at least 20 questions to be asked. Submit the biography and the list of questions to your instructor with the finished story.

CHAPTER ELEVEN / TEAMS WITHIN THE TEAM

A daily newspaper is different things to different people. To the reader, it is something to be skimmed for timely information and entertainment, kept a day for reference, then discarded. To a disciple of Marshall McLuhan, it is merely a point on the global grid of mass communications, linked to other points by wire services, syndicates, and intermittent telephone connections. To a printer, it is a factory product composed of paper, ink, and information. And to editors and advertising executives, it remains a daily miracle. It is a battle against time which they always win—or at least fight to a draw—despite the odds. The product of this battle contains more words than the average novel, yet the bulk of it may be produced in as short a time as two hours.

Behind this daily miracle are the efforts of an astronomical number of individuals. It is truly the product of teamwork, externally as well as internally. The newspaper's own labor force may range from fewer than 100 persons for the small daily to more than 1,000 for many metropolitan publications. But in addition, each newspaper has the indirect help of at least hundreds of thousands. And these are only the people who feed it information; the figure doesn't include those who provide equipment and supplies. The individual reporter and the local sources are only the starting point; each newspaper also has the potential help of all the reporters working for other newspapers and broadcast stations to which it is connected through wire services. Editors also have the help of those who work directly for the wire services and syndicates as well as those who sell their output to these middlemen. And the advertising department has the help of clipping services, national and local advertising agencies, their suppliers, and merchants who prepare their own copy.

It would be misleading, however, to overemphasize the newspaper's role as part of a global system. No newspaper uses more than a fraction of the information available to it each day, nor does it transmit more than a few of its best stories to newspapers elsewhere. Despite the importance of national and international connections, the daily newspaper in the United States remains primarily a local enterprise. It gathers most of its information, both news and advertising, from the immediate community. It screens, interprets, and reassembles this information, then returns it to the environment from whence it came.

THE PUBLISHER AND THE DIVISION CHIEFS

Because all newspapers perform the same functions, they are organized internally in much the same manner. The standard plan often is compared to a military organization, with each member of the team having a clearly defined area of responsibility and authority. But this analogy is incomplete and slightly misleading. Newspapers depend on creative talent, and most are far more democratic than any military organization. Dissent is welcomed and arguments are commonplace—until a decision is reached. At that point, militarylike discipline takes over, and the organization demands instant and almost mechanical obedience to its senior officers.

The standard organization consists of many small teams organized into four major departments that create and distribute the product. *Advertising* and *news-editorial* provide the informational input, *production* or *mechanical* puts it on paper, and *circulation* gets it to the reader. These assembly line departments are served—and to a large extent supervised—by the *business office*, which handles personnel and payroll, purchasing, billing, and general accounting. A medium-to-large newspaper also will have various housekeeping departments: building maintenance and janitorial service, vehicle maintenance, plant security, and perhaps a cafeteria staff.

The total operation is overseen by a publisher or general manager who is either the owner or the direct representative of the owners. In military terms, this person is the commanding general, concerned more with overall strategy than with tactical details. Although publishers may carry the double title of editor and publisher, they are seldom involved in the operational decisions of the news-editorial department. They are primarily business people, and they may give their news staffs free rein unless circulation suffers, spending gets out of hand, or the editors jeopardize the company by getting into a libel suit.

Publishers aim to increase the company's profits. They can achieve this by (1) increasing the sale of advertising, which accounts for 70 to 90 percent of the income; (2) increasing circulation to a point where they are justified in raising the rates they charge for advertising; or (3) reducing costs. Most publishers constantly work in all three directions.

After establishing broad guidelines, publishers leave most of the day-to-day operating decisions to division commanders: the advertising director, the managing editor, the mechanical superintendent, and the circulation manager. The newspaper's success is determined largely by the competency of these executives and their ability to function harmoniously as a team. Although the common goal is a strong newspaper, each department head is likely to have personal ideas about how it best can be achieved. Editors and advertising executives traditionally are at odds over (1) the amount of space that can be devoted profitably to news, and (2) the distinction between legitimate publicity and nonnews puffery. They are united, however, on one point: both would like later deadlines than production and circulation executives consider practical. And in one respect, the heads of all four operating departments may think alike: they are all likely to consider themselves the worst abused victims of a cost-conscious business office.

If morale is high, all employees in the organization's ranks may behave as if theirs is the only department responsible for the newspaper's success. But all are important and equally indispensable. Without advertising, nobody in the plant would be paid. Without production, there would be no product. And without circulation, nobody would see it.

Each of the four major departments has several subdivisions. Advertising is divided into display and classified, and each of these is further subdivided. Production is divided generally into composing and the pressroom, and circulation is similarly subdivided. For the beginning reporter, however, the most important subdivisions are those in the news-editorial department.

THE MANAGING EDITOR AND THE NEWSROOM LIEUTENANTS

The head of the news-editorial department may be called editor, executive editor, or managing editor. The last title is the most common and usually the most descriptive; in all but the smallest operations, the person filling this position is as much a manager as an editor.

Managing editors direct staffs that may range from fewer than a dozen to several hundred persons. And the way they function depends on the amount of help they have. In a small town, the managing editor may have only three or four assistants: a sports editor, a society editor, and one reporter-photographer. The shirtsleeve editor who heads such a small staff must work night and day—laying out pages, editing and heading copy, and writing editorials. In metropolitan situations, by contrast, managing editors may edit nothing. Indeed, the only stories they are likely to see before they reach print are those that raise a basic policy issue or the danger of a libel suit. And instead of composing their own editorials, they have special staffs to write them.

On most news staffs ranging upward from 20 or 30 persons, managing editors are primarily supervisors, mediators, and arbiters. They hire and fire within their department, initiate or approve special projects, keep peace among employees, negotiate problems that involve other departments, and report more or less regularly to the publisher. They also help represent the newspaper to the rest of the profession and to the general public.

The arbitrary, dictatorial metropolitan editor of folklore is a rarity. Most news-editorial decisions are group products, rather than the work of one person. And most of them are developed when the managing editor assembles the key lieutenants—news editor, city editor, state editor, and perhaps others—for the daily story conference. The subeditors describe their more important or more interesting stories, those in hand and those that are expected to develop, and tell how they think each should be treated. Several questions are implicit: Is the story worth front page? Is it exclusively ours? Do we have photos or drawings to go with it? Should it be held for further investigation? Does it require or suggest cooperation between subdivisions? How does it compare with stories being offered by other editors?

Consensus is the goal of the story conference. The editors want to design a package that grades the news according to the best judgment of all. Often the last subeditor to give his opinion is the news editor, whose job is to determine placement and emphasis and to design the front page. When all have spoken, the managing editor either approves the day's general plan or calls for changes. In most organizations, decisions reached at the story conference still are considered only tentative, subject to on-the-spot revision by the news editor if something unexpected develops.

Sometimes the editor of the editorial page joins the story conference, although most likely only as a passive listener with no goal other than to keep informed. The content of the editorial page usually is determined at a separate conference which may include the publisher as well as the managing editor. The opinion editor, therefore, has nothing to be settled at the story conference and may skip it entirely.

Several other subeditors normally are left out of the daily story conference because they function more or less independently of the general news operation. These include the sports editor, home and family or society editor, and the editor of the Sunday magazine. Each may confer with the managing editor only when it seems necessary.

The City Room

Most of the news is written and edited in a large, desk-filled area known as the newsroom or city room. The latter term may be the more common, but it is slightly misleading. The news handled here includes state, national, and international, as well as that generated by the city reporting staff. Indeed, the only special staffs that may be segregated from the city room are those assigned to sports, home and family or "women's" news, the Sunday magazine, and the editorial page.

In the traditional city room, the executives with the most authority are the news editor and the city editor. Both are shirtsleeve editors who normally must be on the job every minute, dealing with news as it develops. Separately or together, they are the operational bosses of the city room, subject only to the supervision of the managing editor. Sometimes the news editor is considered senior to the city editor; more often they rank approximately as equals in the newsroom hierarchy, each senior to the other subeditors, but neither with any clear authority over the other. One reason for this division of authority is the contrasting nature of their jobs. The news editor coordinates the internal operations of the city room, dealing with finished copy and directing the work of copy editors and printers. The news editor usually has no direct control over the external newsgathering. The city editor, by contrast, faces outward into the community, dealing with events that are not yet stories and directing the work of the city reporters.

EDITORS WHO FACE OUTWARD

The city editor is the most powerful of all subeditors who primarily watch the outside world and make certain that everything of consequence is covered. The two other outward-facing editors found in every city room are the state editor and the wire editor. Here is how they operate:

City Editor—Most of the newspaper's general reporting staff—beat people, special writers, and general assignment and rewrite personnel —are under the direct supervision of the city editor. This may constitute more than one-fourth of the entire news-editorial crew. The number may range from two or three reporters on the small daily to more than 100 on the larger metropolitan staffs. The more common range is from a half dozen to perhaps 50.

The city editor's job is to make certain that all regular beats, all

continuing stories, and all unexpected developments are covered completely and accurately. This requires careful record-keeping, frequent
contact with each reporter, a well-developed news sense, and the
ability to improvise under pressure. It also requires the city editor to
monitor the competition night and day. At the office, the city editor
or an assistant usually listens to a radio that monitors all emergency
frequencies. The city editor is the newspaper's No. 1 reporter, more
concerned about getting the story than about what happens after it is
written. Although the city editor or an assistant may read each story
that the city staff produces, any editing may be restricted to matters
of accuracy, policy, libel, and taste. The city editor in the larger
operations seldom is concerned with the finer points of style or grammar, nor does he or she often write headlines.

The city desk is the newsroom's busiest command post, much like
the communications center of a police department. Reporters are
constantly stopping at the desk to ask instructions, report their progress, or check out of the office. The telephones seldom stop ring-
ing. And in a metropolitan newsroom, the city editor frequently
keeps in touch with various staff members by radio, teletype, or facsimile. He or she may need two or more assistants on duty at all
times merely to keep records and help manage the traffic.

The city desk keeps two basic records: (1) the daily assignment
sheet, which lists the reporters, their beats or general areas of responsibility, and the more important stories expected of them that day;
and (2) the log, a list of completed stories and photographs ready for
the news editor's consideration. As each story is completed, it is
crossed off the assignment sheet and entered on the log. Periodically
the news editor may call for the log to see what is available, or he
may keep a separate log for personal use.

In addition to these two forms, each of which may be only a
single sheet, the city editor also uses a futures file. At the minimum,
this consists of 44 file folders: 31 representing the days of the month,
12 representing the months, and at least one for future years. The
primary contents of this file are clippings that relate to future events.
Each local story of consequence—especially those that include announcements of future events—is clipped, dated, and put into the
appropriate folder. Then, at the beginning of each shift, the city
editor lifts out that day's folder and makes a list of events to be covered and continuing stories that require further investigation. At the
end of the month, next month's futures are transferred into the daily
file. And, near the end of the year, next year's futures are transferred
into the monthly file.

The value of the futures file is that it serves as a safeguard against
overlooking any story about which the newspaper has published advance notice. It is no help at all, of course, in covering the unex-

pected, and the danger is that the city editor may be tempted to rely too heavily on it. Bookkeeping may seem easier than imaginative, aggressive newsgathering.

The city editor's domain is defined by local interest, rather than geographical limits. Typically, statehouse and Washington bureaus report to the city desk. And most of the special assignments that call for extended travel originate at the city desk, if not at the managing editor's office. Any major story anywhere, if it contains sufficient local interest, may be considered fair game for the city reporting staff.

State Editor—The state editor functions much like the city editor, except that he has far less control over his staff. Often they are merely voices on the telephone or by-lines on stories that arrive by mail.

The state editor is responsible for covering the outlying communities in the newspaper's circulation area. Some state editors control a network of several bureaus manned by one or two full-time professionals who report to the home office by teletype or facsimile. Others, usually in the smaller operations, have few if any trained reporters; they are limited to "stringers" (correspondents paid according to the length and placement of their stories), and these often are small-town housewives who send most of their copy to the office by mail.

In many of the smaller operations, state editors are primarily rewrite people, spending most of the time on the telephone. They may send all their copy through the universal desk, editing none of it themselves. In larger operations, a state editor may have a staff of rewrite people. And the state editor may edit and head all state copy, even to the point of laying out one or more state pages. Regardless of the size of the operation, the state editor gets out of the office occasionally to cover a few stories in person. He or she also may have to travel to recruit new correspondents or solve problems that develop in outlying bureaus.

State editors keep a log and a list of developing stories much like the records kept by city editors. They also must keep a futures file and be prepared to pursue a story by telephone if some member of the far-flung staff falters. In addition, they have one bookkeeping chore that is heavier at the state desk than at any other: they must measure the copy the stringers produce to make certain those people are paid the right amount.

Wire Editor—Unlike the other outward-facing editors, wire editors have no staffs and therefore no power to make assignments. Their job is to read the copy that arrives by teletype from the Associated Press, United Press International, and any supplemental services, and to make certain that the newspaper is covered in those areas that lie beyond the normal range of the city and state editors. In the smaller newsrooms, much of the copy they handle will be from other cities in the same state. In the larger organizations, wire editors may virtually ignore any state copy because they can be fairly certain that other editors already have the story. If the newspaper dominates its state, the wire editor may be concerned only with national and international news.

Metropolitan wire editors see more stories—and use fewer of them—than anyone else in the city room. Every five or ten minutes, the wire editor may receive as much copy as the city editor sees in an entire shift. And if the newspaper has a strong state desk and its own Washington bureau, it may use less than 2 percent of the copy it receives from wire services. The wire editor's job is to select the *best* 2 percent, which is then offered to the news editor for publication. This means wire editors must understand national and international affairs. They also must read fast enough to keep up to the minute on major developments, and they must be particularly alert to stories that should be shown to the city editor, sports editor, or state editor for possible development of a local angle.

The metropolitan wire editor and his small-town counterpart function in vastly different ways. In a large operation, the wire editor must read so much copy from so many wires that he or she can do little more than become familiar with the general content of each story and the relative merits of the differing versions offered by competing services. Headline writing and word-by-word editing must be delegated to others. In smaller cities, where the newspaper may subscribe to only one service, wire editors often must lay out pages, write headlines, and edit their own copy. They also may be responsible for much of the syndicated copy that arrives by mail. Small-town wire editors usually double as news editor and are responsible for the makeup of all general news pages. In such a situation, they work closely with printers and face inward as much as outward.

Although wire editors have no power to make assignments, sometimes they can make their influence felt by telephoning special requests, suggestions, and inquiries to the nearest wire service bureau. Whether the requests are honored depends largely on whether they happen to be in the interests of the other clients or member newspapers.

EDITORS WHO FACE INWARD

The largest number of subeditors in the traditional metropolitan city room have nothing to do with gathering the news. Indeed, their job begins where the reporter's ends. They take the copy produced by the city, state, and wire desks; assign it a position in the paper; edit it word by word, and write headlines for it. They deal mostly with printers and with each other, rather than with reporters. Here's how they operate:

News Editor—In the traditional city room, news editors see every major story that comes from the city, state, and wire desks. They evaluate each story, determine the amount of space it will require, then assign it a headline size and a place on a page dummy. Because of the volume of work, the news editor may concentrate on the front page and have two or more assistants who dummy inside pages. Another assistant may be posted full time in the composing room to make certain that headlines and stories fit and that the printers follow the news desk's instructions. If news editors lack assistants, then they must divide their time between the city room and composing.

News editors are perhaps the most deadline-conscious of all editors. Theirs is the responsibility of seeing that copy flows smoothly to the composing room, that each page is closed on schedule, and that everything is ready to go at presstime. Regardless of what is happening at the city desk or wire desk, the news editor must produce a paper on schedule. And often that schedule requires a completed page dummy every five minutes.

Little if any actual editing is done at most metropolitan news desks. News editors will, if they happen to notice it, correct an error, but detailed editing is not their primary concern. The news editor's desk is a planning station, a central point where the general news package is brought together. Most of the detailed editing is done at the universal copydesk.

Slot and Rim: the Old Universal Desk—The horseshoe-shaped universal desk has vanished from many city rooms, but the nomenclature that evolved from its physical appearance lingers on. The head of the desk—the supervisor—is called the *slotman* because he or she sits (or once sat) on the inside of the horseshoe. The assistants, more properly called copy editors, became known as *rimmen* because they sat outside the horseshoe. Today they may sit at several small desks still arranged in horseshoe fashion or all may sit at one long table. In the traditional method of handling copy, which is fast disappearing, rim editors write all the headlines and edit every story that goes into the general news columns. As stories arrive at the universal desk, the slotman deals them out across the rim, equalizing the workload and trying to assign each story to the editor best qualified to handle it. When the rim editor finishes, the headline and edited story go back to the slotman. If he is satisfied, it is sent to the composing room; if the headline fails to measure up, the slotman tosses head and copy back across the rim with the order to try again. The clarity and tone of the newspaper's headlines depend largely on the slotman's standards and his determination to enforce them.

The old-fashioned copy editor's only physical tools were a supply of soft-lead pencils, a pastepot, and scissors. Much of this has changed. Instead of handling stories on paper, the modern copy editor may see them as images on a cathode ray tube. And instead of using a pencil, he or she may use a keyboard to make corrections and write headlines.

In many city rooms, the universal desk has been eliminated. Instead of routing all copy through the news editor and one central copydesk, the current trend is to use three or more smaller copydesks: one for city, one for state, and one for wire news. This places the copy editor closer to the people who write the news and allows him or her to develop a better understanding of a specific class of copy. The result has been to reduce errors committed by editors who didn't understand what they were handling.

Departmental Editors

As many as half of the news-editorial staffers may function independently of the news editor's centralized operation. Most of these are assigned to sports, home and family or "women's" news, the Sunday magazine, and the editorial page. Another independent is the financial editor, who handles market news. The farm editor also may be independent, and some newspapers have other independent departmental editors, depending on special needs. A typical example is the petroleum editor, a fixture on metropolitan staffs in Oklahoma and Texas.

Specialized departments vary greatly in both size and methods of operation, but they have at least four things in common: (1) each has a specific space reserved for its particular use, (2) each collects its own news without help from the general reporting staff, (3) each dummies its own pages and sends its copy directly to composing without routing it through the news editor, and (4) all members of departmental staffs must edit as well as write. Here is how some of the departments operate.

SPORTS

The sports department usually occupies a portion of the city room or a space nearby. The reason is that stories important to sports may move on the general news wires, or a story developed by the sports staff—for example, a betting scandal—may merit front-page consideration. It is desirable, therefore, to place sports staffers where they can consult with the news editor at any moment.

In the smallest cities, sports is a one-man department—and that one man sometimes must call on other staff members for help. He can hardly cover the Big Game, take all the phone calls reporting other games, edit and head wire copy, and dummy one or two pages without assistance. In such a small operation, the entire news staff may have to write some sports stories, and the wire editor may have to dummy the pages.

In larger operations, the sports department functions like a miniature city room, with its own news editor, rimmen, stringers, and rewrite staff. Unlike the news editor and the people at the universal desk, however, sports staffers tend to think of themselves primarily as reporters. And most metropolitan sports editors are careful to make sure that desk assignments are rotated frequently and no sports writer is kept inside for more than a few weeks.

One peculiarity of sports departments is their reliance on part-time help, especially on weekends when activity is heavy. The typical part-time sports writer is a high school or college student whose duties are limited to taking incoming calls and writing only the most routine stories.

HOME AND FAMILY OR "WOMEN'S" NEWS

What once was called society copy has undergone such a change in the last two decades that one can hardly define it today. The once-common label of "women's" news is in disrepute and often no longer used. In some newspapers, the page or section is called "People"; in others, "Living Today." Indeed, there are perhaps a dozen or more common names for the section. The label may cover anything of interest to either sex: politics, the arts, a sports event, population control, or poverty.

A sampling of the content of one "People" section shows two stories about convicts (men), one about college fraternities (not sororities), one about the life of a mugger (male), and one on objectionable telephone calls (made by men). The only safe definition of news for this section is that it is whatever the editor says it is. And the section editor—who sometimes is a man—seldom turns down an attention-getting story, no matter what the subject.

The package still contains stories of engagements, weddings, club activities, and fashions, all apparently inescapable holdovers from the old-fashioned society page. It also is likely to contain recipes and advice to homemakers and the lovelorn. But the trend is to handle these staples as briefly as possible, thereby gaining space for a broad range of feature material that will appeal as much to men as to women.

The typical home and family or "women's" section of a middle-sized daily is almost entirely a local product. It may use no wire copy, and usually has a minimum of syndicated material. Unlike sports and general news, it contains few urgent or fast-breaking stories. Indeed, many of its stories are written several days in advance of publication, and the deadline for the Sunday section may be as early as Wednesday. Because of the broadened scope of news for this section and the emphasis on semitimeless feature copy, these departments have attracted some of the best magazine-style writers in the newspaper business.

Except in the small towns where country correspondence remains a fixture, the editor for this section seldom uses stringers. Nor is there likely to be part-time help. The department, which is usually about the same size as the full-time sports staff, normally is self-sufficient.

THE SUNDAY MAGAZINE

Although newspeople commonly talk of *the* Sunday magazine, many metropolitan newspapers publish more than one—and not necessarily all of them are distributed on Sunday. These are produced in a variety of ways. One staff may edit two or more magazines, or each supplement may have a separate staff. The staff may be large enough to produce most of the magazine's content, or it may rely heavily on free-lance contributions and syndicated material. The newspaper may print its own supplement, or it may send the copy to a commercial printer. Generally, however, all locally produced Sunday supplements have a few things in common: (1) the copy deadline ranges from several days to as much as a month before the distribution date, (2) the percentage of photography is much larger than you find on general news pages, and (3) at least some free-lance contributions are welcome.

A few Sunday supplements are almost entirely staff produced. Such a staff may include several columnists and feature writers and one or more full-time photographers, some of whom travel extensively. More often, however, the magazine is produced by only two or three editors who draw from many sources: amateur photographers, free-lance writers, wire services and syndicates, and members of the general reporting staff. To hold down costs, it is common practice to assign book reviews to anyone who will accept a copy of the book—which the newspaper receives free—as payment.

Because of the long lead time between deadline and publication, the Sunday magazine is restricted to stories of a semitimeless nature. It is an attractive department for the writer-editor-photographer who is more interested in feature copy than hard news.

THE EDITORIAL PAGE

Newspapers not only separate news from opinion, but they separate the staffs as well. Often the editorial page staff is not even on the same floor as the city room and sports. More likely the opinion staff occupies a suite of semiprivate offices in an out-of-the-way part of the building where there are few distractions.

The people who write a metropolitan newspaper's anonymous editorials often perform double duty as by-lined columnists. Unlike the average reporter, who seldom writes fewer than a half dozen stories a day, the editorial writer-columnist is under no pressure to produce copy in volume. The quota may be only one editorial a day, with the emphasis on thorough research, depth of thought, and persuasive presentation. Each word is carefully considered, and a lead editorial may go through several drafts before it is approved by the editor of the editorial page. Even then, it may be amended by the managing editor or the publisher.

A strong opinion staff is composed of writers who already have proved their ability as reporters of government and economic affairs. They tend to be older and better educated than city room reporters, and many have advanced degrees in history, political science, or economics. Many continue to gather facts by doing their own legwork; others rely largely on library research and the reporting of the city staff.

The editor of the editorial page often is merely the senior writer and presiding officer at the daily editorial conference. He often delegates the detailed deskwork—heading syndicated columns and making up the page—to a junior member of the staff. Another common practice is to rotate the makeup responsibility much as the sports department does.

Variations of Reporting Jobs

In Chapter 4, all reporters were classified broadly as beat, general assignment, or rewrite personnel. Although this system of general classification still applies, it is inadequate to describe the variety of talents, tasks, and methods of operation that the beginner soon will discover.

SPECIAL WRITERS

Practicing journalists may find it difficult to draw the line between a special writer and a beat reporter. Yet there is a subtle difference in the way a special writer functions and often a considerable difference in background or education. The specialist is an authority in a broad subject field, such as agriculture, aviation, music, medicine, the physical sciences, drama, the fine arts, education, or business. This person may have an advanced degree or simply have developed specialized knowledge on a beat. Many specialists never planned to be writers; they may have been high school teachers, government employees, or even actors before turning to journalism.

Specialists may or may not have a beat. They undoubtedly have regular sources of information, but they may have no specific list of offices at which to call each day. A specialist's success depends on keeping abreast of developments in a particular field no matter where they occur. Such writers may spend much of their working time poring over trade, technical, and scholarly journals. If they are recognized authorities, they may be relatively independent of the city editor's control; they are expected to know enough about their subjects to cover them without guidance. Although specialists are primarily writers, they may be called editors—for example, farm editor, aviation editor, education editor, etc.

Specialists often travel considerably, attending national conferences and conventions, space launchings, or major concerts or play openings. Unlike generalists, who seldom know what tomorrow will bring, specialists usually can plan their travels far in advance.

STAFF CORRESPONDENTS

The staff correspondent may be either a specialist who covers some portion of the government at the statehouse or in Washington or a generalist who covers a small community or a large geographical area for a regional newspaper. A correspondent may be the Cheyenne bureau of the *Denver Post* or "our man in the Middle East," who lives in Beirut and covers several nations. Whatever correspondents are, they are seldom seen in the city room; they do all their writing somewhere else and transmit their stories to the home office by teletype, telephone, mail, or facsimile.

Correspondents may work for the city editor, the state editor, the foreign editor (if the newspaper has one), or the newspaper as a whole. They may even serve a group of newspapers all owned by the same company. Like the special writers in the home office, correspondents have a large measure of independence. They are expected to cover their area with a minimum of guidance, and several days may pass without specific instructions from the editor. Sometimes the instructions they do get are extremely terse; the lone Washington correspondent for two Southwestern newspapers once was told only to "go to Atlantic City and cover the Miss America pageant."

Usually the correspondent's beat is a specified geographic area, although this often coincides with a special subject field, as in Washington or a state capital. The correspondent is by necessity a generalist who can get a variety of stories under a variety of conditions, but he or she also may have a specialist's education.

Some correspondents are lone operators whose skills include photography and the ability to punch a story by teletype. Others are primarily news executives with large staffs.

STRINGERS

Stringers are correspondents who are not full-time members of the staff. They are paid according to the amount of published copy they produce, rather than the number of hours they work. Typical pay scales in the early 1970s ranged from 15 to 30 cents a column-inch, often with bonuses for front-page copy.

A stringer may be a generalist who works for the state editor, a specialist who reports only to sports, or a rural housewife who serves only the "women's" editor of a small daily. Typical stringers include college students, high school teachers and coaches, courthouse employees, and reporters who are employed full time by newspapers smaller than the one they string for. Your own managing editor may be a stringer for a wire service or a national magazine.

FREE-LANCERS

Unlike stringers, who have written or oral agreements with the organization they supply, free-lance writers or photographers submit most material on speculation. Often they are strangers to the editors, perhaps only names on feature stories that arrived by mail. Or perhaps a free-lancer is a tourist who happens to have photographs of a violent accident. Sometimes he or she is a voice on the telephone, a journalist working elsewhere who has run across a spot story of interest to this particular newspaper and knows how to make $10 to $50 by placing a collect call to the city editor.

Many free-lance writers and photographers point their work toward the Sunday magazine section, where payment usually is higher than in the general news columns. A few proven feature writers attain near-correspondent status; some even have contracts to supply a specified number of features each month.

THE INVESTIGATIVE TEAM

Apparently the way to win a Pulitzer Prize is to get assigned to an investigative team. That's how four of journalism's top reporting awards were won in 1973. The winners were the *Washington Post,* for a continuing series of revelations that grew out of the burglary of Democratic national headquarters; the *Chicago Tribune,* for an investigation of massive vote fraud; the Knight Newspapers' Washington bureau, for reporting Senator Thomas Eagleton's medical history; and the *Sun Newspapers of Omaha,* for exposing Boys Town's unused financial resources of more than $200 million. Most of these stories required months to develop. And in each case the investigation was conducted by a team of two to five persons.

The trend toward formal investigative task forces first surfaced in the mid-1960s. As the idea spread, some metropolitan newspapers made long-term investigations a regular practice, keeping two or more teams busy simultaneously. This often created a city room atmosphere of cloak-and-dagger secrecy. Reporters disappeared and went underground. Tapes, signed statements, and microfilms of documentary evidence were kept in special safes. Members of the investigative teams became the new elite. And their fellow reporters often had no idea what they were up to.

Two things were new about this: (1) the creation of *ad hoc* task forces assigned to a single project, and (2) the growing acceptance of the notion that more than a few stories were worth months of effort. Investigation itself was nothing new; in a sense, the best stories always have been "investigative." Nor was teamwork a revolutionary concept; the entire news staff always has functioned as a team, especially on major stories. Editors merely formalized something they had been doing intermittently—and often haphazardly—for years.

As investigative reporting has grown, so has the demand for reporters with special skills. Editors, like the FBI, have been especially interested in recruiting people with a knowledge of law or accounting. Some of the best investigation, however, has been conducted by people with no more training than that of any beginning police reporter.

Shared Service Departments

News-editorial normally shares two or three special departments with advertising. These, which may or may not be under the administrative jurisdiction of the managing editor, are photography, the art department (if one exists), and the library.

PHOTOGRAPHY

On small newspapers, reporters may be expected to shoot, develop, and print their own photographs. At the first step up the ladder, the newspaper employs a darkroom technician to do the developing and printing. The next step is to divorce reporting from photography and hire two or three full-time cameramen.

A metropolitan photo staff usually consists of at least eight to ten persons and often many more. When the staff is this large, the photo chief becomes an administrator whose job is to make sure photographers are in the right place at the right time, fulfilling the assignments received from the editors and the advertising department. Sometimes this is made easier by assigning one or more photographers full-time to the advertising department and one or two more to the Sunday magazine. The staff also may include one or more photographers who shoot nothing but color.

Despite the tendency to relieve reporters of photography on the larger newspapers, camera skills remain almost a necessity for every journalist. No cost-conscious editor will send both a reporter and a photographer on a distant assignment if one person can do the job. Photography, therefore, is especially important to the reporter who hopes to be a foreign correspondent.

THE ART DEPARTMENT

The newspaper that must operate without staff artists—and this includes most of the approximately 1,750 daily newspapers in the United States—often is severely handicapped. The editor may not realize it, however, until he is forced to retouch a photograph himself or visit the advertising department to find somebody capable of drawing a map. This shortcoming of American newspapers is in sharp contrast to the situation in Australia, where hand-drawn art is considered an important editorial ingredient.

For the art departments that exist in metropolitan American newspapers, the primary routine task is that of retouching photographs to provide better tone separation. Artists also may regularly help design special pages, such as the cover of the Sunday magazine. But they can do much more for the editor who recognizes their potential. They can provide quick maps to pinpoint the location of a disaster or portray the scene of a crime, fashion sketches for the "women's" pages, cartoons to illustrate offbeat human interest stories, and graphs to explain government budgets and economic stories. They also can provide visual coverage of a trial from which photographers are barred.

Because editors tend to describe themselves as "word people" or "photo people," they sometimes overlook the possibility of illustrating a story with drawings. The beginner who recognizes art potential in a story would be well advised to mention it to the editor. An illustration might add enough clarity or impact to warrant front-page position.

THE LIBRARY

A newspaper library sometimes is called the morgue because of all the "dead" information it contains. But it can be a lively source of facts when you need them fast.

The three basic components of every morgue are (1) the clipping files, (2) bound volumes of the newspaper's back issues, and (3) reference works. In the small daily, these may be scattered throughout the plant. The more recent bound volumes may be kept in the advertising department, with older issues stored in the basement. The clipping files probably occupy a corner of the newsroom, and most of the reference works probably are kept on a single shelf in the managing editor's private office. The only encyclopedia may be in the publisher's office. Large newspapers, of course, maintain far more extensive libraries, which often occupy an entire floor. Staffed by professional librarians, they contain a wide variety of reference works, including almanacs, atlases, encyclopedias, medical and scientific dictionaries, foreign language dictionaries, state statutes, city charters, regional histories, specialized directories, and such periodicals as *The Congressional Record* and *Facts on File*. A newspaper may even have its own law library. And in addition to preserving its own back issues on microfilm, a medium-sized newspaper may subscribe to microfilm files of *The New York Times.*

Even the smallest morgues usually contain *Who's Who in America,* a state directory of public officials, and a sound regional or state history. And the clipping files offer a wealth of biographical data on local newsmakers, often accompanied by "mug shots." The clipping files also can supply election statistics; fiscal background on government; records of major crimes, trials, disasters, or anything that made big headlines in the past. It is common practice to clip every local story of consequence, and no reporter should tackle an unfamiliar subject without first checking the clip files.

Because newspaper libraries differ so greatly, as a beginning professional you should become familiar immediately with your own morgue's resources—and its filing system. In the smaller organizations, you will have to find your way through the files without help.

LEARNING FROM THE TEAM

Beginners who go to work for a metropolitan newspaper often are given a stylebook and a tour of the plant, then placed under the supervision of the city desk. There they learn to open the mail, answer the telephones, keep the city editor informed about their activities, and check regularly to see if there is more work. If they are restricted to rewrite chores, they may begin to feel that the world is indeed a small place.

Reporters who begin their careers with a small daily are in some ways more fortunate, although they may get less pay. In the small newsroom, everyone must be able to do everything, and beginners quickly get a variety of experience. They may need to be as much photographer or editor as reporter, and they almost certainly will have to help the sports editor. In addition, reporters on a small daily are in an excellent position to see the entire team—what there is of it —in operation. They see the managing editor writing editorials and worrying over the budget, and they overhear the managing editor's arguments with the advertising manager. They see the wire editor laying out the front page, heading all the wire copy, and handling the markets. They observe the city editor functioning as his own star reporter, and they overhear the "women's" page editor's attempts to mollify the bride's mother. Nothing is hidden, because it all happens in one room.

After six months on the job, the small-town reporter may be far more versatile than his metropolitan counterpart. Big-city reporters, however, usually must meet higher standards of literacy. And to some extent they can overcome their lack of varied experience by observing other members of the team, adopting their methods, and using their resources. They can build their own futures files, explore the library, and above all learn who does what in news-editorial. Then, when they need help, they will know where to go to get it.

SUGGESTED ASSIGNMENTS

1. Interview one of the top executives—publisher, business manager, mechanical superintendent, or managing editor—of your local newspaper and write a feature story about technological changes the newspaper has adopted in the last five years. How have these changes affected manpower in the production department? How have they affected deadlines? How have they affected editing and the flow of copy? Search for a news peg; what further changes are being considered?

2. Write a personality profile of a veteran reporter. Does he consider himself a specialist? Or is he a generalist? What is his educational background? What jobs has he held? Has he won any awards? Ask him to describe his most interesting assignments.

3. Interview a wire service executive and describe the organization's state or regional operation. How many newspaper members or clients does the system serve in the state? How many radio and television stations? How has the service changed recently? What further changes are planned?

4. Investigate the local market for free-lance sales and write a "how-to-sell-it" feature. Include prospects for stringers. Check with the sports, state, city, and Sunday editors. Don't forget to ask rates for straight news, features, and photos.

CHAPTER TWELVE / A QUALIFIED FREEDOM

In 1644, John Milton's *Areopagitica* stated the case for a free press in words that have become basic philosophy in the English-speaking world:

> And though all the windes of doctrin were let loose to play upon the earth, so Truth be in the field, we do injuriously by licensing and prohibiting to misdoubt her strength. Let her and Falsehood grapple; who ever knew Truth put to the wors, in a free and open encounter

Milton, writing his polemic as a letter to Parliament, argued that no man is qualified to determine truth or falsity for all of society. It was this belief that inspired the First Amendment to the U.S. Constitution:

> Congress shall make no law respecting an establishment of religion, or prohibiting the free exercise thereof; or abridging the freedom of speech, or of the press; or the right of the people peaceably to assemble, and to petition the government for a redress of grievances.

Some people believe wrongly that this gives the press a freedom that amounts to license. But no historical evidence indicates that the founding fathers meant any such thing. The traditional interpretation is that they meant only no prior restraint—no licensing or censorship. Any Americans, trained journalists or not, may publish whatever they please. No authority can stop them. But this in no way prevents the courts from holding them accountable after the fact. They still must answer to the laws of libel, privacy, contempt, and copyright. They still must avoid advertising a lottery if they want to retain their second-class mailing privilege or broadcast license. And they are almost certain to go to jail if they incite a riot or print counterfeit money.

Freedom of the press, therefore, is a *qualified* freedom. In many sensitive matters, ranging from personal reputation to national security, it must be viewed as the freedom to publish at your own risk.

MAJOR LEGAL RESTRAINTS

The risks of publishing are shared by everyone in the organization. No matter what your job may be, you are legally responsible for the content of every story you handle. Conceivably you could be sued, fined, or sent to jail if a story violates the law. In practice, most civil actions name only the publisher, but you still are obliged to protect the publisher if you want to keep your job. In your own interest, you must know as much as possible about libel, contempt, and the right of privacy so that you can quickly alert an editor if you see a violation.

Libel

Libel is published defamation. It is equivalent to slander (oral defamation), but the penalty is potentially much greater because of the possibility of mass circulation and therefore more widespread damage. A defamatory statement is any which tends to hold a person up to public ridicule and contempt, blacken his reputation, cause him to be shunned or avoided, damage his credit, or injure him in his business or profession.

Three elements are necessary to make a statement libelous: defamation, identification, and publication. None is quite as simple as it sounds.

Defamation requires both "a good name" and injury. A person without a good name theoretically could not be libeled, but few lawyers are likely to base a defense on such a delicate point; the law presumes a good name unless the person is an habitual criminal. As for injury, any statement that imputes a crime, low moral character, a venereal disease, or less than normal mental capacity is automatically presumed injurious. It is libelous, therefore, to write that a person is a moron, a lecher, a deadbeat, or a drunk. And it is especially libelous to write or imply that someone is guilty of a felony.

Identification doesn't mean that the injured person's name must appear in the story. If the wording is such that an acquaintance might recognize the plaintiff, he has been identified sufficiently in the eyes of the law. This is one reason why reporters sometimes fictionalize names and other details when they write about retarded persons, alcoholics, drug abusers, and unwed teenage mothers.

Publication can be by words, pictures, or any other signs. It is not restricted to printing; defamation broadcast by radio or television is as libelous as if it had appeared in a newspaper or magazine. Nor is mass circulation required; courts have held that a statement is "published" if only one person other than the writer and the injured person sees it.

CRIMINAL AND CIVIL LIBEL

Libel can be either a crime (an offense against society) or a civil tort (an offense against an individual). The latter is far more common. Generally, criminal libel is defined as any which "tends to incite a breach of the peace." A brave and angry prosecutor might construe this as meaning almost any defamatory statement. As a practical matter, however, most criminal libel actions are restricted to the defamation of dead persons. The reason for this is that a civil suit can't be brought in the name of a dead person, so a criminal action is the only way the family can hope to clear its name. Where does "tends to incite a breach of the peace" come in? The legal explanation is that the libeled person's relatives may have been angered sufficiently to want to horsewhip the editor.

Criminal libel is rare for two reasons. First, the family has nothing material to gain. If the libeler is convicted, he goes to jail or pays the court a fine; the family gets nothing but the satisfaction of seeing him punished. Second, the action must be brought by a public prosecutor, who normally is elected, and few elected officials want to antagonize the press. Unless the family can convince the prosecutor that the libel is blatantly malicious, the chances are that nothing will be done.

In civil libel, by contrast, the plaintiff has a great deal to gain in the form of cash damages. These often can be high enough to put a publishing house out of business. Further, the mere cost of defending a libel suit has a chilling effect. Even though some publishers might be reasonably sure of winning, they usually will try to avoid going to court.

Under the law, anyone connected with a libelous story may be sued. This includes the reporter, the editor on duty (whether or not that person saw the story), the typesetter, and the proofreader. Most suits, of course, name only the person with the money: the publisher. The reporter seldom loses anything but a job and the chances of getting another.

If a plaintiff wins a libel suit, he or she automatically is entitled to *compensatory* damages. These may be any amount from a dollar to several thousand—whatever the judge or jury considers reasonable. If the plaintiff can prove actual monetary loss as a result of the libel, as professionals and businesspeople often can, he or she also may qualify for *special* damages. And if malice is involved, the court may award *punitive* or *exemplary* damages. These often amount to hundreds of thousands of dollars, so publishers take special pains to show lack of malice. One tactic is to publish a retraction, which is not a complete defense but serves to mitigate against punitive damages. Another way of showing good faith is to fire the reporter who was responsible.

THE THREE CLASSIC DEFENSES

News reporters commit libel every day, yet they are seldom brought to court. This is because the publisher has a legal privilege to print many defamatory statements and a solid defense for many others. In short, a statement can be libelous but not actionable.

The first line of defense in many instances is *qualified privilege.* In this defense, neither the truth of a statement nor the fact that is defamatory is at issue; the publisher merely cites the right to report any information that is covered by *absolute privilege.* This includes public records, court testimony, and anything a congressman or state legislator says on the floor of the legislature. The theory behind absolute privilege is that truth in a democracy is more important than personal reputation, and therefore no witness or legislator should be subjected to a slander suit for speaking freely. Under qualified privilege, the same protection is extended to those who report such information.

Qualified privilege recently has been extended to statements made at meetings of city councils, school boards, and lesser government agencies. Sometimes it also is claimed as a defense when the reporter is quoting a public official in the performance of his duties, but here the defense is extremely shaky. The best course is caution; make sure the board or council you are covering keeps an official transcript or tape recordings of its proceedings, and avoid defamatory remarks by public officials. Stick to the record. Remember, too, that privilege vanishes when a statement is expunged from the record. If a judge says, "Strike that," don't use it.

Another traditional defense is the doctrine of *fair comment and criticism.* Under this doctrine, courts recognize the right of journalists to criticize any performance or work of art that is offered for public approval. This is a particularly valuable defense for drama and literary critics, columnists, editorial writers, cartoonists, and sports writers. Sarcasm, irony, even ridicule are acceptable—as long as the criticism is restricted to whatever is offered for public approval. The rule is that you may criticize the work or the performance, but not the person. However, this distinction becomes blurred when the target of criticism is a politician who offers himself for public approval.

Fairness is an important element of the defense of fair comment. Writers should be qualified to judge whatever they are criticizing, and their opinions must be based on the facts and not motivated by malice. Editors, if not lawyers, deem it unfair to criticize amateur perform- ances and works of art by the same standards they apply to profes- sionals. It is one thing to criticize a Broadway show, quite another to criticize the high school senior play.

After a case comes to trial, the best—and the only absolute—defense is *truth without malice*. To qualify for this defense, a statement first must meet the legal test of truth; hearsay evidence attributed to its source won't work. If the source commits slander, then you commit libel when you quote him. Nor is the word "alleged" any help; if you call a person an alleged murderer, you still have called him a murder- er. Further, a statement can be absolutely true and still not qualify; you still must show lack of malice. You must demonstrate that it was published "for good and justifiable ends" and not "motivated by wicked and evil purpose." If the story is truly newsworthy—if it is in the public interest—you should have no difficulty proving lack of malice. And if it is also accurate in every detail, you have an ironclad defense.

TIMES V. SULLIVAN AND ITS EXTENSION

In 1964 the U.S. Supreme Court took a major step toward liberal- izing libel law when it ruled that a public official cannot recover damages for a defamatory falsehood "relating to his official conduct unless he proves that the statement was made with 'actual malice'— that is, with knowledge that it was false or with reckless disregard of whether it was false or not."

The defamatory falsehoods that led to this historic ruling had ap- peared in a full-page advertisement in *The New York Times* on March 29, 1960. It was signed by a group called the Committee to Defend Martin Luther King and the Struggle for Freedom in the South. It contained several inaccuracies in its account of police actions in Montgomery, Alabama. Among them were the assertions that police had ringed the Alabama State College campus and had padlocked the school's dining hall in an attempt to starve student demonstrators into submission. It also said that Martin Luther King had been arrested seven times, whereas actually he had been arrested only four times.

The advertisement triggered nearly $3 million in libel suits against the *Times*. One of the first cases to be tried was that brought by L. B. Sullivan, commissioner of public affairs for Montgomery. Sullivan, who wasn't named in the advertisement, contended that the word "police" referred to him because everyone knew that he was in charge of the police. An Alabama jury awarded him $500,000, and the Alabama Supreme Court upheld its judgment. The *Times* then appealed to the U.S. Supreme Court and won a reversal.

Times v. *Sullivan* eliminated the necessity for proving truth as a defense when the libeled person is a public official. The court stipulated only that, as in the older doctrine of fair comment and criticism, the libel must concern only the official's public conduct, not his private life, and the remarks must not be a knowing lie or a reckless disregard of the truth. In effect, it excused a defamatory falsehood committed in error as long as the publisher had taken "normal precautions" to determine its accuracy. The court did not, however, define "normal precautions."

Through later decisions, what had become known as the *Times* doctrine was extended to cover nonpolitical public figures and candidates for public office as well as those already holding such offices. Then, in 1971, the Supreme Court took what appeared to be the ultimate step: it extended the rule of *Times* v. *Sullivan* to private persons. Some journalists announced that the law of libel had been repealed. This, however, was an exaggeration. It also proved to be premature.

What appeared for a few years to be the ultimate extension of *Times* v. *Sullivan* came as a result of statements that Radio Station WIP broadcast about George A. Rosenbloom of Philadelphia. The station said Rosenbloom, a distributor of nudist magazines, was involved in "the smut literature racket," that his books were obscene, and that he was a "girlie-book peddler." After he was acquitted of a criminal charge of selling obscene materials, Rosenbloom sued WIP and was awarded $25,000 compensatory damages and $250,000 punitive damages. But the Pennsylvania Court of Appeals overturned the judgment, and the appellate court's ruling was upheld by the U.S. Supreme Court in *George A. Rosenbloom* v. *Metromedia, Inc.* The Supreme Court said there could be no libel judgment to private individuals for discussion of matters of public or general concern unless the individuals could prove knowing or reckless falsehoods.

It made no difference, at that point, whether the injured person was a public figure or an ordinary citizen. The important yardsticks were (1) whether the *subject* was of public or general concern, and (2) whether that publisher or broadcaster had taken "normal precautions" to determine that the statement was true.

In 1974, however, the Supreme Court again drew a line between the public figure and the ordinary citizen. Some editors and scholars jumped to the conclusion that the Rosenbloom decision no longer applied, that the law of libel essentially had been rolled back to *Times* v. *Sullivan*. Again they exaggerated the effect of a single ruling. The Rosenbloom rule was sharply modified, but it was not overturned completely. What the court did, in *Gertz* v. *Robert Welch, Inc.*, was to draw a line between the private person who injects himself into a newsworthy situation and the person who is drawn into the spotlight through no action of his own. The person involuntarily pulled into the spotlight, the court ruled, can collect damages for libel if he can prove that the publisher or broadcaster was "negligent" or careless. The plaintiff need not, however, prove actual malice as defined by the *Times* ruling. As for the definition of negligence, the court left that to the states.

The central figure in the 1974 ruling was Elmer Gertz, a Chicago attorney who had been retained in a civil suit brought against a policeman convicted of murder. The John Birch Society featured Gertz in an article in its magazine, *American Opinion*. The article charged that the policeman's criminal trial was a frame-up, that it was part of a Communist campaign, and that Gertz was one of the people behind the frame-up. It called Gertz a Leninist, a Communist fronter, and an official of two organizations described as Communist. Gertz sued for libel and was awarded $50,000 by the trial jury, but the judge overturned the award. The Court of Appeals upheld the judge. The U.S. Supreme Court, however, sided with the jury. The court said that Gertz, as an attorney in a civil action, had done nothing to inject himself into the public spotlight.

NO EXCUSE FOR NEGLIGENCE

Few libel suits result from name-calling or what a layman would define as malice. Many, however, are the result of negligence that at least borders on what the Supreme Court has defined as "actual malice"—reckless disregard of whether the story is true or false. A man named Hunter is accused of a felony, and the reporter writes "Fisher." Fisher sues. Or the reporter omits "Jr." after a man's name. His father sues. Or somebody switches the complaining witness's name with the defendant's in a minor police story. Or the identifications under a photograph are transposed. Or the address comes out wrong in a story of a vice raid. Or a reporter accepts something defamatory from a previously reliable source and fails to check it. The list of possibilities is endless, but they all add up to the same thing: failure to check names, addresses, and other second-hand information.

The law generally offers no excuse for such negligence. A publisher can only print a retraction in an effort to avoid punitive damages, then hope to settle out of court.

Privacy

While the number of libel suits has decreased in the last few decades, the number of suits for invasion of privacy has grown. This poses a particular problem, primarily because (1) the courts have yet to determine where the public interest ends and invasion of privacy begins, and (2) truth is no defense in privacy.

The belief that every human being has a "right to be let alone" is nothing new. It is at least as old as the English common law principle that every man's home is his castle. We have the law of trespass, laws that limit official search and seizure, laws that protect business and commercial secrets, laws that partially control wiretaps and other forms of electronic surveillance, and many state statutes that try to define a general right of privacy. Yet the entire body of law on privacy leaves many questions unanswered. Exactly where do you draw a line between a public meeting and a private meeting? And how much of the information stored in government offices—in public documents which may be published without fear of a libel suit—still might be construed as an invasion of privacy? What sort of records may a person insist be kept confidential?

A few points are relatively clear:

1. The First Amendment applies only to *expression;* it is no protection in the collection of news. In getting a story, reporters have no more right to invade a person's home than anyone else has. Nor may they open another person's mail. The first is trespass under the common law, the second a federal offense.
2. Raw police (or FBI) files are not public records and therefore are not protected from either libel or privacy suits.
3. In many states, it is legally permissible for reporters to make tape recordings of their own telephone conversations without telling callers they are being recorded. In other states, consent of both parties is required. Where one-party consent is legally sufficient, the law presumes that any person speaking with a reporter does so at his own risk; the fact that he does so implies consent to the use of his words. Ethical reporters, however, will tell callers their conversations are being recorded, regardless of whether their consent is required. And, of course, a reporter can't tap anyone's phone but his own.
4. A person's name or photograph can't be used for monetary gain without his consent. A photograph that can be used legally as news becomes an invasion of privacy if it is reprinted later in an advertisement. For this reason, photographers are advised to get the person's signature on a model's release form if there is a possibility that the picture may be used in an ad or on a magazine cover.
5. The right of privacy ends when a person consents to publication or when he publishes the information himself. Consent is implied if a person agrees to an interview.
6. A public figure surrenders some of his claim to privacy. The plaintiff most likely to sue successfully is the ordinary person who isn't normally in the news.

7. Anything newsworthy that happens in a public place or in full view of the public is legally privileged. You may write about it or photograph it with impunity. But you are invading privacy when you use a telescopic lens to photograph something the public can't see.

The best protections against a privacy suit are (1) overriding public interest and (2) consent of the person named or pictured. If public interest can't be demonstrated and you don't have consent, the best course is not to publish it.

Contempt of Court

Contempt is willful disobedience of public authority—usually a court or a legislative body—and is punishable by fine or imprisonment. In some forms of contempt, a hearing is required. In others, judges may simply say "I find you in contempt" and impose whatever penalty they like, functioning simultaneously as prosecutor, judge, and jury. The law gives judges this extreme power so that they may keep order in the courtroom and help assure a fair and impartial trial.

To understand how the law treats a contemptuous act, you must know whether it is (1) civil or criminal and (2) whether it is direct or indirect. You also must know, if you are dealing with a state court, whether state statutes recognize these distinctions. Some states don't.

Civil contempt perhaps is best defined as passive noncompliance—ignoring an order by a judge, grand jury, or legislative committee. A common example would be refusing to divulge a source of information at the judge's order. The "remedy"—legal scholars refuse to call it punishment—is an indeterminate jail sentence designed to force compliance. The offender is said to "carry the keys to his prison" because he may be released whenever he agrees to do as the judge says. Because it is not considered punishment, the jail sentence is not subject to pardon.

Criminal contempt is an overt act—such as disorderly conduct or insulting behavior—which disrupts decorum or obstructs the administration of justice. It is punished by a fine or a specified term in jail fixed by the judge. The offender, however, can be pardoned.

Direct contempts are those committed in the presence of the court "or so near thereto" as to interfere with the administration of justice. The phrase "so near thereto" need not be interpreted geographically; it can cover an act anywhere that is closely related to the case at hand. A judge may deal with a direct contempt summarily, acting as his own prosecutor and jury. And courts have held that the First Amendment's guarantee of free speech and a free press does not apply to direct contempt.

Indirect contempts are those committed outside the presence of the court and so loosely related to the case at hand that no judge can apply the "so near thereto" rule. Acts of this nature have at least some protection under the First Amendment. Further, the judge must hold a hearing in a case of indirect contempt, and the defendant may even request a jury trial.

Some contempts are easily recognized. Photographers who take pictures in a courthouse corridor in defiance of a judge's order are clearly guilty of criminal and direct contempt. They can be jailed on the spot. And reporters who defy an order to identify a news source are just as clearly guilty of civil and direct contempt. They can be locked up until they comply or until the judge relents. These are risks that every journalist understands.

Acts outside court, however, are more difficult to assess. Suppose a newspaper publishes the details of a grand jury investigation before it is completed. Or suppose the newspaper publishes an editorial criticizing a judge while a trial is in progress or an appeal is pending. Are these contemptuous acts? If so, are they direct or indirect? It all depends on how the judge interprets that phrase "so near thereto."

A judge may hold that it is direct contempt to publish testimony that he ordered stricken from the record. He also may hold that it is direct contempt to publish a defendant's previous criminal record. Indeed, contempt is whatever a judge says it is.

A contempt citation can be appealed, of course, but often a reporter must serve time pending the appeal.

Copyright

Copyright gives authors or publishers an exclusive property right to their work for 28 years, renewable for another 28 years. Anyone who reproduces the material—an article, a play, a motion picture, a telecast, a song, a photograph, a portion of a book—without permission may be sued for infringement of copyright.

Most magazines and many major newspapers are copyrighted, yet reporters may use information from these and other copyrighted sources without fear if they follow a few simple guidelines. The reason is that copyright applies only to the literary or artistic form—the arrangement of words or symbols—not to the facts or ideas they express. You may use factual information from any source, as long as you are careful to paraphrase and borrow sparingly. Professional courtesy also requires that you credit the source, unless it is a standard reference work such as an encyclopedia.

Regardless of copyright, simple prudence dictates that you should never accept as fact anything that is broadcast as news or published in a competing newspaper. If it can't be verified but the fact that it was reported is in itself news, use it cautiously and only with attribution. Say only that CBS or the *Times* reported it, not that it actually happened. And be sure to paraphrase.

Because copyright is intended primarily to protect artists, you are far more likely to get into trouble by reproducing quotations from a novel or a play than by lifting a phrase from a news story. It is especially dangerous to use verses from a poem or a song, or to reproduce a copyrighted photograph.

Lottery

Federal law forbids anyone to advertise a lottery, and in many states it also is illegal under state statutes. The penalties include fine, imprisonment, and loss of a newspaper's second-class mailing permit. The final penalty usually is regarded as the most severe because it could put many newspapers out of business. This often must be explained to the publicity chairmen of various organizations who wonder why reporters won't mention their raffles, door prizes, and bingo games.

A lottery is composed of three elements: consideration, chance, and a prize. *Consideration* can be anything required of the contestant —the price of a ticket, trading at a given place, even walking to the rear of a store whether anything is purchased or not. *Chance* means that skill is not a factor; poker and bridge, for example, are not entirely games of chance. A *prize* may be anything of value, regardless of how little.

Because of the difficulty of defining consideration and drawing a firm line between chance and skill, most editors refuse to mention anything that even remotely resembles a lottery, even though it is permissible to name winners after the fact.

SELF-IMPOSED RESTRAINTS

No law says reporters must write all the news that is in the public interest; indeed, the First Amendment has been interpreted as guaranteeing the right to remain silent as well as the right to speak. Nor does any law say reporters must separate fact from opinion. No law forces them to stay out of politics or refuse gifts from promoters. No law requires them to exercise good taste in reporting news of crime, vice, and violent death. Yet ethical reporters do all of this and more because of the requirements and restraints that journalism itself imposes.

The self-imposed rules by which journalists live reflect the profession's collective interpretation of what is right or wrong, what is in the public interest, and what is fair to the individual. One might say they are the way journalism combines the Miltonian doctrine of a free press with the Golden Rule. They have been listed in broad terms in the Canons of Journalism of the American Society of Newspaper Editors, the Code of Ethics of the Society of Professional Journalists, and the National Association of Broadcasters' Television Code and Radio Code of Good Practices.

The basic premise of all journalistic codes is that freedom of the press is a *societal* right, rather than an individual privilege. It exists only to serve the public's right to know. Therefore, those who own, manage, and serve the press are morally entitled to do so only as they perform responsibly and abide by the rules of fair play. And in their own interest, they must remember that what society has given, society can take away.

Journalists are generally agreed that their primary missions are to (1) publish complete and accurate information about everything that is in the public interest and (2) defend freedom of the press so that they can *continue* to publish. They also are committed to the broad principles of fairness and good taste, but there have been many disagreements over what these terms imply. Does fairness mean that both sides in a controversy must be given equal space and equal headline treatment when the editor is certain that only one side is saying anything of consequence? Does good taste mean that we should never publish a picture of a corpse, or that all suicide stories must be kept off the front page? Does the ethic of neutrality mean that reporters are forbidden to join a political party, or only that they are forbidden to campaign actively? Where do we draw the line between the rights of the individual and the rights of society, or between interpreting and editorializing?

No code yet devised can answer all the ethical questions that arise regularly in publishing. But perhaps reporters can develop some of their own answers by first looking at what they owe themselves, then examining their obligations to each person with whom they deal.

The Reporter

Freedom of the press is directly proportional to the freedom of the individuals who serve it. The first responsibility of all reporters, therefore, is to protect their own independence of thought and action. They must be indebted to no one and committed to no cause other than that of reporting the news thoroughly, accurately, fairly, and impartially. They must avoid any activity that even appears to be a conflict of interest. For their own integrity, reporters must:

1. *Refuse gifts, favors, or free travel.* They should accept nothing of value from anyone but members of their immediate families and their employers. Christmas gifts and tickets from promoters must

be returned. Champagne flights and other junkets must be refused. Even dinner invitations should be suspect.

2. *Avoid political involvement.* Like other citizens, reporters may register political preferences, but they are barred from seeking office, actively campaigning for any candidate or cause, or soliciting money. They also should avoid any nonpolitical community service which might inhibit or bias their professional activity.

3. *Be judicious about secondary employment.* Most editors consider it acceptable for reporters to supplement their incomes by freelance magazine writing or serving as correspondents for another newspaper or a wire service. But moonlighting as a publicist or an advertising copywriter is off limits. Even jobs which appear totally unrelated to journalism should be scrutinized carefully. It's better to work for only one employer and demand a salary that makes moonlighting unnecessary.

4. *Refuse special treatment in the news.* Ethical reporters never use the news columns for personal benefit. They neither promote themselves nor try to conceal news which might damage them. Ideally, they should conduct their personal lives in a way that keeps their names out of the news; but if they become involved in a crime, a scandal, or a minor embarrassing incident, they must be treated like anyone else. Journalism cannot maintain its credibility if it protects its own. Nor can reporters maintain their freedom if they conceal information that could make them subject to blackmail.

The Reader

More than any other person with whom reporters deal, the reader represents the whole of society. The reader, after all, is everyone. Therefore, reporters usually serve society best when they serve the reader.

But what constitutes proper service to readers? Is it giving them what they want? Or is it giving them what thoughtful and unbiased professionals think they should have? Is it truly in the best interests of the readers to publish comic strips, personal advice columns, and extremist political opinions—all of which they seem to want? Or do these staples merely pander to the lowest common denominator?

At the higher echelons of publishing, where the total package must be considered, the definition of reader service is a matter of unending debate. But for reporters, it can be narrowed down considerably. Service means giving readers what they have come to expect in the news columns—timely, factual information. The readers want news—not pornography, propaganda, ancient history, or even serious education—and this is what the reporters give them. Reporters owe the readers:

1. *A complete and accurate account of anything that affects their personal welfare.* Threats and opportunities automatically are top priority news.
2. *Within the bounds of good taste, any other news that interests them.* Significant personal involvement is not the only yardstick of news value. Readers deserve thorough coverage of events, ideas, and situations that may never touch them. And they deserve at least an occasional look at the lighter side of life.
3. *Balanced, neutral reporting of controversy.* The readers must be able to rely on the reporter to present all sides of an issue, not just those the writer agrees with. Whenever possible, an opinionated statement should be balanced with its opposite in the same story. If a person who figures in a controversy declines to speak or is unavailable for comment, readers should be told so; they must be assured that the reporter has done a thorough job.
4. *Identification of the source whenever possible.* Even an unsophisticated reader tends to be skeptical of information that comes from unidentified sources. The reporter, too, should suspect a source who declines to stand behind his words publicly.
5. *Correction of published errors.* A substantial error of fact that is allowed to stand uncorrected is a breach of faith.
6. *Respect for normal standards of taste.* Reporters should avoid words that might be considered obscene, and they should try not to portray a life of crime or vice as attractive. In stories of death and violence, reporters should omit details that might make the reader physically ill.

The Person in the News

Everyone who figures in the news deserves fair and impartial treatment. On the surface, this seems a simple obligation. It would appear that all reporters need do is treat everyone equally and, like the law, presume that all are innocent until proved guilty. After all, reporters usually discharge their obligation to the person in the news in the same way that they discharge their obligation to the reader, by presenting the facts without judgment. If someone is offended—and someone often is—reporters always can fall back on journalism's favorite justification: "I don't make the news; I merely report it."

But every professional knows it isn't that simple. To begin with, the disclaimer that reporters don't make the news is at best a half-truth. Editors and reporters do, to a great extent, determine which facts are newsworthy and which aren't. And, within the larger framework of the law, they are the final judges of what is fair and what isn't. They alone must constantly balance the public interest against the rights of the individual; they alone must decide what to publish and what to leave out. And they can do this fairly only if they have a series of firm guidelines—a news policy under which everyone is treated equally.

Policy is the way an organization defines news; it stipulates the way certain stories shall be treated. It may decree, for example, that no automobile accident is to be considered news unless someone is killed or seriously injured. Or it may say that all misdemeanors shall be ignored, or that no suicides shall appear on the front page. Policy tells reporters when names and addresses shall be used and when they shall be omitted, and whether euphemisms are to be employed in certain stories. It also extends to issues which are more a matter of good business than morality; for example, many newspapers omit the familiar "in lieu of flowers" in obituaries because they don't want to antagonize florists. And still others have a rule against naming a hotel where a suicide has occurred.

Each newsgathering organization has its own policy, and no two are exactly alike. Few have ever been published in their entirety; more often the policy is a part of the newsroom's oral traditions. Newcomers to a staff may be briefed on the major rules or maybe left to discover them by observation. Indeed, they may be told that "our policy is whatever the editors say it is." And they may never become aware of some of the finer points unless they run afoul of them.

Perhaps no policy rules are universal, but here are a few of the more widely observed guidelines as an editor might list them:

Names and Identification—Don't name rape victims, welfare recipients, or retarded persons. Don't name juvenile first-offenders unless the charge is murder. Don't name a person being questioned about a crime until he is formally charged. Don't use race as a means of identification unless it is necessary so that the reader can fully understand the story. Don't identify a suspect in a criminal case as a veteran; many men are veterans. Don't name the make of automobiles in accident stories; don't use any trade names unless absolutely necessary.

Kidnapings—Don't write anything that might further endanger the victim's life. Normally this means cooperating fully with investigating officers.

Plane Hijackings—Treat them like kidnapings.

Suicides—Keep them short and omit the gory details; think of the family. If death was by poisoning, don't be specific about identifying the poison and don't tell how it was obtained; we don't want to give anyone else a recipe. Unless the victim is a public figure or took his or her life in a public place, the suicide should be treated as a routine obituary; keep it off the front page.

Addresses—In writing captions for photos, omit addresses of young women; let's not help the persons who make obscene calls.

Photos of Corpses—Don't publish a picture of a dead person unless the body and face are covered. Photographs of battlefield dead are permissible only if the faces can't be recognized.

Political Charges—Use no political charges from unidentified sources without first consulting the editor. As in a court of law, the accused person has a right to face the accuser. He also should be given an opportunity to reply—if possible, in the same story. If he chooses not to answer, report it. If he insists on a lengthy verbatim defense, tell him to write a letter to the editor; we will use only news in the news column.

Divorces, Marriage Licenses, Births, Hospital Admittances and Dismissals, and Misdemeanors—All will be treated in list form, and no names will be omitted for any reason whatever. We can make no exceptions without destroying our credibility. If someone objects, explain that it's our policy to print the public record, and that everyone is treated alike.

The Source

News sources are rather special people. First, they are our most thorough and critical readers. Second, they often figure in the news themselves. Third, if they are conscientiously neutral and co-operative over a long period, they may come to be treated almost like unpaid members of the staff. Reporters, therefore, owe their sources everything they owe the reader and the person in the news—and a little more.

A reporter's primary obligation to the source is, of course, to honor any agreements. Any information accepted "off the record" must remain so. Any promise to conceal the source's identity must be kept, regardless of the legal consequences. And if a reporter agrees to withhold a story until a certain hour, he or she is honor-bound to withhold it; should another agency break the release time, the reporter can only inform the source and ask to be released from their agreement.

But to be entirely fair, reporters owe their sources one thing more: a clear explanation of why they behave the way they do. Sources must understand why reporters refuse gifts, why they are so reluctant to make promises, why they can't serve as publicity chairpeople, and why they can't mention a raffle. Sources must understand which names can't be used and which must be published at all costs. In short, sources must be given a continuing education in the law and ethics of journalism and the individual newspaper's policy. This is more than being fair; it is also a way of making them better sources.

The Publisher

No newspaper can long remain free unless it is economically strong. If the business is shaky, it becomes vulnerable to the pressures of advertisers, politicians, and special interest groups. And if a great newspaper suspends publication, all of society suffers. It is in the best interests of society, therefore, for reporters to treat the publisher's business as if it were their own—to do their part to see that the presses roll on time, that the paper contains salable news, and that it is not weakened by unexpected legal actions.

The way reporters serve the publisher best is by aggressively reporting the news—by covering the beat or assignment as thoroughly as possible and by striving for the latest and most detailed information. Regardless of the competition, they try to get the most and the best for their own organization. If possible, they get it first. They meet all deadlines, let the city editor know where they are at all times, and never refuse an assignment. They never tell an editor "That's not on my beat." They do whatever is necessary to get the news printed on time.

Reporters also must realize that to some extent they are public relations people for their organization. People tend to judge an institution by its most visible employees, and few newspaper employees are more visible than the reporters. If reporters are rude, slovenly, or pointedly cynical, the newspaper's public image suffers. Reporters owe it to the boss as well as themselves to project a respectable image.

The advertising side of publishing, although it accounts for 70 to 90 per cent of the newspaper's income, is normally none of the reporter's business. Indeed, professional ethics demand that reporters stay out of it as much as possible. Neither the promise of advertising nor the threat to withhold it must deter reporters from the primary duty of serving the reader. Reporters should, however, be certain that (1) they give away no free advertising in the news columns and (2) they alert editors so that a defense can be prepared whenever something unfavorable must be written about an advertiser.

As long as they work for a given newspaper, reporters are committed to follow its policy to the last detail. If they disagree with a certain ruling—if they think the policy is unethical—they are entitled to protest and try to get it changed. But if the editors stand firm, reporters have little choice. They must either accept the ruling or quit the job.

The Larger Society

Reporters and editors often run into situations which cause them to question one of journalism's basic premises. Does the reader truly represent all of society? Is the public's right to know always paramount? Or is the public interest sometimes served better if certain facts—perhaps entire stories—are suppressed?

Editors tend to agree rather reluctantly that sometimes the readers should be kept temporarily in the dark. Often this is for their own protection. In wartime, for example, it would be dangerous to give readers information that an enemy might use against them; they need not know about troop movements until after the fact. And at times a reporter may have to protect the readers' pocketbooks; it would be a disservice to report all the details of a proposed public project if premature information would inflate land prices and cost more of the readers' tax dollars. An editor also can justify delaying news of a criminal warrant to avoid alerting a suspect that officers are on their way to make an arrest. And an editor can defend the common practice of delaying the identification of dead persons until next of kin have been notified. But in most such cases, editors think primarily of *delaying* information, not suppressing it permanently.

In some routine situations, a specific delay has become a matter of general policy. All ethical journalists, for example, honor release times set by political candidates and public relations practitioners. And in South Dakota, newspapers and law enforcement officers have agreed on what is known as "the six-hour rule" for notifying the next of kin of persons who die violently: newspapers will withhold identifications for as long as six hours; if the next of kin can't be reached within that period, then the names will be published. But these are common and relatively safe situations; in truly dangerous circumstances, each case must be decided on its merits. And history offers only a few guidelines to suggest what kind of information should be delayed or for how long.

Shortly after mid-century, southern editors were faced with a series of difficult decisions as the result of efforts to desegregate schools, public transportation, and food service. If they ignored the efforts, they served neither their general readership nor the blacks who demanded recognition and equality. If, on the other hand, they published timetables for freedom rides and sit-ins, they could be accused of telling white extremists where and when to mass. Most editors took the risk. They published the timetables. And when violence followed, they tried to cover it as factually and dispassionately as possible.

On one front, Oklahoma was a notable exception. Thanks to the influence of E. K. Gaylord, publisher of the *Daily Oklahoman* and the *Oklahoma City Times,* newspeople and state officials agreed to withhold all advance notice of specific timetables for school desegregation. Schools were desegregated quietly and the press covered only the accomplished fact. The result was virtually no violence.

But the Oklahoma experience, successful as it was, provides no principle which editors can apply to all situations. On the contrary, partial suppression sometimes may cause far more trouble than full disclosure. An historic example, the effect of which may never be fully determined, is the way *The New York Times* handled its advance knowledge of Cuban exiles' plans to invade their homeland in 1961. Tad Szulc of the *Times* wrote that the exile force massed in Guatemala was trained and supported by the U.S. Central Intelligence Agency and that an invasion was imminent, but these facts were deleted before the story was published. Szulc's story also was marked originally for a four-column head at the top of the front-page, but *Times* executives reduced it to a one-column head and moved it down from the top of the page.

The invasion went ahead with only one change: President Kennedy backed down on the promise of air support. The result was a disaster for the exiles at the Bay of Pigs.

Two questions have haunted *Times* executives ever since: (1) If nothing at all had been published, as James Reston advised, might President Kennedy have fulfilled the promise of air support and thereby have insured the invasion's success? Or (2) if the full story had been published in proper perspective, would public opinion have forced Kennedy to call off the U.S. sponsorship entirely? These are questions for which there can be no answers.

Editors of the *Times* acted in what they believed to be the public interest. But what constitutes the public interest?

Perhaps Turner Catledge, executive editor of the *Times* during the invasion period, said it best: "When people talk about newspapers serving the public interest, I am sometimes forced to admit that I'm never sure what the public interest is, beyond its need for accurate information."

INDEX